S0-AJK-455

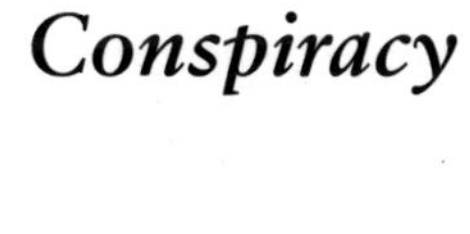

Conspiracy

Conspiracy

Peter Thiel, Hulk Hogan, Gawker, and the Anatomy of Intrigue

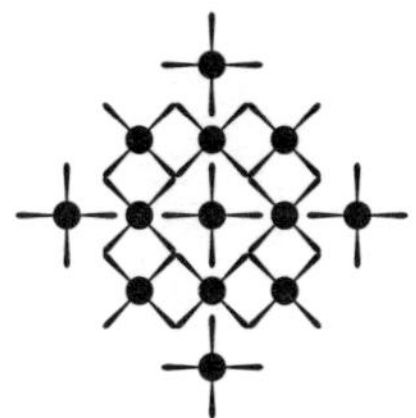

RYAN HOLIDAY

P

PROFILE BOOKS

First published in Great Britain in 2018 by
Profile Books Ltd
3 Holford Yard
Bevin Way
London
WC1X 9HD

www.profilebooks.com

First published in the United States of America in 2018 by
Portfolio / Penguin, an imprint of Penguin Random House LLC

1 3 5 7 9 10 8 6 4 2

Printed and bound in Great Britain by Clays, St Ives plc

A CIP catalogue record for this book is available from the British Library.

ISBN 978 1 788816 083 4
eISBN 978 1 78283 463 2

To all those who are conspiring,
and all those who deserve to be conspired against . . .

Contents

I couldn't stand it. I still can't stand it. I can't stand the way things are. I cannot tolerate this age. What is more, I won't. That was my discovery: that I didn't have to.

—Walker Percy, *Lancelot*

Conspiracy

A Word

This is the story of a conspiracy, the story of a billionaire who set out to make an example of a millionaire, to destroy the man's life's work in response to a cruel transgression made as thoughtlessly as it was quickly forgotten. It is a story of poetic justice on a grand scale, plotted silently for nearly a decade. It is also a book about that controversial word and method—*conspiracy*—which has long terrified and intrigued.

There is an unpleasantness in talking about conspiracies, I'll grant that. Yet *conspiracy* is a neutral word. It depends on what one does with it. Our tendency to shy away from this truth creates a profound ignorance of how things really work, and what it means to be strategic, to be powerful, and to try to shape events rather than simply be shaped by them.

So what then do we mean when we talk about this word? Certainly not imaginative guesses about what goes on in the shadows, or silly theories. Conspiracy entails determined, coordinated action, done in secret—always in secret—that aims to disrupt the status quo or accomplish some aim.

There is a moment in *The Great Gatsby* when Jay Gatsby introduces Nick Carraway to Meyer Wolfsheim, mentioning offhandedly that he is the man who fixed the 1919 World Series. The idea staggers

Gatsby's idealistic young friend. Of course, Carraway knew the series had been thrown. But "if I had thought of it at all," he says, "I would have thought of it as a thing that merely *happened*, the end of some inevitable chain." It was unbelievable to him then, as it is to us now, that a single person could have been responsible for changing the outcome of an event watched by some fifty million people.

In real life, the 1919 World Series was fixed not by Wolfsheim, but with great skill and audacity by Arnold Rothstein, a Jewish gangster. A young lieutenant colonel in the U.S. Army named Dwight Eisenhower eagerly followed the game as the scores came in via telegram, and like everyone else, never suspected a thing. He would remark years later that the revelation of the conspiracy that had thrown the series produced a profound change in his perspective about the world; it taught him never to trust in first appearances.

Nearly a century has passed, and too many of us have not yet lost that Jazz Age naïveté. One longtime Washington columnist wrote recently that years of covering politics taught him one lesson: the legend of Washington as a ceaseless, ruthless, scheming place is simply that, a legend. The truth, he says, is that "No one can carry out complicated plans. All parties and groups are fractious and bumbling." We nod our heads in agreement. We shake our heads in disappointment.

This is a book for a world that has come to think like Nick Carraway, riding in disbelief through life on the wake of conspiracies we won't believe until we see, unable to comprehend why they happen and who makes them happen. This ignorance of how things really work is depressing to me. Because it opens us up to manipulation. It closes us off from opportunities to produce fruitful change and advance our own goals. It is time to grow up.

Nick Denton, whom you will come to know in these pages, is a kind of freethinker who has always held that the things other people are afraid to say are precisely the ones that need saying most. Peter

Thiel, whom you will also come to know, has famously become associated with one question, which he uses in interviews and over long dinners: "What important truth do very few people agree with you on?"

I'll give you mine to close this short preface: Perhaps we have too few conspiracies, not too many. Too little scheming, rather than too much. What would happen if more people took up plotting, coordinating how to eliminate what they believe are negative forces and obstacles, and tried to wield power in an attempt to change the world? We could almost always use more boldness, and less complacency. We could use less telegraphing of our intentions or ambitions and see what secrecy, patience, and planning might accomplish. We could use a little more craziness and disruption, even from the people we disagree with.

This book is my homage to that complicated idea, told in part through the complicated story of one almost unbelievable conspiratorial act.

Please use it wisely.

Introduction

There are no grand, towering bookcases befitting a billionaire in the New York City apartment of Peter Thiel, yet the space is defined by books. They lie in neatly arranged stacks of different heights on nearly every table. Colorful paperbacks and ancient hardcovers about economics, chess, history, and politics fill sets of small, modern shelves in the corners and against the walls.

If you look closely, on the shelf closest to the chef's kitchen and the arched windows that look out over Union Square Park, there is a small white-spined edition of a book by a sixteenth-century political theorist and Florentine diplomat, worn from use. It is not *The Prince*, which many people—rich and ordinary alike—pretend to have read, though it is by the same author, Niccolò Machiavelli. This more obscure volume consists of 142 chapters of five-hundred-year-old musings and analysis on the works of a Roman historian two thousand years deceased. Even the title is boring: *Discourses on Livy.*

Indeed, most of the pages in that book don't matter for this story. Flip past them for now, you can read them another time. But there, buried between notes on how hereditary rulers lose their kingdoms and the effect of noises upon troops in battle, the title of chapter VI in book III stands out refreshingly in its simplicity.

It is just one word: *Conspiracies*.

What follows is Machiavelli's guide for rising up against a powerful enemy, for ending the reign of a supposed tyrant, for protecting yourself against those who wish to do you harm. It is appropriate that such a book sits just within arm's reach of one of Thiel's wingback armchairs and not far from the chess set which occupies considerable amounts of his time. Something in these pages planted itself deep into Thiel's mind when he first read it long ago, and something in Thiel allowed him to see past Machiavelli's deceptive warnings *against* conspiracies and hear the wily strategist's true message: that some situations present only one option.

It's the option available to many but pursued by few: intrigue. To strategize, coordinate, and sustain a concerted effort to remove someone from power, to secretly move against an enemy, to do what Machiavelli would say was one of the hardest things to do in the world: to overthrow an existing order and do something new. To engage in a conspiracy to change the world.

A thousand miles and a few months away, in a Pinellas County courtroom, just such a conspiracy is reaching its climax. A six-person jury delivers its verdict as a towering professional wrestler named Terry Bollea sits in nervous anticipation. When they announce the judgment, Bollea nearly collapses. He clutches his attorney, Charles Harder, who not long before was an ordinary if not obscure entertainment lawyer. In that moment, they both absorb the enormity of the numbers being entered into the record.

At Thiel's prompting, and with his backing, the pair had sued Gawker Media, a New York–based gossip and entertainment empire, along with its founder, Nick Denton, and former editor in chief, A. J. Daulerio, for a handful of claims including invasion of privacy, intentional infliction of emotional distress, and violation of

Florida's Security of Communications Act. Four years previously, Gawker.com published excerpts of a secretly recorded tape of Bollea, known to the public as Hulk Hogan, having sex with his best friend's wife. The tape was eventually stolen and leaked to a wild and impulsive reporter who, in publishing it, was doing what Gawker claimed to do best: chasing the stories no one else would touch.

Thousands of miles across the Pacific, unknown to the public, or even to many of the conspirators, the twenty-something operative who helped engineer this moment watches the verdict on a livestream. Farther away still is Peter Thiel, asleep in his hotel suite in Hong Kong. Peter is alone, as he often is, and it's early in China, but he will take a call from this number at any time. It takes twenty minutes to finally get a connection. The cell reception is terrible. "Did you hear?" No, no, he had not. No one expected a verdict this soon, but neither man is staggered. They had been confident of victory for some time, having already experienced this moment, twice, in expensive mock jury proceedings. All that remained to be decided, as far as Thiel was concerned, was how much it was going to cost Gawker. The final tally? $115 million—$60 million of it for emotional distress.

It is perhaps the largest verdict against a publisher in history and the death blow in a feud that began a decade earlier, bringing with it the culmination of a conspiracy that had run nearly as long. A Florida jury has been used to send a message, used to right a perceived wrong that almost everyone else had forgotten. The message was delivered and now Gawker Media, long considered the invincible renegade internet powerhouse, is left bleeding out on the courtroom floor.

The mortal blow is struck. Billionaire tech investor Peter Thiel has struck it.

It is 2016 and he has shocked the world by doing so. Which is what brought me here, to Thiel's apartment for dinner, in a year in which even the pope has come out to denounce irresponsible journalism as a form of terrorism. I can see the copy of *Discourses* over his right shoulder as he describes his personal war against Gawker in defense of a right he believes it threatened—privacy—and for what that privacy offers—the space to be peculiar, to think for oneself and to live as one wishes. The chef brings the first, second, and third courses as Thiel talks, revealing a painstakingly organized plot—the plan to reassert agency over a situation many believed was unchangeable, to protect something that most of his Silicon Valley peers had written off as an anachronism, but also to destroy an enemy and make the world a little bit closer to his vision of what it should be.

Twenty blocks downtown there is an equally nice apartment belonging to Nick Denton, the former owner of Gawker Media, the former dark prince of the internet himself. Only, this apartment is almost devoid of furniture. It was empty of its owner until very recently, while the courts decided whether he would be forced to sell it in bankruptcy. No man will take your coat at the door and there is no private chef. Nick will open the door himself and he'll make you a drink at his SodaStream.

He is much friendlier and more thoughtful than you would assume for a man who created what was one of the most explosive and rebellious media outlets ever. One that, as it spun out of control, growing bigger and bolder, even he privately began to worry might lead to a suicide. As so many reactionary organizations tend to do, it had begun to drift toward absolutism and nihilism.

A quick scan of Denton's darkly lit apartment confirms that books define it, too. They are built into the architecture itself, lining each window, inset and running up to the thirteen-foot ceilings. Again, one book catches the eye. It's a copy of the works of the Stoic philosopher Seneca, and it's there precisely because of the conspiracy Peter

Thiel had led against its possessor. Seneca is the author you read when your life's work has been destroyed, as Denton's undeniably has. Over the last few years, he has gone from owning one of the most valuable independent websites in the world to being on the wrong side of a $140 million judgment.* He found himself outmaneuvered and outspent by a nemesis he'd deliberately prodded and provoked. It would be now that Denton is looking for the kind of solace needed when your fortunes change, when your seemingly unassailable dominance is suddenly threatened, when you are given an abject lesson in the exercise of power in its most unforgiving form.

Every conspiracy is a story of people. The protagonists of this one are two of the most distinctly unique personalities of their time, Nick Denton and Peter Thiel. Two characters who, not unlike the cowboys in your cliché western, found that the town—whether it was Silicon Valley or New York City or the world's stage—was not big enough for them to coexist. The gravitational pull of the two figures would bring dozens of other people into their orbit over their ten-year cold war along with the FBI, the First and Fourth Amendments, and soon enough, the president of the United States.

It somehow dragged me in, too. In 2016, I would find myself the recipient of unsolicited emails from both Peter Thiel and Nick Denton. Both wanted to talk, both were intrigued to hear I had spoken to the other. Both gave me questions to ask the other. And so for more than a year, I spent hundreds of hours researching, writing about, and speaking to nearly everyone involved. I would read more than twenty thousand pages of legal documents and pore through the history of media, of feuds, of warfare, and of strategy not only to

*Three days after the initial verdict, the jury awarded Bollea an additional $25 million in punitive damages. Denton was liable for $10 million of it personally.

make sense of what happened here, but to make something more than just some work of contemporary long-form journalism or some chronological retelling of events by a disinterested observer (which I am not). The result is a different kind of book from my other work, but given this extraordinary story, I had little choice.

What follows then are both the facts and the lessons from this conflict—an extended meditation on what it means to successfully conspire, on the one hand, and how to be caught defenseless against a conspiracy and be its victim, on the other. So that we can see what power and conviction look like in real terms, as well as the costs of hubris, and recklessness.

And because winning is typically preferable to losing, this book is about how one man came to experience what Genghis Khan supposedly called the greatest of life's pleasures: to overcome your enemies, to drive them before you, to see their friends and allies bathed in tears, to take their possessions as your own. The question of justice is beside the point; every conqueror believes their cause just and righteous—a thought that makes the fruits taste sweeter.

"We live in a world where people don't think conspiracies are possible," Thiel would tell me. "We tend to denounce 'conspiracy theories' because we are skeptical of privileged claims to knowledge and of strong claims of human agency. Many people think they are not possible, that they can't be pulled off."

In these pages, I seek to show you, step by step, not a conspiracy theory but an actual conspiracy as explained by the people who did pull one off. I also seek to show you the consequences and the causes. Machiavelli said that a proper conspiracy moves through three distinct phases: the planning, the doing, and the aftermath. Each of these phases requires different skills—from organization to strategic thinking to recruiting, funding, aiming, secrecy, managing public relations, leadership, foresight, and ultimately, knowing when to stop. Most important, a conspiracy requires patience and fortitude, so much patience, as much as it relies on boldness or courage.

The question that remains: What would a world without these skills look like? And would a world with more of them be a nightmare or something better?

That's for you to decide. In the meantime and for the record, I simply present what happened.

PART I

The Planning

CHAPTER 1

The Inciting Incident

"The beginnings of all things are small," Cicero reminds us. What becomes powerful or significant often begins inauspiciously, and so, too, do the causes that eventually pit powerful forces against one another.

The conflict at the heart of this story is no different. Its genesis is a largely obvious, mostly unremarkable blog post—not even four hundred words long—that outed a little-known technology investor as homosexual. Written by a gossip blogger named Owen Thomas, for a now-defunct tech news website owned by Gawker called *Valleywag*, the piece was published at 7:05 p.m. on December 19, 2007, under a headline that would sear itself into the mind of its subject:

Peter Thiel Is Totally Gay, People.

It wouldn't be fair to say, as some partisans have in the intervening years, that Owen Thomas was some reckless blogger who plucked some private citizen from nowhere for his story. He'd been a reporter for over a decade, and Peter Thiel had a media profile as an investor and an entrepreneur. Thiel had made a fortune as a founder of PayPal and put the first $500,000 into Facebook. The man had previously posed for photographers and agreed to be interviewed by reporters who were covering him or his companies. And it was not disputable that he was, in fact, gay.

Peter admits that his sexuality was no revelation. "I think everyone already knew in 2007," he told me. By that he means that his parents knew he was gay. His friends knew and so did his colleagues. But it was not a fact he advertised. A friend would say that Peter burned to be the best technology investor in the world. To insert "gay" into that, to be seen as the *best gay technology investor*, seemed artificially limiting. Like it was cheating him of something he was desperate to earn. And by his choice, Peter Thiel's sexuality stood as a kept but open secret in the close-knit community of the Silicon Valley elite.

To the modern mind, this reticent gay identity seems like an anachronism, but when you do the math, you quickly realize how different the world was in 2007. The Democrat who would be elected president in less than a year's time was still five years away from announcing his support for same-sex marriage. The woman who opposed him in the primary would take an additional year to come around. 2007 was also much closer to the burst of the dot-com bubble than it is to the present day. Facebook's IPO lay five years in the future and most of the astonishing success of this class of start-ups from Twitter to Netflix still lay ahead.

While Thiel was not no one in late 2007 when the story broke, Peter Thiel was not then *Peter Thiel*. He was not the person he would be at the end of this story, the idiosyncratic lion of Silicon Valley venture capital or controversial political power broker. Thiel was more like all the other technology investors most people have never heard of. Do the names Max Levchin or Roelof Botha sound familiar to the average person? They were Thiel's partners in PayPal. Or the name Jim Breyer? He put a million dollars in Facebook less than a year after Thiel put in his half million. What about Maurice Werdegar, who put in money *with* Thiel in that famous seed round? Few have even heard of these people, let alone cared whom they slept with. They are, as far as popular culture is concerned, as Thiel was then, barely notable. And he was, above all, a quiet, private person.

When one considers Thiel's burning ambitions against this backdrop, and the potential for this *Valleywag* story to be the first thing to broadly define him outside the Valley, one might better understand Thiel's reaction to Owen Thomas's small, unexceptional story and the flippant headline that went with it.

"It was like a full-on attack out of the blue. There was nothing I had ever done to these people in any way whatsoever. On a superficial level, the article was just about outing me," Peter said. It wasn't the outing itself, however, that most got to him, but the second narrative, that he has psychological problems because he didn't want to be outed. "It was never about the Owen Thomas article," Thiel eventually admitted to me. "It was the Nick Denton comment."

In the comments section at the bottom of Owen Thomas's story, Nick Denton, *Valleywag*'s editor and the founder of its parent company, Gawker Media, had posted a few sentences in the form of an accusation that seemed to respond to itself: "The only thing that's strange about Thiel's sexuality: why on earth was he so paranoid about its discovery for so long?"

By normal, journalistic standards, this commentary would be extraordinary. For a founder and publisher to editorialize and speculate from the peanut gallery of his publication's own comments section? Yet by 2007, this kind of combative, adversarial approach to the news and its subjects was standard operating procedure for the somber, perpetually scruffy Englishman with cherubic cheeks, a love of technology, and a passion for gossip.

Even those who hate Nick Denton would describe him as brilliant. Born Nicholas Guido Anthony Denton to a British economist father and psychotherapist mother of Jewish-Hungarian descent, Denton attended Oxford University. He sold his first company, a networking group for people in the tech industry, for millions. When he started his online media company in 2002, his love for tech was at the forefront of his mission: *Gizmodo*, the first of the many sites that would comprise his publishing empire, was a "vertical blog devoted to superskinny laptops, spy cameras, wireless wizardry, and all manner of other toys for overgrown boys. All gadgets, all the time."

Roughly four months later, he launched a new site dedicated to his other, more primal passion: secrets and gossip. He named it Gawker. Technology may have been Denton's first love, but many would say this—his lust to expose, to reveal, to lob bombs—was Denton's *true* love, a side of him that ran parallel to his urge to build. He would name his celebrity site *Defamer* (one blogger joked, "Why not go all the way and call it 'Defendant'!"), and he would name his porn site *Fleshbot*, but it was Gawker that would stick as the name of the parent company, since it so well described the editorial ethos of Denton's online empire and captured the pathos of its founder perfectly.

Gawker's first editor, Elizabeth Spiers, was paid $2,000 per month for twelve posts a day, seven days a week. Her job was to mock the club of New York elites she had never been invited to join. Her job was to, with a kind of humorous contempt that's come to be called *snark*, dismiss people and institutions as laughably unimportant, even as, in writing about them, she was in fact admitting how important they actually were (and that perhaps, deep down, she'd like to join them someday). Denton had a knack for recruiting talent like her, and for cultivating their voices as he did with Spiers and, eventually, Owen Thomas. He liked young writers with drive and wit, and a gift for pointing at hypocrisy and vulnerabilities that brought audiences quickly and cheaply. Within six months, Denton's sites were pulling in more than 500,000 page views a month. Within a year, the blogs were making more than $2,000 per month each; within three years they were estimated to be generating at least $120,000 in advertising revenue per month. A little over ten years into Gawker's run, its revenues would be nearly $40 million a year and the sites would have more than 40 million readers a month. Denton had struck a rich and dark vein. He had harnessed a modern, digital take on the old tabloid sensibility that, George W. S. Trow once observed, requires a sort of "back and forth of loathe and love of old authority." This pinging between self-pity and self-importance would be Gawker's secret formula.

"As a publishing entrepreneur who built an operation out of nothing, I had to go where the energy was," Denton would say. That energy was mostly the energy of disillusioned youth, of outsiders criticizing insiders. In being *anti* this and that, and rarely for something else instead. *Mankind has always crucified and burned*, a great playwright once said. *We take a secret pleasure in the misfortune of our friends*, said another wise man. For Gawker it was no secret pleasure but a conspicuous one and to it they added the power of blogging. Nick's instincts were captured and compounded by the economics of his instruments: twenty-something writers with school debt and little income. Overeducated children of Boomers, the children of parents whose idealism became materialism, the writers believed they had something to say because those same parents had told them they were special and important and talented.

Previous generations of writers came to New York City with a dream. This generation came with a bone to pick—for the broken economy, for the collapse of old industries, for the hypocrisy and fakeness that had finally become acute. They wanted a seat at the Algonquin and ended up sharing a bedroom in Bushwick, writing twenty articles a week (nineteen of which no one would read) for $12 apiece. Of course they were pissed. A *New York Times* writer would later dub this ethos the "rage of the creative underclass." A Gawker headline captures it better: "It's OK to Be a Hater Because Everything Is Bad."

The existentialists spoke of *ressentiment*, or the way that resentment creates frustration which fuels more resentment. Philosophers might have said this feeling was pointless, but they knew it was a fearful force. Gawker would revel in ressentiment, of its writers and readers. Like most movements that harness the power of an underappreciated class, the environment was temperamental and volatile, but you could not argue that the results were not also entertaining and forceful. Especially when combined with financial incentives.

Denton experimented with different forms of compensation in the early years, but his most important shift was away from a raw number of posts per day (how many things can you make fun of today) toward page views (how many people agree with what you're making fun of). Denton's mind gravitates toward small publishing innovations like these. His sites were some of the first to post the view count at the top of the article. He notices that his writers obsess over this number, refreshing the stat counter over and over, and begins to pay them accordingly. He puts up a large screen in the office that ranks the writers and the articles based on traffic. He calls it the "NASDAQ of Content," but it's closer to the millennial id. If the untapped energy of young people was his first great breakthrough, this is his second. The first offers the power of being heard, the second provides the power of reach and then of quantification—turning blogging into something you can win. How? By getting the most readers. With what? That's for you to decide.

What Denton did, in effect, was turn writing, social commentary, and journalism into a video game. Writing wasn't a craft you mastered. It was a delivery mechanism. The people and companies you wrote about, like Peter Thiel, weren't people, they were characters on a screen—fodder for your weekly churn. And the people you got to read this writing? They were points. The score was right there next to your byline. Views: 1,000. 10,000. 100,000. 1,000,000. The highest prize, the best ticket to traffic? *Scandalum magnatum*—going after great men and women. But in a bind, and with so many posts to get out each day, ordinary people would do just as well.

Gawker Stalker: Elijah Wood Emphatically Not a Gay
Joe Dolce: Portrait of an Asshat
Danyelle Freeman Sucks: The Marrow Out of Life, in General
Which NYC Food Critic Is an Idiot? (Hint: Danyelle Freeman!)
Morley Safer Is a Huge Asshole
Stubborn Jew Rolled by More Stubborn Jewier Jew
Nightmare Online Dater John Fitzgerald Page Is the Worst Person in the World
Andy Dick Gets the Beat-Down We've All Craved
It's Not That Adam Carolla Isn't Funny, It's That Adam Carolla Is a Dumbfuck
Peaches Geldof's Heroin-Fueled One-Night Stand at Hollywood's Scientology Center—with Pictures

When Gawker creates "Gawker Stalker," a feature that lets anonymous users write in with sightings of celebrities so their locations could be tracked online in real time, or when a Gawker writer in 2007 wrote a piece that began, "When is it okay to hate a 4-year-old? Maybe when the kid's name is Elijah Pollack," and tagged it "The Sins of Their Fathers," they were practicing journalism by tomahawk. And it isn't scoops that the sites were looking for, it was scalps: who can we get, who did something stupid, what are other people afraid to say, and who are they afraid to say it about?

If a piece didn't go hard enough, if there were rumors the reporter wanted to talk about but couldn't justify even with Gawker's thin standards, there was always the comments section to push the story from behind—or the bottom, as it were—and drum up tips and speculation and titillation that might lead to more attention. It had always been Nick's nature to push deeper, to speculate, to needle, to drill down to the interesting stuff—and there was no deeper well of ressentiment than the endless scroll of the comments section.

It was all great fun for him, for his writers. Why wouldn't it be? Especially when the old guard yells at you, and you are the type who takes that as a sign you're doing everything right. Journalists, competitors, and leaders alike criticized this editorial style that Nick had invented. Watchdogs were on the lookout for the first Gawker victim suicide. Some inside Gawker even shared these concerns. But it cannot be said that readers didn't *love* Gawker. There was a unique freeness to what Gawker wrote, a kind of raw unfiltered honesty, an exaggerated way of telling the truth. Peter Thiel is *totally* gay, people! If something was true, if they *thought* something was true, they published it. The writers said the things that people thought in private—they fulfilled their wishes. They gave their readers—the people who made up those numbers at the top of each post—what their own bitterness and ressentiment had always craved but no one had seen fit to give them before.

A movie executive once described the "honeyed sting" of the notorious twentieth-century gossip Hedda Hopper as a black widow spider crossed with a scorpion, weaned on prussic acid and treacle. In a way, that was Gawker, too. The perfect conduit for the envy and schadenfreude and jockeying for power that goes on in this world. It's why their tip lines were never dry.

One of the early slogans for Gawker's sports site, *Deadspin*, was "News Without Access, Favor, or Discretion." To Denton that slogan wasn't just branding. "I would own those words," he would say later, under oath. If there was ever a statement that reflected both the man and his monster, this was it, because this wasn't just Denton's character, this was his editorial policy, too. A close friend would describe Denton as "completely unsentimental, contradictory, and opaque." To some journalists, lacking access or discretion would be a weakness. In Gawker's model, they are shackles to throw off. Without them, writers could do things that other outlets could not. They weren't afraid to burn sources, to name names, to run stolen material, to take anonymous leaks. We don't want to know your real name, they would tell sources, we just want the dirt.

Denton was libertarian in this sense. He treated his journalists like adults, he gave them the freedom they wanted, and he treated the demands of his readers as legitimate. Why else would the man have owned a porn site? "Give the people what they want," Denton said, "as shown by data."

Denton only ever served as editor for one of his sites and for a short time. In November 2006, he took over *Valleywag*—announcing his temporary takeover in a short post. He would say, a little less than a year before the Peter Thiel outing, that the site would be dedicated to publishing "open secrets"—the things that are said between the knowing in private but denied to the rest of the world in public. *Facts. Details. Secrets.* Exactly the kinds of things Peter Thiel considered private, Denton believed belonged to the public, and both agreed there was power in controlling them. "Maybe," Denton later reflected, "because I was gay, I grew up hating open secrets. Usually if someone's gay it's a pretty open secret. Their friends know, their family knows, but out of some misplaced sense of decency nobody talks about it."

"We push the envelope all the time at this site in terms of content and journalistic relevance," a Gawker writer would say, "and what comes with that is the perpetual risk that it would be pushed over the edge at some point." Nick loved the traffic that courting controversy brought, however much at odds it might be with his quiet demeanor. As Gawker Media's owner and bold leader, he reveled in the role of questioning the things everyone else believed to be too dangerous. "There has been no such thing as 'too far' with our titles," he said. "We'll run live maps of celebrity sightings, we'll post photographs of star quarterbacks getting drunk at college parties, we'll 'out' politicians, we'll expose Silicon Valley blowhards. What would be the point in holding back? We're independent, we're not owned by a big media company, we don't have to abide by standards that have been set down a generation ago, we have enough advertising to pay the bills, and we attract a very desirable audience which seems to like the fact that we push things too far."

When the cease and desists and the lawsuits came as a result of this pushing, of taking these risks, Nick fought them, and fought them publicly. At stake was his business model and his image as a fearsome publisher.

In 2005, Gawker ran a sex tape featuring the nu-metal singer Fred Durst, but thought better of it and took the video down within a few hours. Three days later, Durst served Gawker with a cease and desist letter and sued it and a few other websites for $80 million. Gawker responded at first not in court but online, mocking Durst for even trying to sue it: "There's an old saying around the Gawker offices, coined by our wise Hungarian goat herding ancestors: you're nobody until somebody hates you. But we had it wrong. It turns out that you're actually nobody until some other nobody sues you." When they were done making fun of Durst, they told him they would *love* to see him in court. Before long, Durst had sent an apology to Nick's apartment, alongside fresh-cut flowers.

For his bravado, Nick Denton was an incisive reader of other people. What he knew was that most people did not have the stomach—or the cash—to actually take it very far against a media outlet. He felt protected by the moat explained in the old twentieth-century proverb: Never fight a battle against someone who buys ink by the barrel. It's easier to just let the whole thing go.

Nick once fired an editor for not having, as he put it, "any story aggression." This aggression was essential to the operation, legally but also editorially. An early Gawker editor would describe its style honestly, not yet aware of the need for optics and branding: "It's not journalism . . . it's blogging. It's putting rumor out there and seeing what sticks." Accepted in this approach, glossed over because they didn't believe it was their problem, is that millions of people were seeing these rumors and that this fact alone often made them true. Gawker's forte was breaking news, and it rarely let obstacles prevent them from doing so. This mindset was responsible for Gawker's decisions in the years that would follow to take on Steve Jobs over a stolen iPhone prototype, to publish a controversial recruiting video produced by the Church of Scientology, to (correctly) accuse the mayor of Toronto of being a crack addict. It was why Gawker was one of the first to reignite rumors of Bill Cosby's alleged sexual assaults, and published anonymous claims about actor Kevin Spacey and young boys, as well as the misdeeds of the director James Toback and comedian Louis C.K.—stories the rest of the media would come to seem embarrassingly late on reporting. Yet this style would also be responsible for Gawker's decision to out a gay executive of a fashion publication who was being extorted by a porn star, to run clips from a surreptitiously recorded and then stolen sex tape of the wrestler Hulk Hogan, and to report on many other stories they would come to regret. But I am getting ahead of myself.

Gawker was an unstoppable force that had yet to meet its immovable object. "Gawker operated by creating larger-than-life enemies,"

A. J. Daulerio, who began at *Deadspin* as a writer and worked his way to editor in chief at Gawker, explained. They would pick people who seemed attracted to publicity and write about them over and over again as the tips came in. Not everyone warranted an enfilade of hit pieces. Sometimes it only took one well-placed shot to change someone's life. But if the opportunity was there—Gawker would take it. Gawker reveled in this power, in the character of the All-American Heel. In a way, Nick did, too. The subject of one of those stories would write in to A.J. to complain. Daulerio replied about two hours later in a tone that would make you think it was an established game they were both playing. "I don't know, man," he said. "It's all professional wrestling." Gawker writers wrote like they were in a cage match against the world. And whether the blows were real or fake, well, it all depended on where they landed on you.

Is it any wonder that Peter Thiel ended up in Nick Denton's crosshairs? Nick, with his love for technology and gossip, and his equally strong disdain for secrets. Peter, the keeper of secrets, with his prominent position in technology investing and his bias toward privacy. Does it not make sense that they would become, as the writer Ernest Lehman put it in one of his short stories, "two bodies in space, repelling and attracting, forever swinging about each other in sickening orbit from which neither could escape"? It was only a matter of time before Nick assigned one of his writers to do a post on Peter and put their trajectories on a collision course.

"Thiel makes me sick!" Nick would explain casually in a chat with Owen Thomas, as he pushed him to write more stories. There was that infamous story aggression. Denton knew there would be interest in a Thiel story, even if Owen Thomas wasn't sure.

"I knew Thiel was gay. I mean, I am gay," Owen explains. "I have enough friends in San Francisco. But I didn't think about it as an open secret until Nick mentioned this to me." Once he did, though, the rest was academic. Owen Thomas worked for a site whose mission was to publish open secrets. This kind of thing was exactly what he was contracted to do. And he did a lot of it. In two years at *Valleywag*, Thomas produced 3,962 posts (roughly six a day). A freelancer when he wrote this first piece on Thiel, his mandate was material *and* page views. Every freelance writer is on an extended job interview, dreaming of a pathway to salary and benefits, and posts like this one about Thiel were how you got on that path at Gawker. Moreover, his job was to publish what he believed to be true. His job was not to think about people's feelings or their private personal balancing acts. His job also required, at least in part, that he override that natural human tendency Denton said he always disliked—that misplaced sense of decency.

The post itself was classic Gawker, the Gawker whose ideal story Nick Denton had described as the one that two journalists gossiped about at a bar over a drink, the thing they could say privately that a buttoned-down editor wouldn't *let them write*. As a result there was not a single named source in the entire article, but there was a strong point of view. "Thiel was publicly and socially out," Owen said later, "but it was his money men who didn't want him to talk about it. I thought that was kind of gross." Owen said later that he had sources inside Thiel's hedge fund who had passed him rumors that Thiel hoped to keep his sexuality secret long enough to raise funds in the Middle East. Is that not a newsworthy angle for the article—a justification for talking about a personal matter? Perhaps if you can prove it. It should be said that there is not a word of that proof in the article, not even anonymously sourced. There's no mention of any attempt to contact the subject of the piece, either—no consideration of asking the person who is being outed why they might have decided to live life this way. There is also no accompanying sense of empathy, no evidence that the journalist understands that the subject is a real person and what their feelings might be, or that the subject is entitled to have any. In the place of these things is the Gawker trademark, something that would be described perfectly in a *Valleywag* memo a few months later, which asked for "one glint of nastiness per post." There is a relishing of what Thiel would point out as a sort of stated and unstated second narrative in Owen's piece, "that the person has psychological problems because they didn't want the article to be published, for some strange reason they don't want to be outed."

"I believe I wrote it with the right journalistic intention, for the right reason," Owen said of the piece. "If some readers didn't take that away from what I wrote that's a failure of mine as a writer and I always think I've got things to learn." That intention, that capture of the Gawker ethos and that conceivable failure between perception and reality, would intersect in the real world, where Peter Thiel was winding down from an otherwise forgettable Wednesday only to find suddenly that a polite fiction, really *omission*, in his private life had been exposed.

Totally gay. Definingly gay. Within twenty-four hours, thanks to Denton's comment, he would also be *strangely, ominously gay and suspiciously secretive about it*. Denton had encouraged others to speculate about why Thiel kept his sexuality a secret. Was Peter hiding his private life because it contradicted his political views? Was there something wrong with him? *Was Thiel just weird?*

It did not end there. This was just one post in a pattern on a rapid cycle. Within a day, another *Valleywag* writer would satirize Owen's post, this time outing Thiel not for being gay but for being an Ayn Rand fan. Another from Owen would put a photo and a name to Thiel's boyfriend, then a trader at the global investment management firm BlackRock. Combined, Gawker's articles on Thiel in 2007 and

2008 would receive more than half a million views and further cement Gawker Media's reputation as the site that would "say the things other people wouldn't say."

And with that we would have a *casus belli.*

While a specific animus toward Thiel may have invigorated the reporting and Denton's push for more stories, the nature of the reporting, specifically its tone, had little if anything to do with Peter himself. It was simply a reflection of the rules that had developed inside Gawker Media in the five years since Denton began this entrepreneurial journey in his living room. The article was remarkable only for how unremarkable it was in the scheme of Gawker's history; it had published and would publish very similar things, many worse things about many more people.

Perhaps Peter should have understood this, that it wasn't about him. Perhaps he should have had thicker skin. But he didn't. What he did understand and what he did believe was that once these articles had started, they probably weren't going to stop. So in that post at 7:05 p.m. on a Wednesday in December, Gawker had made an enemy, it had started a process—a process bigger and more epic than everyone involved.

As Cicero said, the beginnings of all things are small, and so was this one. At its beginning, at the impetus, there was simply something one person thought should be public that another thought was private; that one person thought was funny and that the other believed was serious.

I don't want them to know. It's not their business. It's not who I am. It's not how I want them to see me.

He is upset. His boyfriend is upset, upset that he is upset. Thiel's frenzied mind races now, as it had for others written about by Gawker. The instinct to curl into a ball. The hope that this will go away. The anger at the unfairness of it, the randomness of it, the needless impoliteness of it. The sense that someone was doing this for sport, as part of a game. That someone had this power and wielded it so capriciously . . .

It is from these kinds of thoughts that conspiracies are born.

CHAPTER 2

Deciding to Act

There is an old Scottish motto: *nemo me impune lacessit*. No one attacks me with impunity. Plots of revenge and justice plots both begin, in their own way, with a transgression, against a person or the whole. And then someone deciding that they aren't going to take it.

The distinction between a conspiracy and a feud is as much in the time it takes for one to spring into action as it is in the type of action that one takes. In a fight, one responds to a punch by throwing a punch. In a conspiracy, one holds their punches and plots instead for the complete destruction of their antagonist, while often intending to escape with knuckles unbloodied and untraceable prints.

Fights *break out*. Conspiracies *brew*.

At the moment we first find Peter Andreas Thiel in this story, he is forty years old and in the middle of an astounding rise. His path was in some ways traditional—Stanford to Stanford Law to judicial clerkship to high-powered law firm—but it was also marked by bouts of rebellion. At Stanford he created and published a radical conservative journal called *The Stanford Review*, then he wrote a book that railed against multiculturalism and "militant homosexuals" on campus, despite being both gay and foreign born. His friends thought he might become a political pundit. Instead he became a lawyer. Then one day, surprising even himself, he walked out of one of the most prestigious securities law firms in the world, Sullivan & Cromwell, after seven months and three days on the job.

Within a few short years, Thiel formed and then sold PayPal, an online payments company, to eBay for $1.5 billion in July 2002, the month that Nick Denton registered the domain for his first site, *Gizmodo*. With proceeds of some $55 million, Thiel assembled an empire. He retooled a hedge fund called Clarium into a vehicle to make large, counterintuitive bets on global macro trends, seeding it with $10 million of his own money. In 2003, Thiel registered a company called Palantir with the Securities and Exchange Commission. In 2004, he would found it in earnest. The company would take antifraud technology from PayPal and apply it to intelligence gathering—fighting terrorism, predicting crime, providing military insights. It would take money from the venture capital arm of the CIA and soon take on almost every other arm of the government as clients. That same summer, just around the time that the Gawker blogs found their footing, Thiel placed a $500,000 convertible note into the hands of a twenty-one-year-old Mark Zuckerberg, becoming Facebook's first major investor. A half million was a bit less than 1 percent of the fortune Peter had taken out of PayPal, his first company, or perhaps a year's salary had he not left that law firm.

In 2005, he starts Founders Fund with two former PayPal partners; it would go on to take stakes in Airbnb, Lyft, Spotify, and additional rounds in Facebook. Its assets would grow to more than $3 billion. The returns he was posting as a VC astounded the market, but it's Clarium that occupied the bulk of Thiel's time in the mid- and early aughts, and initially appeared the most promising. It posts a 29 percent return in 2002. It goes up to 65 percent the following year. At the beginning of 2008, less than a month after having his private life made public by *Valleywag*, Thiel decided to move Clarium's headquarters to New York City. Most report the story as a logical move designed to ride the rocket of success closer to where the money lives. Owen Thomas would speculate that there were other reasons, that "romantic reasons" were the real factor, and use the legitimate news story as an opportunity to out Peter's boyfriend. By summer, the hedge fund's assets swell to close to $8 billion, putting Peter, as a friend would tell *The New Yorker* about that moment, on the cusp of quietly achieving his personal ambition of entering the pantheon of all-time great investors.

Before that could happen, the bottom begins to fall out, for Clarium and for Thiel. In April, he cofounds the Seasteading Institute with Patri Friedman, the grandson of economist Milton Friedman, to "empower people to build floating startup societies with innovative governance models." Their efforts would be described as "techie island fantasies" by *Wired* and a "lawless Utopia" by *Valleywag*. By the end of 2008, Clarium takes a wallop as the markets tank, and it ends the year down 4.5 percent. The following year would only get worse. Thiel sits down to write a piece about the future of libertarianism for the Cato Institute in April, expects a decent reaction—at least a conversation—and instead finds himself in a crossfire of contempt and laughter. "The Education of a Libertarian" is not a bad piece; in another era, published in a newspaper, let's say, it might have been controversial for a day, but now it was etched into the permanent record. What was supposed to be a meditation on "the challenges faced by all classical liberals today" becomes quote-porn for haters. A comment about how the expansion of welfare benefits and the right to vote for women have not been kind to libertarian causes at the ballot box (since the only thing rarer than a libertarian is a female libertarian) tees up a *Valleywag* headline: "Facebook Backer Wishes Women Couldn't Vote." The line about whether "freedom and democracy are compatible" sets him up to look like a sort of technofascist. Owen Thomas, returning once again to mock Thiel, would use the piece to question whether Thiel was on drugs, an inference he said squared with rumors Gawker had heard about Thiel, particularly "while he was fitfully coming out as a gay man." Simultaneously, investors are pulling their money from Clarium. By July, assets under management have shrunk to well under $2 billion. The fund ends the year down 25 percent. And 2010 is no better—down another 23 percent with less than a billion under management, most of it Peter's own money.

A person unused to the spotlight, Peter finds himself blinking and reeling from the exposure, both financial and personal, and what he views as its consequences. In the midst of a third straight losing year, he "escapes New York," according to Gawker, shuttering Clarium's Manhattan headquarters and returning to the relative safety of San Francisco and the quirk-friendly Valley.

Gawker's not the only one that is making fun of him now, not the only one writing about him. Other outlets follow their lead, and the comments would haunt him every time he would do anything notable. Thiel does not like the attention. He feels a slipping of control, the changing tide of media that was washing over American culture. Taking your lumps for very public bad bets on the market is one thing. That's the cost of doing business in the hedge fund world. But now he can't even talk about politics without being made to sound like some drug-addicted fag? What is this? And whose fault is it? Who should be blamed? Nick Denton. *Valleywag*. They did this to me, he thinks. Gawker is responsible for all this.

"The external image of them was that they were super powerful. I was scared of them for years and years," Peter would say. In an interview he gave a month after his immediately infamous Cato piece was published, Thiel told a reporter that he felt *Valleywag* and Gawker were like Al Qaeda. He didn't understand how and why people would treat other people like that. To his friends, to the people he worked with, whenever Gawker would come up, he would refer to it as the MBTO—the Manhattan Based Terrorist Organization.

Most people, when they find something they don't like, do that. They call it names. They complain. They make it bigger than it is, make it representative of some larger trend. They think someone should do something, but never them. *Not me*. It's a classic collective action problem: we know things are bad, but they only affect each of us a little bit. So who is going to take care of it for us? Plenty of people believe in the theory of so-called great men of history, but who believes *I am that great man*? There is ego in that, silliness even.

The economist Tyler Cowen once observed that at some point in the 1970s, Americans went from being the country that took literal moonshots to being the people who waited patiently in long lines for gasoline. It's not completely accurate, of course, but it is a criticism that resonates with Thiel as he sits in his office at the Presidio one day looking at the Golden Gate Bridge and wonders if people will ever build something like that again. Do people even have the arrogance anymore? To test the limits? To try big things?

What's more, there is evil in not acting, too. To assume that a bad situation will resolve itself or that someone else will resolve it for you. Gawker was once just a blog with a few thousand page views, and then a few million—and now the rest of the media was following with their own blogs. As Thiel sat in meetings in his offices, another Gawker article about him or one of his companies would be the topic of discussion. Thiel would be raising the concerns that have always riled conservative minds: Where would this go next? Is this a trend? Can it be stopped? When Kierkegaard called gossipy newspapers dogs for the public's amusement in 1846, he did not say it with any sort of bemusement. In fact, they had driven him mad with anger. He had thought they would bring an end to all he cherished.

A century later, the reigning king of media was a tabloid columnist named Walter Winchell. Winchell had begun as a small-time showbiz columnist and grown, unchecked, until his work was consumed by some 50 million people in the United States alone. Including his radio broadcast and his infamous daily column, which was syndicated to more than two thousand newspapers and known simply as "The Column," Winchell reached two-thirds of the adult population.

The column was mostly fake news and prurient gossip. When it wasn't trafficking in rumors about the sex lives of celebrities, it peddled bogus stock tips, pushed government propaganda sourced from J. Edgar Hoover, and accused mostly innocent people of being Communists, Nazis, or homosexuals. And that's just the stuff that Walter Winchell actually wrote—a huge portion of the material in the column was directly submitted and written by press agents.

A 1940 *New Yorker* exposé once fact-checked the column and found that "of the 131 items in which individuals were named, fifty-four were completely inaccurate, twenty-four were partly inaccurate, and fifty-three were accurate." The writer then tells the story of a hypothetical executive considering a career move. On the man's mind is not his family, not his employer or his future employer, not what kind of work he can do, not even his own personal happiness—but how the move might be portrayed by the gossip columnist. *What will people think? What will Walter say about it?* The writer calls this the "Winchell Jitters." The subtle but cumulative effects of this phenomenon are real. Harried by the barbs of small-minded writers, who can do their best work, who can think of anything but their reputation and the risk of missteps?

"When personal gossip attains the dignity of print, and crowds the space available for matters of real interest to the community," future Supreme Court justice Louis Brandeis wrote in the *Harvard Law Review* in 1890, in a piece which formed the basis for what we now know as the "right to privacy," it "destroys at once robustness of thought and delicacy of feeling. No enthusiasm can flourish, no generous impulse can survive under its blighting influence." Brandeis's words reflected some of the darkness of Kierkegaard's worries from fifty years earlier and foretold some of that sullying paranoia that was still to come fifty years in the future. Thiel had read this article at Stanford. Many law students do. Most regard it as another piece of the puzzle that makes up American constitutional legal theory. But Peter *believed* it. He venerated privacy, in creating space for weirdos and the politically incorrect to do what they do. Because he believed that's where progress came from.

Imagine for a second that you're the kind of deranged individual who starts companies. You've created cryptocurrencies designed to replace the U.S. monetary system that somehow turned into a business that helps people sell Beanie Babies and laser pointers over the internet and ends up being worth billions of dollars. Where others saw science fiction, you've always seen opportunities—for real, legitimate business. You're the kind of person who is a libertarian before that word had any kind of social respectability. You're a conservative at Stanford. You're the person who likes Ayn Rand and thinks she's something more than an author teenage boys like to read. You were driven to entrepreneurship because it was a safe space from consensus, and from convention. How do you respond to social shaming? You *hate it*. How do you respond to petulant blogs implying there is something wrong with you for being a gay person who isn't public about his sexuality? Well, that's the question now, isn't it?

By the time Thiel had been outed by *Valleywag* at the end of 2007, he'd already begun to understand how that sexuality was at least part of who he was. People close to him knew about it, and clearly so did some people not close to him. Still, and not uncommonly, he felt stifled at the idea of being defined by this orientation, and it could only add to the frustration Thiel felt that Gawker, that Nick Denton, had been the one to set the terms of his identity. "The way in which Gawker handled these things was always in a purely polemical character. I think these categories are tricky even with the best of intentions. They easily go just terribly wrong in the hands of the MBTO," he says. There must have been a way that Gawker reminded Thiel of the self-righteous people he had been railing against since he was a conservative polemicist in college: the people who claim the moral high ground, who claim to be about freedom of choice, but who bully everyone who doesn't choose their way of freedom. For a complicated man with specific opinions about complex ideas, one might suspect that the gravest threat Gawker posed—why it seemed to him to be a form of terrorism—was the tendency for its trenchant, snarky reporting to become reductive and to cause collateral damage. Thanks to Nick Denton, now no matter what he did with his life, Peter would always be "Peter Thiel, the gay ___________." He may have been the only one who cared, but it must have eaten at Thiel the next year when he was named to *Out*'s Power 50 list, along with Nick Denton. Being defined by the very thing he wished to keep private, landing twelve spots *ahead* of the person who'd forced him to disclose that private fact?

Thiel saw Gawker not so much as a revolution but as anarchy masquerading as a movement. He saw it as cruel and unfair, but also a toxic force in intellectual life and free society. There's a way he clearly overreacted to being outed; it was a true fact and it likely would have come out at some point anyway. Yet in another way, the more he thought about it, the more he could see it as an element in a larger trend. It wouldn't be one article, it would be a cluster of them. Not just about him, but about people like him, too. "My main objection to Gawker is still this moral individual one—that they hurt individuals—but there is a cultural critique, too, I think. It's the kind of thing that's contributed to this sort of incredible homogenization,"

Peter says. What he fears is a culture that would deprive him of the freedom to think, to articulate his strange views, and what that might mean in Silicon Valley with its inestimable collection of strange people with equally strange views that have produced some of the greatest technological innovations and accumulations of personal wealth in the history of the world. And he feared more articles, too—more "Peter Thiel is totally __________, people."

These are the essential beginnings of a conspiracy. First, a slight of some kind, which grows into a larger dissatisfaction with the status quo. A sense that things should be different, and *will be* different, except for the worse, if something doesn't change. But then comes a second step, a weighing of the stakes. What if I do something about this? What might happen? What might happen if I do nothing? Which is riskier: to act or to ignore?

History is uncertain on this question, as were the people in Peter's life, the ones trying to tell him that there wasn't much that could be done. Peter would, at one point, pass me a copy of *The Fifteen Decisive Battles of the World* by Sir Edward Shepherd Creasy, the book he had read as he'd mulled his options over.

The epigraph to the chapter on the Battle of Valmy quotes Shakespeare:

> *A little fire is quickly trodden out,*
> *Which, being suffered, rivers cannot quench.*

The Battle of Valmy was an attempt, in 1792, by the powers of Europe to put down incipient revolution in France. Had they succeeded, the Reign of Terror might never have happened, Marie Antoinette and Louis XVI would have kept their heads, and Napoleon would not have been unleashed against the world.

Simple enough, except they did not succeed. The attempt to tread out the flames by the Prussians gave the French Revolution exactly what it wanted and needed: resistance. The French soldiers cried *Vive la Nation!*, rallied, and defeated the opposing armies. In victory, they abolished the monarchy and relieved the king and queen of their heads.

You rush in to stamp out the sparks and end up fanning them into flames. This is the risk.

In retrospect, sympathy, let alone understanding of this crossroads, is in short supply for a billionaire like Peter Thiel. But a rich man has feelings, just like a poor man, worries and fears and opinions like a regular man. The difference is that the former has a way of thinking that he ought to spend his money doing something about them. And rich men don't tend to like feeling small, feeling that same powerlessness they had once felt at a young age that had driven them to accomplish the things they had accomplished.

This buzzing frustration, this warmness in his cheeks is not a familiar feeling to the adult life of Peter Thiel. His anger is at odds with the cautious mind that is his nature; he is not a man prone to being ruled by his emotions. If someone asks him a question—say, about some controversial issue of the day—he does not simply react with an opinion, or pluck a conclusion from nowhere. Instead, he begins with, "One view of these things is that . . . ," and then proceeds to explain the exact opposite of what he happens to personally believe. Only after he has finished, with complete sincerity and deference, describing how most people think about the issue, will he then give you his opinion, which almost always happens to be something radically unorthodox—all of it punctuated with liberal pauses to consider what he is saying as he is saying it. Even when he does describe his opinion, he prefaces it with "I tend to think . . ." or "It's always this question of . . . ," as if what he is about to tell you is simply capturing where his opinion falls the majority of the time when running a thought exercise on the topic, as if he is always in the process of deciding what he thinks. And this is simply the process for articulating what he *thinks*.

And now he is thinking, Should I do something about this?

The conspirator who does not wish to be ruled by, to be run to ruin by, their emotions must engage in some version of this process. *No man attacks me with impunity* is well and good, but also a recipe for diving headfirst into a feud or a boondoggle. Instead, it's the careful consideration of the costs and benefits that separates the successful conspiracies from the regrettable ones—or the pyrrhic ones.

Not that there aren't baser motives as well. The reason and the *real reason*. If Thiel can shake that feeling of anger and hurt, he can't help but sit down and estimate the potential costs of Gawker and its coverage on his business interests. An inaccurate story about Facebook might derail its IPO or acquisition talks. One of his comments—and he knows he is going to keep making them—could be taken out of context, forcing him to resign from a board seat—or causing a founder to decline to work with him. A call from Gawker to its readers for rumors about Palantir could deprive the company of a major government contract. Public sentiment could be turned against one of his pet projects.

The downside risk might be in the billions of dollars. This is not an absurd estimation. In May 2007, an erroneous report by *Engadget*, a *Gizmodo* competitor, temporarily knocked $4 billion off the market cap of Apple. There had been a feud between one of Thiel's business partners, Sean Parker, and the venture capitalist Mike Moritz. There was a kernel of real conflict between the men, but the public nature of the feud, spurred on by Gawker, costs Peter's fund millions in commitments. The kind of mathematical equation someone like Peter might consider would look something like this: if there is a 20 percent chance that Gawker will cost me $1 billion, then it makes perfect sense to spend up to $200 million trying to prevent that from happening. Negative expected value—it's a calculation Wall Street guys make every day.

Sources around Thiel agree this is the math he would consider, in fact almost to the exact number. He, of course, denies that: "The simple cost-benefit calculation is that you don't do it. You don't do what I did." By that he means the risk of getting caught, and making things worse, is too high.

So at first the math says, you know, don't do anything. Just ignore it. Let it go. Listen to your friends.

"It's not like I started this in late 2007 right after the article. It was years of this, even after they laid off of me, they'd gone after people I knew, and it was, just, this is never going to end," he would explain. But still, a man can hope. A man can be patient. A man can fool himself for a while.

There are, of course, better and easier ways to make money, and to protect money, than conspiring against a media empire that has a record of roughly dispatching its challengers. Besides, Peter Thiel already had a lot of money. And it must have kept him busy. Suitors are knocking to buy Facebook, their offers creeping up from millions to a billion to *billions*. He had put $30 million of his partners' money and his own money into Palantir, and the company was busy chasing computer hackers and Chinese espionage rings.

Why should Gawker be his problem? Does he even have the time to try to solve it if it is?

Yet this is also what he is supposed to say—you never admit that it was about money. But if he looked beyond Gawker's potential cost to him in dollars to the cost to society in total, the math changed. What are the potential risks to his partners and friends? To the global economy? What is the societal cost of the "Gawker jitters"? If the continued effect of *Valleywag* is that it makes Silicon Valley 1 percent less ambitious, what is that cost? If one suicide is prevented and that person could have been a great founder or could have had one great idea? For every dollar in revenue that Gawker makes, how much economic value is it destroying, for Peter and for other people? And so even if this attempt is quixotic and impossible, even if it runs a real chance of making things worse, if you believe those things matter, if you're crazy enough to see yourself as someone who has the power to shape the world, doing something about Gawker might also be logical and justified.

Twenty-five hundred years ago, Thucydides would say that the three strongest motives for men were "fear, honor, and self-interest." Fear. Honor. Self-interest. All covered.

Which is the truest of them for Thiel? Does it matter?

Someone had begun to think seriously that something needed to be done and believed that he might be the person to do it.

CHAPTER 3

Turning to Conspiracy

Machiavelli said that conspiracies were *weapons of the people*. Only princes could afford to send an army against another army, he observed, but a conspiracy is available to every man. Which is why it is usually the desperate who turn to conspiracy and why the powerful fear them so much.

It's the self-perceived underdog who resorts to the so-called special means of evening the playing field, as the British did when they rushed to get onto a war footing in the late 1930s against a more heavily armed and ascendant Germany. It is the weaker party who relies on secrecy and surprise and "low tactics." Because they have to.

From 2007 to 2011, Peter Thiel is thinking about the "Gawker problem," as he had come to call it, and the language is illustrative. It's a problem. A *social* problem. A *cultural* problem. The MBTO. He's talking about Gawker not just intellectually, but about what can be done about it. He would discuss it in the office, he would discuss it with fellow tech moguls. Over dinners, he would ask the smartest people he knew. "For a number of years, after the various articles, the response was 'There's nothing we can do,'" he says.

The only suggestions they have are conciliatory. Learn the game, start to play it. Get thicker skin. Cozy up. Feed the machine gossip about your friends. Trade morsels about other people to replace the ones they have about you. Tamp down on behavior you might not want to see made public. Nick Denton would explain later that many of Thiel's peers in the Valley had come to accept this very arrangement, sending in tips to Gawker's tip line. It's the logic of two campers and the bear—you don't need to be faster than the bear, just faster than the other camper.

In early 2008, Peter reached out by way of a friend to an unusual and dapper attorney named Eddie Hayes. In addition to being a capable lawyer, Hayes also served as literary inspiration to the author Tom Wolfe, was a friend of the late Andy Warhol, and is a talented actor who played Robert De Niro's lawyer in *Goodfellas*, as well as De Niro's attorney in real life. He is a notorious and well-connected "fixer" who has been a confidant and problem solver for actual mob bosses, celebrities, artists, and politicians. His infamous slogan, "I can get ya outta anything!," must have called out to Thiel, and so too did his connections in New York media. It is on Eddie's advice that Peter makes his first attempts to play ball, to work through those traditional and pseudo-traditional channels. Beginning that year, Thiel would make the first of what would ultimately amount to more than $1 million in contributions to the Committee to Protect Journalists. It's one of the simplest and oldest options: let's see if some of my money might soften this antagonism between us.

Eddie sees that Thiel's main problem isn't a legal one, it's that he's an outsider: not only does Thiel not like playing the game, he doesn't even understand the game. So Eddie begins making introductions, first to Choire Sicha, Gawker's editor in 2003 and again in 2007, as well as to other journalists whom Thiel ought to meet.

It would be the meetings with Choire Sicha that would be most revealing, for both of them. At the first in late May 2008, and the second on an early morning two weeks later, Choire is bubbly and gregarious. Thiel is already secretive and defensive. He had spoken to Choire to arrange their meeting only through intermediaries and requested that it be held in Thiel's apartment. "Peter's view of these things was almost European," Choire would say. "He asked, 'Why would anyone write these things about anyone? Why would anyone write about anyone, *at all*?' He saw this writing as mean—almost a form of business hostility—and he was looking for insight about why anyone would do this." Choire would remark later about how much Peter reminded him of Nick. Each of them seemed to be living in his own sci-fi novel, and human connection did not come readily for either of them. Encouraging Peter to get to know more people in New York, Choire urged him to follow Hayes's advice and to actually spend time with and meet some of the writers at Gawker as a way of humanizing his image. Peter's response was that "if I talk to them, it will be worse."

Choire could only nod silently to himself and think, *you're probably right*, as events would soon prove. Through Choire and Hayes, Thiel is also introduced to Ryan Tate, who in 2009 became the editor of *Valleywag*. At a wine bar in Palo Alto, Peter Thiel sits down with Tate and supposedly says, "See, I do negotiate with terrorists." In their meetings, Choire relented and began to give Peter some of the information that Peter had wanted about Nick, a man with whom he had made no secret of his own love-hate relationship. "The only thing Denton lives for is gossip," Choire would tell him. *It's almost pathological.* These things that are so big for you are very small to gossip writers, he said. A friend and writer would say in an interview around this time, "There's no point in writing about Nick if you can't get to the fundamental problem of his nihilism." Selfish people are easy to understand. They act on motives. It's when we begin to see that something deeper than self-interest is at play, that they cannot be made to see reason, that we begin to despair of ordinary means of resolution.

Another idea comes Peter's way in a series of long conversations with another frustrated billionaire who had seen himself made into one of Gawker's favorite targets, Napster and Facebook cofounder Sean Parker. Parker had seen his feud with Mike Moritz made public, he had seen untrue rumors published about himself and his friends on Gawker. So he suggests to Peter: Could we just buy the company? Could we buy it and change the editorial direction? Could we buy it and shut it down? The idea is as interesting as it is inconceivable. Mainly because Nick isn't selling, nor is he looking to hand the operation over anytime soon. "I imagine doing what I'm doing now for a very long time," he had told a reporter in a profile about Gawker in 2006. He doesn't seem to need more money, or want it. This is what Nick *lives for*, Choire Sicha had told Peter. And even if they could raise the money to buy Gawker Media, what then? They've just rewarded precisely the behavior Thiel wants to stop, created a gold rush for it.

To Thiel, Denton's unending lust for secrets, for attention, his strange insistence that he was a technology entrepreneur and not a journalist, and his need to be feared instead of respected were tells of sociopathy. "It's super unclear how to negotiate with sociopaths," Thiel said.

"At the time, it felt like a crazy uphill battle, you know, even with all the financial resources," Thiel would say of this period of consideration. "It was the nature of the thing. Gawker's power in part came from pretending that it was more powerful than it was." Once that power dissolves, as it would eventually by Peter's doing, it's difficult to remember how that once was the view.

But it was the view.

Alexandre Dumas once wrote that the king of the press has a throne everywhere. As Gawker's page views went from thousands to millions and then to billions annually, as the rest of the media rushed to court his favor (or avoid his disfavor) and copy Denton's business model, he began to accumulate both real power and perceived power.

Power through his access, through his platform, through his ability to break stories that other media outlets would have to follow, and through his own growing wealth. From 2007 to 2009, Nick Denton was spoken about in the way Machiavelli said that people would speak of a powerful prince—with "a thousand fears and a thousand hesitations." Few would think to consider Peter Thiel that way.

No one had challenged Gawker and won. In fact, almost no one had ever challenged the American media, period, and won. After the series of famous *Washington Post* stories by Bob Woodward and Carl Bernstein about the Watergate scandal in 1972, President Nixon not only fails to destroy the paper's publisher, Katharine Graham, he destroys himself in the process and officially ends the traditional deference between the press corps and the presidency. Barbra Streisand sues to remove a picture of her house from the internet, and not only does she lose, but more people see the photo than otherwise would. It is a behavioral phenomenon that gets dubbed, fittingly, the Streisand Effect and has stood as a warning since: the media always wins in the end.

Neither Nick nor Gawker was easy to talk to or influence. Denton kept his company independent for precisely this reason. The writers relished the fact that there were few editors, few publicists, few executives, few adults sticking their nose in things, trying to make the site more palatable or business-friendly. Those who came to Gawker with a complaint or believed they were being treated unfairly tended to see the opposite of whatever Margaret Thatcher saw when she met Mikhail Gorbachev: "I like him. We can do business together."

It is interesting that Nick and Peter come to be in conflict with each other, because despite any public or power differential, they are at first glance so similar. Both rich. Both foreign born, both immigrants who chased the American dream. Both gay men with elite educations. Both free-market libertarians who distrust the "system."

Both builders—entrepreneurs. These are two men who get pitched the same deals, who have money in the same banks, who occupy the same rarefied air of the 1 percent (more like .01 percent in reality). They are perhaps the only two people on the planet, one person who had studied them closely observed to me, who might actually identify as plutocrats. Both socially awkward, opaque, firm, who accomplished the same things as young men, which made them rightfully believe that they were special and extraordinary. Both take a quiet thrill in doing the things you aren't supposed to do.

There's a picture of Thiel in prep school uniform in South Africa, a blazer and shorts, carrying a briefcase instead of a backpack, with knee socks on. At eight, he has the look of someone who has already seen enough of the world to know what bullshit is, and to know that he's smarter than most of the people he has met, including the adults. And if Denton wasn't even more private than Thiel, hadn't obscured his own childhood even more than Thiel, we'd probably find a similar photo of him, another young outsider, another kid who doesn't like being told what to do, making the same look.

Yet it is clear that as similar as the two men were, something ate at one about the other. Owen Thomas's headline in 2008: "Does Nick Denton Wish He Were Peter Thiel?"

One of the most profound intellectual influences on Peter Thiel is a French thinker named René Girard, whom he met while at Stanford and whose funeral he would eventually speak at in 2015. Girard's theory of mimetic desire holds that people have no idea what they want, or what they value, so are drawn to what other people want. They want what other people have. They covet. It's this, Girard says, that is the source of almost all the conflict in the world. Is this not the source of the tension between Denton and Thiel, not because they are so different, but because they are so similar?

Still there is a chasm between them, the power differential that put one in position to out the other. Growing into his role as a maverick publisher, Nick Denton had through the years developed the confidence of a journalistic gangster, a man who didn't just flirt with the edge, he got married and built an impressive home there. Perhaps he hadn't made as much money as Thiel, but his profile and his impact were more immediately and culturally recognized. Perhaps he assumed that Thiel felt powerful and would brush the attacks off. More likely, perhaps Denton assumed that Thiel would recognize that this was the game. That this was a tax on successful, rich people—being mocked and teased online. Or perhaps it was simply the traditional arc of the bully who becomes empowered the more he picks on others, grows to like the feeling it creates, and the longer he goes unchallenged, the more he comes to convince himself the status quo is tolerable for everyone involved.

And if it isn't, what to do? The conspirator asks: Can anything be done?

"At some point, Thiel's stance hardened," Denton would later observe of the period after Thiel had reached out to Hays. "I came away after thinking there was nothing to do here," Peter would tell me about his meetings with people on the periphery of Gawker in 2008, 2009, and 2010. You might say that it was not that diplomats on either side of the issue failed, but that their respective powers held irrevocably opposing positions which no amount of conversation could possibly bridge. The conflict between Denton and Thiel was not simply ideological, it was personal and timeless, anthropological in the way that it was about far more than either of them. At a certain point, no amount of bargaining could have made Thiel happy, just as it couldn't have made Denton happy. He could never have toned down his coverage for the sake of someone else's feelings—even his own.

So if nothing would be possible through traditional channels, was there some other way to address this power disparity? To even the playing field? To exert leverage? To draw attention to the unfairness of the situation that will force action?

Many years later, a young girl would find herself in a position not unlike Peter's, despairing of the growing power of the right-wing troll Milo Yiannopoulos. Controversy was only fueling his celebrity. Traditional remedies had not been effective. And the man was legally allowed to say the things he was saying. So she takes it upon herself to solve this problem. Listening to hours and hours of his interviews, she found something Milo had said that went far beyond what most people had instinctively recoiled from, something his fair-weather allies and even his friends would not be able to ignore: comments he'd made about very young boys having sex with much older men. Their release coordinated with a conservative group, and then quickly distributed to the rest of the media, the clips would set in motion a cascade of events. Within the week, Milo had lost his book deal, had resigned from his powerful position at *Breitbart*, and was essentially laughed out of popular culture as a pedophile apologist. Less than a year later, his powerful backers had publicly disowned him, too.

But there is no such leverage against a Nick Denton.

"Nick is a tough guy to get revenge on," A. J. Daulerio would explain. "The traditional ways, like smear campaigns, won't work for Nick. One thing I learned from him was to keep all your shit out, in public, and ultimately, that's a protective shield." In one exchange in the comments section over a gooey viral article that had an unhappy ending, Gawker writers and Denton debated publicly the kind of issue that most newsrooms would talk about only in private whispers: whether they were obligated to debunk stories that were shared widely on social media. Denton said they probably should. The editor replied, "If and when that happens our traffic will crater. . . ." Denton would explain in an interview with *Playboy* that this kind of radical honesty was partly a defense strategy: "The easy way to insulate yourself against snark is to preemptively snark. Snark before anybody else does. That's a kind of classic defensive humor. Make fun of yourself before somebody else does and lower everybody's expectations. . . . I lower everyone's commercial expectations. 'Oh, nothing to see here. There's no business here. This thing has the revenue of a hamburger stand. We have no journalistic ambitions. If we ever commit journalism, it's by accident.'"

Gawker's public image served as a kind of abatis, a sharp, intimidating preliminary line of defense. It wasn't impossible to overcome, but it did make you think twice about getting tangled up with it. Which Nick Denton depended on—the business wouldn't work if everyone they wrote about followed up with a lawsuit or leveraged their contacts to get him to rein in reporters. The result for Peter Thiel, then, was a kind of helplessness. He couldn't easily hold Gawker accountable for what he saw as bullying, or chasten it with public criticism; he couldn't even embarrass Nick or Owen Thomas if he had wanted to, not the way you could with an ordinary group that accepts the rules of society. One can't shame the shameless. Gawker had embraced a role that meant it didn't have any. It had preemptively made itself next to impossible to criticize. It was the bully that had convinced people it was the underdog, and was so confident in it, it even told everyone that's what it was doing.

"I came to believe that the nastiness of the internet was not a function of a technology or various things that have gone wrong, but the function of one particularly nasty media company led by a particularly sociopathic individual and that if I defeated Gawker, it would actually change the media landscape," Thiel would say. It was the point where he transitioned from thinking someone should do *something* to thinking that that something was more than could be accomplished in a few private meetings arranged by a fixer.

One will come upon situations in life where it becomes increasingly clear that the normal playbook will not work. No working out of differences. No backroom deals. We reach the point where we believe that the normal remedies will not be enough. Where we are significantly outmatched or unsympathetic. We reach a point where even the out-of-the-ordinary remedies will not suffice. The kinds of situations that even an Eddie Hayes can't get us out of.

It is here that we begin to look beyond the playbook, to create our own. It's this frustrating ground that births the conspiracy.

"At the end of the day, Hayes convinced me there was nothing to do within 'normal' channels and pushed me toward either doing nothing or doing something outside the 'normal' channels—and we chose to do the latter, starting in 2011," Peter would say.

It is always revealing to see how a person responds to those situations where he's told: "There's nothing you can do about it. This is the way of the world." Peter Thiel's friend, the mathematician and economist Eric Weinstein, has a category of individual he defines as a "high-agency person." How do you respond when told something is impossible? Is that the end of the conversation or the start of one? What's the reaction to being told you *can't*—that no one can? One type accepts it, wallows in it even. The other questions it, fights it, rejects it.

This choice defines us. Puts us at a crossroads with ourselves and what we think about the kind of person we are.

"Anyone who is threatened and is forced by necessity either to act or to suffer," writes Machiavelli, "becomes a very dangerous man to the prince."

And Peter Thiel was driven into a desperate position, of and not of his own making, that had started with a matter of his identity and become about a deeper identity. Now he had not only decided to act against Gawker, but he would *conspire* to destroy them.

CHAPTER 4

Assembling the Team

Machiavelli writes that a conspiracy without any coconspirators is not a conspiracy. It's just a crime. This is also basic legal principle. If you kill someone by yourself, in the heat of the moment, it's murder. If you meticulously plan it with someone else beforehand, that's conspiracy.

Lee Harvey Oswald almost certainly assassinated John F. Kennedy by himself. What he hoped would happen as a result is unclear. John Wilkes Booth *conspired* not only to assassinate Abraham Lincoln, but working with Lewis Powell and George Atzerodt also aimed to assassinate Andrew Johnson and William Seward. It was a coordinated attempt by Confederate sympathizers to usurp the United States government. It's not simply a single crime, but a crazed, desperate effort to turn back the tide of a lost war.

In his definitive book on the subject of strategy, Lawrence Freedman writes that "combining with others often constitutes the most strategic move." By definition, the first move in the act of a conspiracy is the assemblage of allies and operators: your coconspirators. Someone to do your bidding, to work with you, someone you can trust, who agrees with you that there's a problem, or is willing to be paid to agree with the sentiment that it's about time *someone, somebody* did something about this. Each hand doesn't need to know what the other is doing, but there needs to be more than one set.

Thus, Thiel's vague idea to do something about Gawker is concretized into conspiracy on April 6, 2011. It began unremarkably, when Thiel traveled to Germany to speak at a conference and had dinner with a student he'd met on a tour of a university a few years before. Peter arrives, driven in a black S-class Mercedes, the same model he has idling outside with a driver, twenty-four hours a day, seven days a week, wherever he is in the world. From the hotel emerges a short, fit young man of indiscernible origin. Aside from his Ivy League education, the young man has at this point achieved next to nothing. But Peter attracts these types—mostly men early in their potentially ascendant careers—and puts them to good use: investing in them, giving them advice, placing them in start-ups, assigning them important roles in his operations. This specific young man in Berlin we shall refer to as Mr. A, the pseudonym that almost everyone involved in the conspiracy refers to him by.

Mr. A is not just young, but ambitious, ambitious in a way that makes observers slightly uncomfortable, that makes him stand out even among the cadre of upstarts in Peter's orbit. It's not fame he wants, or money either, or even to create the next big tech company. He read Machiavelli at thirteen. He's fascinated by power and knows that Peter is a means by which he can wield it.

There is a scene in the movie *The Assassination of Jesse James by the Coward Robert Ford*. At the beginning, in the woods, Robert Ford, played by Casey Affleck, illustrates this phenomenon. He thinks the outlaw Jesse James is a great man. He thinks that he, himself, is a great man, too. He wants someone to recognize that in him. He wants someone to give him an opportunity—a project through which he can prove his worth. It just happens that Frank James would size the delusional, awkward boy up in the woods outside Blue Cut, Missouri: "You don't have the ingredients, son."

In contrast, Mr. A is ambitious, but it's paired with self-confidence, social adeptness, and a clear sense of what Thiel wanted. Even so, the prospect of meeting with Thiel is intimidating: his stomach churning, every nerve and synapse alive and flowing. He's twenty-six years old. He's sitting down for a one-on-one evening with a man worth, by 2011, some $1.5 billion and who owns a significant chunk of the biggest social network in the world, on whose board of directors he also sits. Even if Thiel were just an ordinary investor, dinner with him would make anyone nervous. One quickly finds that he is a man notoriously averse to small talk, or what a friend once deemed "casual bar talk." Even the most perfunctory comment to Thiel can elicit long, deep pauses of consideration in response—so long you wonder if you've said something monumentally stupid. The tiny assumptions that grease the wheels of conversation find no quarter with Thiel. There is no chatting with Peter about the weather or about politics in general. It's got to be, "I've been studying opening moves in chess, and I think king's pawn might be the best one." Or, "What do you think of the bubble in higher education?" And then you have to be prepared to talk about it at the expert level for hours on end. You can't talk about television or music or pop culture because the person you're sitting across from doesn't care about these things and he couldn't pretend to be familiar with them if he wanted to.

They are seated to dinner at Restaurant Tim Raue promptly at 8:00 p.m. A reservation has been called ahead, a good table secured, in a restaurant that has hosted Obama, Merkel, and other world leaders. This was Berlin, not far from Checkpoint Charlie, but it could have been New York, Los Angeles, London, Brussels, Tokyo. It's quiet, filled with the kind of global elites who need to know that wherever you are in the world you get your two-Michelin-star-quality sautéed brussels sprouts and pork belly. Feigning confidence, Mr. A glances at the menu and orders the eight-course tasting menu. Peter beckons the sommelier over to order wine. He asks what kind of wine Mr. A likes. Hearing Riesling, he makes his request: "We'll have a bottle of this one." It's the second most expensive Riesling on the menu.

The butterflies settle. The conversation has wound itself down naturally and now there is nothing left but for Mr. A to seize the moment. This moment that few get. The chance for a pitch that can change your life. There is something popular with ambitious people called the "briefcase technique." You don't show up to a meeting with a few vague ideas, you have a full-fledged plan that you take out of your briefcase and hand to the person you are pitching. Even if nothing comes of this plan, the person on the other side is knocked over by your effort, so impressed by the unexpected certainty that they cannot help but see your usefulness to them. Mr. A unlocks that figurative briefcase on the table: "Okay, I know what you think about Gawker, here's what I am proposing. . . ."

Thiel had spoken about Gawker many times. He had spoken about it in interviews, he had complained about it to friends. It had come up in passing in conversation when Mr. A and Thiel had first met a few years before. Now sitting at this table in the city that birthed a thousand Cold War plots and counterplots, Thiel finds that first successful return of those many trial balloons. Ambition and opportunity have collided and the kid in front of him is proposing a solution to that problem that Thiel has set upon trying to solve: Peter should create a shell company to hire former investigative reporters and lawyers to find causes of action against Gawker. Gawker has written thousands of articles about thousands of people; it must have made a mistake somewhere. Mr. A's proposal is more than just an idea, it's a comprehensive, structured plan: he has researched some names, he has a timeline and a budget.

Three to five years and $10 million.

Peter replies with one of his customary pauses. The silence hangs there, one second, two seconds, ten seconds, and like so many others before, Mr. A wonders if this suggestion is crazy, if he has blown his chance. And then Peter begins to talk, interrupts himself as he does, as if he still needs time to decide his own thoughts, and then repeats the words he has been told by so many others, so many times—that there was nothing that could be done. Has Peter come to believe this? Is he testing the young man before him?

Here is where the ambition and naïveté of youth are so powerful. Mr. A responded with words that were absurd for someone of his age, someone who in fact knew little about the world except from what he had read and learned in school. Except he was right and the words he spoke were the type a man like Thiel could not resist. "Peter, if everyone thought that way, what would the world look like?"

"Just hearing that was so refreshing," Peter would say later, "because of course what you always heard were these incremental things that wouldn't quite do it." Yet Gawker is hardly a pressing issue in 2011. *Valleywag*, the site that had written about Peter, has been temporarily shuttered. Mr. A is then in the position of convincing the healthy man how bad it is to be sick. He picks a seductive angle for Thiel then. He isn't talking about defense—not simply righting a wrong that had been done to him, or insulating his own business against someone with a grudge—but something that feels more noble and inspiring than that. It is more than the servant whispering to Darius, "Master, remember the Athenians." It is *Peter, think about all the people they've hurt. It's going to keep happening.*

It's only going to get worse. If you—the billionaire—can't do anything about it, who can?

Peter had seen many ambitious upstarts out of what Alexandra Wolfe called the "eternal freshman herds" of Silicon Valley. But Mr. A is different. Multiple people, describing him to me, borrowed Robert Caro's description of LBJ as a young man: a *professional son*. Lyndon Johnson knew how to identify a susceptibility for protégés in older successful people and then make himself into theirs. Mr. A had that. In fact, he would self-identify with the label of professional son, too.

The professional son understands what every father wants—a progeny worth his time, someone to invest in, someone who can further his legacy. The professional father wants to see his greatness given a second body—a younger one, with more energy, with the benefit of his hard-won experiences. Peter was then not married, and he has no children. There is a loneliness there.

Rooted in every conspiracy is often shared loneliness, a smoldering frustration or bitterness. Of not being listened to. Of the world not understanding. Two people come together and this smoldering becomes the small flicker of a flame for the first time. *Someone shares this with me. I am not alone.* Two is more than one and can become three, four, five quickly. And so across the table at that restaurant in Berlin, the conspiracy begins.

It would be a mistake to confuse Peter's pondering Socratic-ness for uncertainty. His mind, for all its detours and considerations, ultimately meanders toward precision, the kind that calculates down to the ten-thousandth decimal point in ordinary conversation. He is the kind of man who might make a multimillion bet without hesitation. It's only if you ask him a question about an arcane point in Russian literature that you get the long pause of consideration. *He wouldn't want to just spout off.* But if he thinks he has some deep idea about human nature, about the market, he'll go all in.

In this case, after a few hours with a person he knew only socially, at a meeting that ended in a hotel bar at 3:00 a.m., Thiel committed up to $10 million on an uncertain venture. There is much brainstorming left to do but he has given the green light. Thiel has committed to pursuing a conspiracy through the most untraditional of means—not with the help of some PR specialist; not with some grizzled political operative who knows how to grease palms or lobby the right lawmakers; but by investing entirely in a person who had literally not accomplished a thing in his life. When the CIA plots the overthrow of some foreign government, they don't turn to the most junior agent and say, "We'll follow your lead."

As with many alliances, the two have differing motives. Thiel seems to be alternately compelled by a sense of justice and an interest in doing the impossible. To him, Gawker is a vicious thing, a cultural problem that he can solve. To Mr. A, it is, at least at first, simply an opportunity. Rich Cohen once wrote that "one definition of evil is to fail to recognize the humanity in the other: to see a person as an object or tool, something to be put to use." Gawker's writers were certainly guilty of that sin, but getting into that black car with Peter, Mr. A had a similar evil in his heart. Destroying Gawker was just a way for him to make his mark. To be the professional son. To show a big and important person that he had the ingredients to do something equally big and important.

It was paramount to Peter that he not be associated with the plot in any way. Some would later argue that this is inherently deceitful, but I'm not sure why that would be so. The hiring of the anonymous cutout is not just practical—a young kid will attract less attention, he is the messenger who can travel here and there without notice, and is a billionaire really supposed to do all the work himself?—it is more a matter of strategy. If Thiel wishes to set a precedent with the Gawkers of the world, it is better that it appears the *world* is sending that message and not someone with a personal score to settle. It would be better were it to appear that whatever fate befell Gawker happened not because some rich person had brought it about, but because it was a matter of justice and fairness and karma. This would mean that Thiel would never be associated with the events he is about to put in motion, that the public will have no idea who was ultimately responsible. Strategically, practically, Mr. A represents those things. He is also, more simply, there to take the fall if something goes wrong.

With his first hire, Thiel's conspiracy is stronger, by virtue of simply existing, yet it is also naturally weaker. This is the risk of combining with allies. The strategic benefit of adding a new coconspirator comes at the cost of substantially increasing the chance of getting caught. While you do want to find the right people . . . you typically want as few of them as possible.

A few weeks later, Mr. A finishes his exams, graduates, and flies home to see his parents on one of the last planes he will board with an economy ticket. He is excited, yet he cannot say a word about why—to them or anyone. Within a week, he is with Peter at his home in New Zealand. The planning begins. The whirlwind of travel will not stop until he is nearly thirty.

The image of Silicon Valley is that the start-up comes together quickly, from idea to minimum viable product to world-changing business in a montage of exciting steps. In truth, like conspiracies, it takes a little longer. The path can be meandering. PayPal's anti-fraud insights took several years to become Palantir. Thiel had registered the name before he truly founded the company that looked for outside investment. Even Peter's hedge fund had been something he'd started before PayPal and only came back to after PayPal. Thiel calls this the *prehistory* of a company, of a conspiracy.

The two conspirators meet again that summer at Peter's home in San Francisco, beginning a routine that would become a compartmentalized piece of their lives for the next half decade: meetings at one of Peter's homes to strategize. Regular phone calls to check in. Their discussions would confirm a theory that both Mr. A and Thiel had developed independently. "Gawker's modus operandi was to have hurtful speech with no repercussions because they believed that the court system didn't work, that the people had no access to it," Peter said. Thiel and Mr. A are both law school graduates, but in their meetings they had concluded that any legal testing of this theory would require the addition of someone who had actually passed the bar, and then they would need to bring into the conspiracy the lawyer who would represent them in the cases they might bring. Because the United Kingdom has long been seen as more favorable to lawsuits against publishers, Mr. A begins to research the case law. Finding this angle promising, he goes to London to interview law firms and get legal advice—hoping to find a partner. At a set of swanky law offices near the Museum of London he is told that revenge cases were not their forte and that such a scheme was unlikely to succeed. The firm suggests some American firms that might have a taste for blood, including some based in Los Angeles. One stands out. Even the name is more fitting for what Thiel and Mr. A are trying to do: *Wolf* Rifkin.

Wolf Rifkin is a powerful law firm, but let's just say it's considerably less classy than the Brits who had made the referral. Its office is above the headquarters for Krav Maga Worldwide. The main tenant in its building in West Los Angeles is Wonderful Pistachios. Sandwiched between the headquarters for a self-defense system renowned for its brutal counterattacks and a massive distributor of nuts that are notoriously hard to crack was the perfect law firm for Peter Thiel.

Almost a year after his own meeting with Thiel, Mr. A meets with an attorney named Charles Harder to potentially recruit him into the conspiracy. Charles Harder is tall and thin with sandy blond hair then and now smeared with gray at the temples. He's prone to the occasional Jackie Chiles–esque rhetorical flourish: "It's repugnant, I think it's unethical, I think it's immoral, I think it's disgusting and filthy." He has the tan and the blue eyes that only Californians seem to have. He dresses in that Beverly Hills chic of jeans and a plaid button-up that still somehow costs hundreds of dollars, but there is no doughiness there, it's the lean body of a former athlete. In many ways he is the opposite of Thiel—stylish, at ease, upbeat, and gregarious. Before this case, his name was unknown and unseen outside *Hollywood Reporter* articles about lawsuits that George Clooney filed against electronics companies for using his image without permission. As recently as 2009, Harder was fighting on behalf of celebrities to get their domain names back from squatters. His own website celebrated domain name wins that year for Kate Hudson and Sandra Bullock and Cameron Diaz and Sigourney Weaver, and not much else.

Mr. A finds himself confiding in this unlikely coconspirator, a lawyer whose name isn't on the building, who had no outsized reputation, explaining, "I have been charged to take down a major media outlet by a group of wealthy individuals who will fund causes of action. Would you be interested?" The answer is yes, Harder is interested. Very interested.

Mr. A takes a certain pride in this little lie, the use of the word *individuals* instead of individual. Throughout the conspiracy, he would try to refer to Thiel as "my principals"—implying that there was some consortium of backers involved. Mr. A believed it was much less likely that Harder would demand to speak to them, to go over the head of this twenty-something, if it was much less clear whom he would be going to. And finally, the plurality of benefactors gave Mr. A a certain duplicative freedom. If money was slow, he could blame the delay on coordination problems. If he was unsure of something, he could buy time to deliberate. He could use the illusion of a group for pressure, as cover for different opinions, for expressing doubts, and for anything else he needed.

And what does Harder see in this twenty-something who has come into his office, who alternates between fantastical certainty and obsequious flattery? He sees the same thing that Peter Thiel sees in the professional son: an opportunity, energy, raw potential, and talent. Even if he is skeptical of the venture, Harder sees something less glamorous but much more real than conviction or righteous anger: billable hours. In the language of the legal profession: churn, baby, churn.

From here begins the dance of recruitment, the sussing out of intentions without revealing too many of your own. How much can Mr. A share without saying the name? *Gawker*. How enticing can he be about his financial position without making himself seem like a deep-pocketed mark? He would have asked simple questions: What do you know about this company, Gawker Media? What do you think about them? How do you work? Harder would have asked some of his own: What does success look like for you? Why are you doing this?

Harder doesn't ask directly, not then, not ever: Who is behind this? He seems entirely comfortable with being the hatchet man for an unknown entity with unknown motivations. He could have been working for a dictator or for Gawker's competitor just trying to damage a rival. Mr. A would say that Harder's strength was *compartmentalization*: he was content with his role on the team. He could manage the inherent difficulty of serving two masters, his clients and his *client*, without violating his obligations as a lawyer, and knew how to keep those obligations from ever conflicting with each other.

This compartmentalization is key to a conspiracy. Not everyone can be in charge. Mr. Harder works for the clients whose bills are paid by Mr. A, who works for Mr. Thiel (while Mr. Harder does not know who Mr. Thiel is). Not everyone can know every element, or give their opinion on all of it. Not every decision can be explained or needs to be. At some point, some people's job is just to answer the phones, to press the buttons, to shred the documents, to argue in court, because that's what they are paid to do. They are paid to do *a job.*

But that's the nice thing about lawyers: as long as you're paying them, they're usually good with whatever terms go along with it. Compartmentalization *is* their job. It's how they represent people who are guilty, how they file long motions they know are unlikely to be successful, how they can patiently keep secrets that they'd otherwise love to be able to share.

Harder was nearly twenty years into his legal career when he was first approached. Though he often worked on celebrity cases they tended to be for routine matters, not exciting criminal proceedings or blockbuster cases, and when you're retained to enforce rights of privacy and publicity on behalf of your clients, it tends to follow that they don't want you grandstanding in the media on their behalf, building a profile as you work for them. His last appearance in the *New York Times* had been in 2001, about a case for a client who had been let go from an ad firm almost immediately after she left her new job to join it. Harder won two months' back pay. It's not exactly the kind of victory that marked the career of lawyers like Marty Singer, whom Harder had once worked for, and whom the *Times* had called the "Guard Dog to the Stars." A lawyer who *had* publicly fought cases over celebrity sex tapes, who tangled with Gawker once on behalf of Rebecca Gayheart and the actor Eric Dane when their tape had run on Gawker and managed to eke out a small settlement, without an admission of guilt. So why not hire Singer? Because Peter Thiel and Mr. A didn't want someone who was content to settle, or another lawyer who knew the standard Hollywood saber-rattling routine. They wanted someone who would win. Now, in mid-2012, they appear to have that man.

In the search for collaborators, hunger is an essential qualification. While it's dangerous to conspire with people who have a lot to lose, you can't conspire without someone who is afraid to bet on themselves, who isn't willing to take a big stake on something that very well could fail. Where these two traits overlap there is often a sweet spot: the man or woman who has something to prove *and* something to protect, the strong sense of self-belief coupled with that killer instinct.

It's these two, Mr. A and Charles Harder, one much older than the other, who will do the bulk of the work and both walk this delicate balance of hunger and competence. In the business of bringing down Gawker, Mr. A was the president, Harder was the CEO, and Thiel the majority shareholder who expected his men to mind his money and find the returns he is after. This is the model he likes to operate. Early in the two companies he cofounded, PayPal and Palantir, Thiel would install strong CEOs and leaders. He relies on what might be called the plenipotentiary model—empowering trusted, skilled people on his behalf to execute the bold vision he has created. In Mr. A and Harder, he needed representatives whose judgments were close enough to his own that he could be confident in his ignorance of specific issues and deploy them to the places he couldn't go, trusting them to discern which decisions were important enough to be made by Thiel alone.

For someone who walked away from one of the biggest law firms on the planet, it is with some irony that the conspiracy would create, as his third company, a law firm. But Thiel is a big enough and demanding enough client that within the next six months Harder will leave Wolf Rifkin for his own shingle, Harder Mirell & Abrams LLP. The conspiracy itself is its own kind of company. One made up of three men, with differing motivations but a shared ambition and an accepted vision—to leave a mark, to do something that was said to be impossible.

A start-up is, in Peter's definition, "a small group of people that you've convinced of a truth that nobody else believes in." This is a fitting definition of what has assembled here as well. More people would be added as time passed. Allies and enemies of enemies would be brought into the fold. But all of it would proceed from the shared belief of these three men that the destruction of Gawker might be possible. Now they had their first decision to make together: *how*.

CHAPTER 5

Finding the Back Door

We are often taught that successful strategy is a matter of boldness, but it has also always been the case that it's as much a matter of patience and due diligence as it is of noticeable action.

By early 2012, nearly five years have passed since Peter Thiel was unceremoniously introduced to Gawker Media and its polemical ways. It hadn't taken too long after that Wednesday in December for him to decide that something had to be done, but it had taken four full years since then to conceive of *what kind of response might even be possible*. Thiel founded and sold PayPal in considerably less time. Now he has finally made some progress, but just barely. A team has been assembled: Mr. A has been enlisted; Harder has been identified. A hire and a half. That's it. But this is good.

"With patience and resources," Mr. A would come to say often on his weekly calls with Peter, "we can do almost anything." Tolstoy had a motto for Field Marshal Mikhail Kutuzov in *War and Peace*—"Patience and Time." "There is nothing stronger than those two," he said, ". . . they will do it all." In 1812 and in real life, Kutuzov gave Napoleon an abject lesson in the truth of that during a long Russian winter.

The target, Nick Denton, is not a patient man. Most entrepreneurs aren't. Most powerful people are not. One of his editors would say of Denton's approach to stories, "Nick is very much of the mind that you do it now. And the emphasis is to get it out there and be correct as you can, but don't let that stand in the way of getting the story out there." Editorially, Nick Denton wanted to be first—which is a form of power in itself. But this isn't how Thiel thinks. He would say his favorite chess player was José Raúl Capablanca, and remind himself of the man's famous dictum: To begin you must study the end. You don't want to be the first to act, *you want to be the last man standing.*

History is littered with examples of those who acted rashly in pursuit of their goals, who plunged ahead without much in the way of a plan, and suffered as a result. One could argue that the bigger of Nixon's two blunders wasn't his attacks on the Democratic Party but the decision to go after Katharine Graham and the media, and yet both decisions were the product of a fundamental lack of patience and discipline. Or consider the late head of Fox News, Roger Ailes, who responded to a series of Gawker articles and attacks by allegedly hiring private detectives to follow the reporters around. Not only did he find nothing of practical value, but these heavy-handed tactics came back to embarrass and discredit him at his most vulnerable moment. In fact, two weeks after the news of this disturbing conspiracy broke, he would be dead.

How ought one do it then?

We might think again of Eisenhower who, as president, held considerable power, certainly more than the opponent before him: Joseph McCarthy, then at the height of his power as a demagogue. Though most Americans would come to see Eisenhower as the kindly, friendly "Ike," they did not realize that beneath that exterior was a cunning strategic mind that knew how to wield power without raising alarms and was, if anything, a patient plodder. And that the first part of powerful ability had its roots in that awakening he had from the ignominious defeat of the Chicago "Black Sox" to the Cincinnati Reds in 1919. He decided not to rush in or take things at their first appearances. Seeing that opposition and publicity were what gave McCarthy his power, he looked for a better opportunity. Eisenhower began to work behind the scenes, directing and pushing for others to limit McCarthy's power, stripping the man of allies, using his own allies to criticize him, removing opportunities McCarthy would have liked to take advantage of. It's because of this use of the "hidden hand" that McCarthy never knew that the president was working against him, and so when Eisenhower crushed McCarthy, and crushed him completely using the man's weaknesses against him, it would be decades before historians could even piece the evidence together.

So the user of special means must scorn the obvious—ignore the conventional wisdom and voices from the sideline. Eisenhower watched as McCarthy attacked his closest friends, pocketing at one point a full-throated defense of George Marshall that he must have wanted to give so badly, because while it might have scored public points against his opponent, it wasn't the *right* strategy.

"It's almost limitless what one *could* do," Mr. A says, musing on all the theoretical angles of attack they brainstormed in meetings at Thiel's house and in late-night phone calls. Given the resources he had to draw on, the limitlessness of the options is nearly true: they could have bribed employees at Gawker to leak information, or hired operatives to ruin the company from the inside. They could have directed hackers to break into Gawker's email servers. Someone could have followed Nick Denton and, while he dined at Balthazar one morning, stolen his cell phone. A team could have attempted to bug the Gawker offices. You could fund a rival website, operate it at a loss, and slowly eat away at the razor-thin margins of Gawker's business. Or create a blog that does nothing but report on gossip about Gawker writers—returning the very pressure and scrutiny they'd put on other people. "There are things that were very tempting, an eye for an eye, tooth for a tooth. Retributive justice," Peter said. "But I think those would've ultimately been self-defeating. That's where you just become that which you hate." The victory would be pyrrhic, too, easier but at a higher personal cost.

A decision was made to eliminate the strategies that would either be illegal or fall into any one of a number of gray areas. For instance, Thiel could have easily hit Gawker with many meritless cases that he never expected to win in order to bury the company in legal bills, but how effective would that really have been? It's a brute-force tactic that ignores the strategic value of exploiting your opponent's fundamental weakness—if one could be found. "There were all these things that you could be tempted to do and it's not clear they would work any better. So we decided very early on we would only do things that are totally legal, which is a big limitation. But it forced us to think really hard about what to actually do," says Peter. "We were comfortable taking a very aggressive legal posture, just entirely within the system."

As they had decided from the outset, Thiel would not be a claimant in any of these cases and, equally early, Thiel claimed to be interested only in litigating and funding claims that could be expected to survive appeal, were they fortunate enough to reach a positive verdict. "We had the idea early on that there must have been any range of legal violations," Peter tells me, echoing the thrust of Mr. A's pitch to him in Berlin the previous April, "but I wanted to find a cause of action that wasn't libel." Harder agrees; legally it's the strategically wise move, so they decide to avoid cases related to libel or defamation.

Libel and defamation cases are notoriously hard to win in the American legal system. They are fraught with First Amendment complications where the bias is always toward the publisher and the burden of proof on the claimant—especially if he or she satisfies the "public figure" standard—is overwhelming. A private citizen has to prove only negligence on the part of the publisher. A public figure has to prove "actual malice"—that the publisher either knew beforehand that its statements were false or acted with "reckless disregard" as to the truth of the published statements. This was the issue that rendered fruitless so many of Peter's encounters with sympathetic ears in the years after his initial outing.

"I had conversations with a number of different people over the years—in 2008, 2009, 2010—and they naturally ended with this learned helplessness where you never got to the endgame because the middle game would be too difficult," Thiel would say. "You bring a lawsuit and you get crushed. And I had enough of those conversations with enough people in Silicon Valley to conclude that there were a lot of people who maybe were vaguely thinking about it, but when you tried to concretize what to do . . . it's like, you know, *can't quite do it*."

There is a chance, of course, that Thiel is lying. Maybe there wasn't this vexed minority in the Valley suffering helplessly in silence. Maybe he had tried the other options first and they didn't work. Perhaps he really did hire private detectives to follow Nick Denton around and they found nothing. But there is no evidence he did or even considered it. That was one of the benefits of his patience: he wasn't angry anymore, he didn't need people rallying to his side. He wasn't thinking of revenge, but of accomplishing something that would stick.

"Peter is the kind of opponent you'd want," a friend would say about Peter's insistence on operating from principle, "except that you wouldn't want him to have unlimited resources." It is certainly the exception and not the rule that a conspiracy chooses to operate within the law—to use something as constraining as the legal system as their theater of operations. Then again, most conspiracies are defined by a certain desperation. Most do not begin with unlimited resources, most are not led by entrepreneurs who have an aptitude for organization and have, on retainer, a staff of brilliant legal minds. The jungle fighter doesn't choose guerrilla warfare from an array of strategies laid out in some glass-walled conference room. He must wield the only weapons available to him, however nasty and dirty they may be. Yet he, too, must make ethical choices, and draw his own lines.

Just because you decide to operate along a line of interior ethics, however, doesn't mean you're stupid about it. You don't have to disclose your intentions, for instance. No one said the fight needs to be *fair*, or that punches should be pulled. The search for weakness remains. The exploitation of that weakness is still the aim. You're just also looking to be able to say, as Mr. A believed he could, "The organization fell apart because of their own internal unethical conduct. We conducted ourselves with the utmost moral rectitude." The degree to which one succeeds or fails in this endeavor tends to determine not only how well one sleeps at night, but also how the public ultimately views who was in the right. Ethics don't win the war, but they do help keep the peace.

The shared truth of the conspirators is the belief that there is some legal means to get at Gawker. Charles Harder is first hired essentially as a consultant to actually test this hypothesis, to put exploratory muscle behind the goals and theories thus far batted about by Peter and Mr. A in their year of brainstorming and visits. It's his job to independently confirm what Gawker's Achilles' heel might be, so that if it falls—*when it falls*—it's under the weight of its own weakness. Ten thousand dollars is wired from Peter's people to Mr. A. Mr. A wires it to Harder. The scheme is under way. They don't yet know what their big move will be, but they are moving toward the move.

Harder is vaguely familiar with Gawker, in the way that every entertainment lawyer would be. Firms he has worked for in the past have sent their fair share of cease and desist letters on behalf of clients. Lavely & Singer, where Harder had worked several years before, had sued Gawker and negotiated a small settlement in a sex tape case, but he had not been involved. There was much to learn. Associates pored over close to a decade of articles, making phone calls, seeing what they could find. What can they do that is meritorious, effective, strategic? What are the weaknesses in an opponent that, as a matter of policy, airs its own dirty laundry and has, to this point, escaped every legal challenge and scandal? What vulnerabilities does Gawker have that other media outlets don't? Where, far from the favorable and insurmountable protections of the First Amendment, has it made mistakes? Has it overreached and made itself vulnerable?

Gawker's financial structure is complicated. It's based in the Cayman Islands, and it has a Hungarian-based subsidiary to which it sends millions of dollars annually. There are very few shareholders. It constitutes multiple sub-LLCs. All of this for the explicit purpose of reducing tax and legal liability. All of this also creates potential legal weaknesses. Had Gawker bent the law far enough to get itself into trouble?

Gawker's websites often link to websites with products for sale from which they take a small sales commission. There are arcane but mostly ignored laws about disclosing this relationship. Perhaps Gawker has not followed these rules properly or finds itself in violation due to differing local interpretations. Perhaps its lack of disclosures makes it vulnerable to regulation or prosecution in certain states. Could an oversight leave it open to prosecution or complaints?

Gawker is not a public entity, but a few employees and friends own shares. Could there be some sort of shareholder action to bring against the company? Or could acquiring shares bring the company's inner dealings and finances into play? A controlling share or control by proxy could be established, and Nick could be replaced—or the strategy of the company shifted. Was there an opening to do this?

Is Gawker dependent on certain patents or patent violations that could be purchased and then sued over? Is Gawker in violation of employment laws? Are there workplace infractions that could be exploited?

Each of these strategies had potential. Each needed to be explored, probed, and possibly eliminated. Only some would work, perhaps only one would work. "The gating resource here was not capital," Thiel said. "The gating resource was the ideas and the people and executing it well. It's not like lawsuits haven't been brought in the past. It's something that's been done, so we were required to think very creatively about this space, what kind of lawsuit to bring."

Most of the ideas do not stand up to scrutiny, or to Thiel's ambitions. A slap on the wrist from the FCC about affiliate commissions will accomplish little. Exploiting the financial misdeeds of the company would likely require an inside man, and this would be nasty, deceitful business. It wasn't just a question of which strategy might actually win, it was also figuring out which one could actually do real damage.

"It was important for us to win cases," Thiel said. "We had to win. We had to get a large judgment. We did not want to bring meritless cases. We wanted to bring cases that were very strong. It was a very narrow set of context in which you could do that. You did not want to involve political speech, you did not want to involve anything that had anything remotely connected to the public interest. Ideally, our cases would not even involve the First Amendment at all."

The First Amendment was unappealing not because Thiel is a libertarian, though he is, but because as a strategist he understood that it was Gawker's strongest and most entrenched position: *we're allowed to say anything we want*. It challenges the legal system and conventional wisdom where they are the most clearly established.

Forget the blocking and tackling of proof and precedent. At an almost philosophical level, the right to free speech is virtually absolute. But as Denton would himself admit to me later, free speech is sort of a Maginot Line. "It looks formidable," he said, "it gives false confidence to defenders, but there are plenty of ways around if you're nimble and ruthless enough." That's what Thiel was doing now, that's what he was paying Charles Harder to find.

Someone from Gawker would observe with some satisfaction to me, many years away from this period of preliminary strategizing from Thiel, that if Thiel had tried to go after Gawker in court for what it had written about him, litigating damages and distress from being outed, for example, he certainly would have lost. This was said as a sort of condemnation of the direction that Thiel ultimately did attack Gawker from. Which is strange because that was the point. The great strategist B. H. Liddell Hart would say that all great victories come along "the line of least resistance and the line of least expectation." John Boyd, a fighter pilot before he was a strategist, would say that a good pilot never goes through the front door. He wins by coming through the back.

And first, that door has to be located.

Nothing in a conspiracy happens frozen in time. As Thiel and Mr. A and Harder are looking for possibilities, it is not as if Gawker is idle. The sites are publishing as they always have, making enemies, saying the things that other outlets wouldn't say. In the first year that this conspiracy is picking up steam, Gawker Media would post something like 100,000 articles across its eight sites. Almost none of these pieces see an editor before they go live. In 2012 alone, Gawker would find itself the recipient of multiple leaks of celebrity photos, it would unmask a famous internet troll, it would go after politicians, break technology news, publish controversial first-person essays, repeat gossip, and antagonize the sports world. Most of its posts were ephemeral, simple aggregation of the news and trends of the day. Not all, though.

This was a path Gawker had been on for ten years; in that decade it had published more than a million articles. Certainly much of it was forgettable and the vast majority both legal and ethical. But with that kind of volume, there would almost certainly be some gap, some hole in the line as Denton would belatedly acknowledge. How could there not be? He had designed Gawker to have an insatiable maw—tying it to the limitless appetite for content of the internet. It was founded, remember, by paying writers for each morsel they dropped into it, not how nutritious each morsel was. As technology improved, Gawker simply switched to paying by the page view and then later shifted to unique views—essentially paying by the calorie instead of the crumb.

Contained within Gawker's hundreds of thousands of articles, Mr. A was sure, were the seeds of destruction. How many? One? A handful? A hundred? Thiel had limited him in terms of what the range of violations he was comfortable funding would be, so now Mr. A and Harder would need to *really look*, not for the obvious but for the ones that everyone else had missed.

I recorded my interviews with Charles Harder on a Sony ICD Digital Voice Recorder that I placed between us on a Crate & Barrel coffee table in his offices in Beverly Hills. Because this was California, the recorder had to be there, out in the open. Both parties are legally required to consent to being recorded. Had I conducted the interview in New York, however, I could have kept the recorder in my pocket and not told him about it. But suppose I had recorded him without permission, then used his name and likeness to promote some news exclusive. One might fool oneself that this is journalism, but in fact, it is in violation of several different laws. Depending on where I did this and whom I did this to, the consequences can vary widely. What if I had done something worse? What if I had left a hidden camera in Nick Denton's home when he invited me in? What if I had collaborated with someone who had?

This is the kind of fundamental fact of law Thiel has tasked Mr. A and Harder to find in order to make cases. They were looking for Al Capone's tax evasion, a legal mistake that no one else had bothered to enforce, something dismissed potentially even by the person on the other side of the story. The conspirators wanted valid causes of action that did not involve the simple fact of whether a journalist has a right to say something or not. They wanted examples of Gawker's potentially violating the law, violating a copyright, violating the rights of others in ways that might not be protected under the generous shield offered by the Constitution to reporters and citizens. Not just the kinds of cases that a judge would allow to proceed, but ones that would resonate with a jury of ordinary people in whatever jurisdiction they might find themselves. It was obvious that this was a company that took risks, that regularly ignored what Denton called a misplaced sense of decency, that considered itself rebellious and untraditional, had likely done this many times. The conspirators just needed to find an opportunity to take advantage of.

As the team's data mining efforts—to use the language of Thiel's Palantir—continued in earnest throughout 2012, Peter and Harder and Mr. A would find that their initial impressions of Gawker's misdeeds might have been conservative. They came across more and more evidence that Gawker's sins went beyond snarkiness and mean articles, that Peter wasn't the only person Gawker had outed nor was he the only one whose privacy they had treated so flippantly. It began to look like he had actually gotten off easy.

"Anderson Cooper Is a Giant Homosexual and Everyone Knows It": 500,000 page views. "10 People Who Need to Finally Come Out of the Closet": 160,000 page views. They read in profiles of the company that Nick owned a pornography site that would host celebrity sex tapes and images which Gawker could link to (and that this site, *Fleshbot*, was responsible for 5 percent of the empire's total traffic). They learn that Nick actually used to tell people jokingly that he was a pornographer for a living. They find a tweet Nick posted while Gawker Media was in the middle of fighting a lawsuit over one of those tapes: "If you don't want a sex tape on the internet. Don't make one." They found that while he was editor in chief, A. J. Daulerio ran a tape of a college-age girl having sex on the dirty floor of a bar bathroom, and when the girl begs repeatedly over email for him to take it down, he tells her simply, "I'm sure it's embarrassing, but these things do pass." (Eventually realizing the optics of his position, A. J. did take it down.) They find that Gawker's female writers relished going after people, too, particularly other women: "Christina Hendricks Says These Giant Naked Boobs Aren't Hers, But Everything Else Is": 280,000 page views. "Olivia Munn's Super Dirty Alleged Naked Pics:": 680,000 page views. They discover that Gawker had paid $12,000 for photos of the penis of quarterback Brett Favre and had run the story despite the protestations of the woman he had allegedly been sending them to, running her name when she asked them not to. Gawker ran it, admitting that there was a "possibility" the photos weren't even of Brett Favre: *4.9 million views*.

The conspirators surmise that these kinds of stories weren't accidents but part of a policy, part of a strategy. Their suspicions are confirmed when they read a public memo from Denton to his staff in mid-2010 that says, "The staples of old yellow journalism are the staples of the new yellow journalism: sex; crime; and even better, sex crime." And, as Nick would tell *The Atlantic*, looking back on some of his sites' earlier posts, his regrets came not from publishing these types of stories, but from bothering to defend them when criticized.

"We should have just said our interest was voyeuristic. 'We did this story because we thought you would like it. We thought it was funny, so we thought you would think it was funny too.' And there was a tidal wave of traffic and attention."

Printouts of these stories came to Mr. A and he would brief Thiel on the worst of them. "The more I studied the organization, the harder it was to find good," Mr. A explained.

It was obvious, too, that this process was accelerating, which was not exactly a bad thing if you were sitting on the outside looking for a weakness that could be exploited, or hoping for your enemy to make a fatal mistake. More posts being written, more writers being hired, Gawker's swagger and sense of untouchability growing. It was almost a matter of fact that this could not continue without eventually causing serious trouble. A Gawker writer once explained why he liked working at Gawker, what drew him there: "Ultimately, I would rather work at a place that's bold enough to fuck up than one that is too afraid to ever risk it." This is all well and good, up until the point that someone with resources begins to painstakingly examine those mistakes with an eye toward attaching serious consequences to them. It's fine if those fuckups are small. But what if Gawker was just bold enough to unwittingly hand its enemies the perfect opportunity to destroy it?

Peter seems to have a preternatural ability to sense which lever to pull, what angle is the best approach, and it's almost always something radically different from what your average person would select. He wasn't looking for an opportunity to score a few points against Nick Denton, but trying to locate some singular button that would be the man's undoing. An investor tells me that with each investment, Peter Thiel likes to ask: What do I know about this company that other investors don't know? In other words: *Do we have an edge?* It's only with some sort of informational asymmetry, goes the thinking, that one can not only beat the market but dominate it, and get the kind of return that takes a $500,000 check and turns it into a *billion*.

The edge here is believing that the strategy every other would-be Gawker foe had dismissed as too obvious or too difficult is actually possible. It only seemed difficult because no one had ever truly committed to trying, nor had any individual actually had the resources to test its simple hypothesis. Even most wealthy celebrities don't have the resources or the stomach to roll the dice on a legal strategy that costs $550 an hour. And with a career as sensitive to public opinion as theirs, with opportunity costs as high as theirs, could they afford to get sucked into a knock-down, drag-out fight with the outlet that will say anything and everything? The overwhelming belief of their enemies, as was true of Walter Winchell decades before, was that to sue Gawker was to touch pitch.

Gawker had built this calculation into its approach. First, technicalities in the law were irrelevant because few would ever want to pursue them. Second, they had great lawyers on retainer in case anyone was crazy enough to try. Third, Gawker had held, for some time, a million-dollar insurance policy that covered nothing but defensive legal bills. It had a $250,000 deductible, but it stood there as a kind of cosmic reinforcement that allowed the company to know it could fight back aggressively and throw its weight in print and in legal motions if it ever came to that. This scared people. And that was the point. Gawker was an independent media company, owned mostly by Nick himself, not News Corp or Disney or some other large parent company that could afford to pay out lots of money in settlements or decisions. It was in Gawker's interest to intimidate people from trying to get very far. Which is probably why, as Peter observed, no one had tried. No one knew if it was actually impossible to beat Gawker in court. Gawker had taken this uncertainty to mean something else, too: that no one ever would challenge them, and that if someone did, the challenger was destined to lose.

It had been in front of an audience in 2009, as he was quietly exploring the Gawker situation, that Thiel had been asked about one of his strange investments that many people were sure would not work out. "That's a good thing," he said. He liked hearing that criticism. "We don't need to really worry about those people very much, because since they don't think it's possible they won't take us very seriously. And they will not actually try to stop us until it's too late." Here he must have been thinking the same thing again, finding opportunity in an avenue that his opponent not only didn't take seriously, but had become quite naturally confident about. Those flowers on Denton's desk from Fred Durst had seen to that, and the few token settlements and the aggressive press releases about Gawker's other cases had formed an impression in Gawker's collective mind. We weren't wrong to run this, Gawker said after one settlement in 2010, "because we already had won an important decision from the court striking large parts of the plaintiffs' damages claims." Denton and his lawyers were agreeing to take the post down a year after running it, only "to avoid the burden of further litigation."

But Thiel now believes that Gawker's impression of its own strength is based on the quirks of past events and not the fact of law. This belief is an edge, hardly a black one, but a real edge nonetheless. And he's going to test it. "Given the same amount of intelligence, timidity will do one thousand times more damage in war than audacity" is the dictum from Clausewitz. The reverse is true as well. It's Thiel's investment strategy: with the right conditions, a little boldness will make much more progress than timidity will ever protect. So here Thiel finds his first edge: a willingness to try. To prove something in the court of law, to a jury.

This is slow business. It's not glamorous. It's expensive. There's no visible sign of momentum. It's not even obvious to anyone else, including your opponent, what is at stake. But what this option trades in immediate gratification and public validation, it receives in the potential for long-term effectiveness.

This was the team's strategy. Like the moral of Aesop's fable about the tortoise and the hare, slow and steady wins the race. Now all they needed to figure out was which race to run—what was the right case with which to execute their plan.

CHAPTER 6

Tear Out Your Heart

At a certain point in every conspiracy each participant realizes that proceeding will require of them something that little else in their life ever has. What that is isn't willpower or resources or creativity, but instead a certain hardness and viciousness—the hard, unforgiving utilization of power or even violence against other human beings.

There is no other way to say this.

There are perpetrators and victims in a conspiracy, heroes and villains. The chess pieces are not ivory vessels on boards like those that decorate Thiel's homes and offices, they are people. And yet, to further one's ends, these people cannot be treated as people.

To recoil at this thought is natural. While Machiavelli never said—as some might claim—that we must lose that part of ourselves altogether in the pursuit of power, he did say that for the prince who wishes to remake the world to his liking, the natural impulse to be kind, forgiving, and empathetic must temporarily be suppressed. This is not an easy thing to do, even in the face of overwhelming necessity.

By 1939, Franz Halder, a German general, had taken to carrying a pistol so that when he was in the room with Hitler, he might assassinate him. But he could never pull the trigger. He could not reconcile how he could take up as "human being and a Christian to shoot down an unarmed man." In fact, many German generals knew that someone should do it, they wanted it to *have been done*, but they could not do it themselves . . . because it was unethical. Hans Oster, himself a dogged German conspirator against Hitler, would despair, "We have no one who will throw the bomb in order to liberate our generals from their scruples."

Every conspiracy is the story of man sketching out a plan on paper, committing to something in a secret meeting room, and then there is the *and then*. The man believes he has considered any and all reservations, but only when it looks and feels like it will actually happen—when he stands in the same room with the enemy, forced to really do the deed that had been only theoretical before—do the real concerns hit him. Many are stopped in their tracks in that moment, perhaps to the benefit of all involved.

Peter Thiel found himself in a not altogether dissimilar position. He had alternatively explored ignoring and doing something about the Manhattan Based Terror Organization for a long time. But until he hired his team, and sent that initial $10,000 leapfrogging across the circuits of the international banking system, it had all been an intellectual exercise. He had *thought* about bringing about Gawker's destruction via legal and ethical means, but to think and to do are always different things.

Thiel's default state is to embody contradiction. Doing so is what makes him such a brilliant investor, considering each trade and investment anew from a dozen perspectives, seeing what others aren't able to see and doing it on a regenerative basis. A friend would say that "Peter is of two minds on everything. If you were able to open his skull, you would see a number of Mexican standoffs between powerful antagonistic ideas you wouldn't think could be safely housed in the same brain."

His style as a CEO had been deftly adapted to this quirk. At

PayPal, as the CEO, Peter was once required to make the unpleasant decision about whether the company should conduct transactions on behalf of porn companies. As a normal human being, as a Christian, he can see one point of view. As a libertarian, he can just as easily articulate the other, as Nick Denton did when he started *Fleshbot*: give the people what they want. Thiel's solution to this standoff was simple. He called a staff meeting to let the employees decide. In deference to their feedback, it was decided: PayPal would take the money from adult websites but it wouldn't actively seek them out as clients. Moral dilemma averted.

It has been the great collective self-deception of Silicon Valley, and perhaps of our age, that a person can engage in aggressive "disruption" of existing industries while pretending that they are not at least similar to the ruthless capitalist barons of the previous century, that there is not a drop of Carnegie or Rockefeller or Vanderbilt DNA in the whole business. Peter Thiel didn't have to personally fire the bank tellers that he put out of a job at PayPal. He wasn't deliberately driving down the stocks of the newspapers in order to boost the stock of Facebook, even if that was the ultimate effect. He never had to personally sign off on any drone strikes or SEAL Team Six raids at Palantir, even if the data his company handed off made them possible. All the nasty stuff was far from view. The start-up CEO can tell himself that he is a good guy, because from his vantage point he is. We're out here inventing things, or funding people who are. So there might be consequences that ripple through society. How are we supposed to stop that? Of course, these were the contradictions that *Valleywag* had set out to mock and expose. To say to people like Peter Thiel and other billionaires: *You are Jay Gould. You are a robber baron. You're like all the others that ever were.*

But as 2012 dragged on, and as anyone attempting to engage in an ambitious conspiracy eventually finds out, at some point one passes the point of theory and enters the realm of hard reality. Thiel could not tell himself that he was inventing something here, that this was another Silicon Valley experiment, because it was in fact something very real and altogether different from what he had ever done before. As the head of a tiny conspiracy aimed at a single individual and his company, there was no way for Thiel to push any decisions onto other people, either. Nothing could be subject to a vote. This wasn't idle chatter over dinner with a sympathetic young person about how one might take down a media outlet if one was so inclined.

One of the informal mottos of the libertarian community is "Don't hurt people and don't take their stuff." But that is explicitly what conspiracies do, and fundamentally what Thiel's conspiracy had committed to do. It would become increasingly impossible to escape the fact that success as Thiel defined it would involve the destruction of a company that employed many people, people with families, people with no direct involvement in the article about him or similar articles about anyone else. Owen Thomas had left Gawker long ago, and sure, Nick Denton was still there, but there was no going after his business without catching Gawker's accountant and janitor and back-end web developers in the crossfire. To paraphrase Hans Oster, Thiel would have to be the one to throw the bomb that liberated the conspiracy of its scruples and let the consequences unfold.

Could he do it?

The research from the team of paralegals in Charles Harder's office began to bear fruit, giving Peter and Mr. A dozens and dozens of potential cases and plaintiffs to review. Some looked good. Some didn't. Some looked incredible. Here, another dilemma over the chess pieces is made real. Their strategy depended on asking potential plaintiffs to do the very thing Peter Thiel was unwilling to do himself: to go public. To go up against Gawker openly and in the process drag their own often embarrassing business in front of the media once again. Those pictures that Gawker had posted. Those things Gawker had accused them of. That moment that had been turned into a humiliation. For no guarantee of victory, either. Could he honestly ask someone to do this? Would he be able to use someone as fodder like that?

This ability to rope off your human side was exactly how Gawker's writers and editors had learned to function. The writers were, as A. J. Daulerio would describe, "puppies that have been trained to bite—even people who came into the house." Their job was turning part of themselves off, leaning into the lack of empathy, saying loudly the things considerate people would have been driven to soften or say only in a cupped whisper. If you wanted to be a great blogger, if you wanted to succeed in that environment, you had to. "The mortal sin at Gawker," A.J. would tell me, "was *not* running a story that would hurt someone's feelings."

"To be a successful gossip writer a man must have unusual strength of character and a rugged disposition," wrote St. Clair McKelway about the profession as it was being created in the 1940s. "His livelihood depends not so much on talent for collecting gossip items as on an ability to make public what he picks without being disturbed or confused by a softhearted regard for the feelings of the individuals concerned." Is there a truer description of the conspirator who sets out to destroy that gossip writer, deservedly or not?

Peter had selected himself to go after Gawker, to be the hammer of justice as he saw it, and in so doing he, too, was committing to hurt people and to take risks with the livelihoods of people he had recruited. Even to do it along the so-called ethical lines he had drawn, he had to embrace a number of seemingly negative traits. He had to be unforgiving, unrelenting, ruthless, deceptive. If he was to eventually get to his desired position of power over his opponent, he would then have to be unmerciful as he meted out the punishment he felt they deserved.

Nick Denton had understood the need to make a beast of oneself far earlier than Thiel. "My job is to disseminate information and manage an organization that disseminates information," Denton would say coldly in his deposition. "It's up to others to determine the boundaries of acceptable social, ethical, and legalistic norms. . . . It's up to others to have regard for their own emotional well-being. The job of a journalist would be unbearable if one was always to put oneself in the shoes of a subject." In describing Walter Winchell, a friend remarked, "He's not a man—he's a column." There is some of that in Nick. He's a blog. A machine. Thiel had experienced Denton's lack of empathy firsthand, had criticized Gawker for it, and yet there is truth and necessity in it. It helps a man wake up in the morning, gives him the stamina to endure the angry complaints as they come in, the fortitude to ignore the subjects of his writers' stories who plead with him to consider what the articles would do to their lives, and the courage to chase the stories that others would not touch. And now Peter would need to channel a bit of this calculated indifference himself in order to stop it.

"If someone has wronged only you and nobody else, maybe there is a question whether you should forgive them rather than insist on justice. But if there's a pattern of them doing it with many other people, I think that argues in a very different way," Peter would say. "One of my Christian friends told me that he thought it was a really good thing I did this but it might have been morally better to just have forgiven Gawker. You forgive people who do bad things to you and it's morally better to forgive them than to fight them, even though you might get justice by fighting them. I came to think of it like a prosecutor would—at the end of the day it's not just between me and Denton. It was not just personal," Peter said.

We all wrestle with this tension in our own way. In the pages I write here, how much am I willing to let the feelings of the people I am writing about creep into what I am saying about them? How badly am I willing to let other people get hurt to say what I need to say? To proceed, I steel myself against these thoughts, just as Peter inures himself to the prospect of lost livelihoods if he's successful, and Nick pushes away empathy in service of the dissemination of information. I push past any reservations, I try not to think about how my choices might hurt someone else. It's not me who is cruel, hard, unfair. It is the job. I had to do it.

Or so we tell ourselves. *The ends justify the means.*

As he settled on this legal strategy he had worked out through proxy with Charles Harder and awaited the first opportunity to put it into practice, Thiel moved beyond just thinking of himself as an individual responding to an attack from another individual. "It was very easy to think of this as good versus evil," Mr. A would tell me. "The piece that motivated me so much more was that there was a group of people I met in the process of doing this who had been hurt. I thought of what we were doing as heroic," Thiel said. And their confidence in this feeling grew as each day passed, as the mind naturally does once we have chosen a path. It is a slight transition from what Mr. A had said to him in 2011, "If you don't do this, who will?," to something larger and grander, a self-reinforcing process that, once set into motion, almost no amount of talk or reform could have spared Nick Denton. Gawker wasn't just a publisher anymore, it wasn't just an enemy, it was hurting people, ruining culture. It had to be stopped.

This transition is common: one can't see one's choices as simply selfish or personal or one would never have the strength to do what ultimately needs to be done. In the way that it became important for Thiel to see Gawker as singularly bad, the conspirator takes up, often without consent, the mantle of defending (or freeing) a number of other people as his or her real reason for proceeding. It is a sort of self-serving selflessness, a shield against what is to come and the feelings it will provoke.

I think of Sherman's letter to the people of Atlanta, a city he believed must fall for his march to the sea to continue and for the North to win the Civil War. Though he'd once lived in the South, though he had not begun with any strong objection to the practice of slavery, he now saw himself as an instrument of a power that must not be slowed down. To view Atlanta, this city that lay before him and his plans, as the sum total of its people would be to make the whole affair personal, not professional, and thus impossible. "You cannot qualify war in harsher terms than I will," he told them as he rejected their pleas to be spared. "War is cruelty, and you cannot refine it; and those who brought war into our country deserve all the curses and maledictions a people can pour out." When someone categorizes something evil, as Sherman did, as Peter and Mr. A repeatedly did, he implicitly gives himself permission to do what needs to be done to destroy it.

It cannot have been easy for Sherman to demand the evacuation of that city. To see the piles of dead bodies, day in and day out. It was not easy to find himself fighting against former friends, against an enemy he respected, who fought in part for a cause—slavery—which Sherman himself was sadly not all that unsympathetic to. Yet he writes to them that they cannot stop what he is about to do any more than he can. "You might as well appeal against the thunder-storm as against these terrible hardships of war. They are inevitable, and the only way the people of Atlanta can hope once more to live in peace and quiet at home is to stop the war, which can only be done by admitting that it began in error and is perpetuated in pride."

And so Peter Thiel has to make himself the lightning and the thunder that cannot be appealed against, just as all who would attempt to bend society to their will must do. To not do so would imperil the entire operation they have just begun planning. The Count of Monte Cristo would put it better: "What a fool I was not to tear my heart out on the day when I resolved to avenge myself!"

Ah, but what dangerous business this is. This artificial hardening is a dangerous crossroads, a bargain with our primal forces that not everyone escapes or can emerge from with clean hands. William James knew that every man is "ready to be savage in some cause." The distinction, he said, between good people and bad people is "the choice of the cause."

We can see this illustrated in the case of another peculiar, independent thinker named Ross Ulbricht, who around the very same time that Nick Denton and Peter Thiel are jostling toward conflict sits in a dingy apartment in Austin, chafing under constraints he believes are wrongly imposed on adults and the drugs they might like to put in their bodies. He sees oppression not in the media system but in the U.S. government, which he believes unfairly infringes on the liberties of its people. He sits and thinks about what he might be able to do about it, if something can be done about it. In a sprint he codes out the rudiments of what would become the Silk Road, a libertarian-inspired bazaar on the deep web where a man in Ohio can buy ecstasy from a dealer in Odessa. It starts to grow quickly, in part due to a post on Gawker. The planning and the preliminary steps are the easy part, the work of it done from the safety of a computer screen. The process is fun, the rewards are immediate—it's secretive and exhilarating, like a kid sneaking around his parents' restrictions. But this is not kid business, and the savagery soon begins to ooze through. Ross is challenged with questions, with the sticky ethical dilemmas inherent in this small but growing illicit operation. Whom can he trust? Whom can he confide in? What does he do after the first overdose of one of his *customers*? How does he sleep with that on his conscience? And the first time he's told of one user robbing another? Now Silk Road users want to use the site for arms dealing? Can they sell cyanide? Each step, each decision takes one further from the incorporeal realm and into the brutishness of the Hobbesian world. What steps will he take to evade and deceive the police or the agencies that seek to stop him? How will he hide the wealth that has come pouring in? How does it feel to spend money you know came from enabling someone else's suicide? Ross was one day simply sitting in that room, dreaming his plans on a keyboard, and then another day he had to decide whether to order a contract hit on an employee who threatened to unravel his ambitious attempt to change how society works. He can't be stopped, he won't be stopped—what he is doing is too important.

The savagery of ordering not just one murder but six would eventually put Ulbricht in a federal prison cell. Few would come to admire the cause he had been willing to commit such acts for, or appreciate the steeling of his soul that had been required to do it. And indeed he stands now as a cautionary tale, a kind of true story of how one breaks bad.

Yet the paradox is that if one is too concerned about this criticism or these consequences, one will never proceed. Which is what Thiel did, trading in the constructive ethos of his profession as a creator and a patron for this inherently destructive mindset. He did this with some reservations, having long held on to advice once given to him by a friend—choose your enemies wisely, he had been told, because you become just like them—but plunged ahead nonetheless, with a piece of his heart torn out.

CHAPTER 7

Seizing the Sword

Almost every conspiracy is defined by a moment in which the timeline is radically altered, when the conspirators scramble to respond to a sudden change of events. The schedule of the target is changed. The long latent revolution finds its flash point and something to rally around. These moments are not always clear or definitive at the time, but in retrospect it's clear how much it all hinged there—on how they responded to a shift in circumstances or an opportunity that fell into their laps.

In the July 20 plot against Hitler, it's rumors that an arrest of a group of conspirators is imminent that drive members of his inner circle to put their bomb back in the briefcase and slide it under Hitler's conference table for one last assassination attempt. In the Pazzi conspiracy against the Medici in the fifteenth century, a last-minute change means that the assassination will happen at high mass in front of thousands of people instead of in a private dining room in the palace. Caesar, hoping simply to stand for election to consul, is unfairly ordered by the Senate to disband his army and return to Rome. On January 10, 49 BC, he pauses on the banks of the Rubicon, utters those famous words *Alea iacta est*—"the die is cast"—and crosses the river with his army. He is marching on his own country.

To understand this moment in our story, we must go back in time to when Peter Thiel and Nick Denton are first entering each other's orbit. Both are flush and full. They've made their fortunes and are plotting their next moves, trying to build empires. Another man is in the latter stages of his own career, built in very different arenas. His name is Terry Bollea, though you might be more familiar with his stage name from some of those arenas: Hulk Hogan.

Terry Bollea has had an incredible run: the fat, awkward son of a pipefitter, he travels from the docks of Port Tampa, Florida, to become one of the most famous characters in American culture. At twelve years old, he is already six feet tall, and has only one friend: his music teacher. He tries to make a career in music after high school and community college but struggles to support himself. He gets a job loading and unloading cargo at the docks to make ends meet. He begins training to be a wrestler at twenty-three. He gets his first match a year later. He's the young upstart. The older guys don't want him around. He stays at it. It's a story of success not unlike Denton's and Thiel's—but the blue-collar version and with a different ending. He goes from professional wrestler to movie star to icon. He's so well liked he can call everyone "brother" and get away with it.

Terry Bollea is so famous, in 2005, he stars in a reality TV series about his life, and his wife and kids become famous by extension. It's filmed in their $25 million, 17,000-square-foot mansion. His daughter, Brooke, wants to be a singer, his son a race-car driver. His wife demands her chance at the spotlight, too. Everyone in the family is getting their share. The show is a hit. It looks like Brooke might become a singer after all. They're making money. It's been going so well for so long.

But what the gods giveth, they taketh away. By 2006, Terry's marriage is in tatters. His wife hates him, tells him he is too old. She moves from their home in Florida to their place in Los Angeles. While they fight for their marriage over the phone, their son flirts with serious trouble. His daughter's career has cost millions. His body aches from years in the ring. Another set of back surgeries has failed. There isn't much hair left, either.

Appearances are kept up. As long as appearances are kept, a man can keep hope, too. Two dozen years of marriage have rough spots. Things have been bad before. He was no model husband—a good father but not a great husband. He was a celebrity, he'd had his affairs, he'd worked too much, he'd been gone too often. Deep down, he still believed that it could be turned around. This is the man who wrestled André the Giant in front of 93,000 people, who got America's little Hulkamaniacs to take their vitamins, who was a twelve-time world wrestling champion and was inducted into the WWE Hall of Fame at the age of fifty-one. Terry Bollea doesn't give up easily.

It's hope that makes disappointing news so crushing. It leads us to believe that the thing we dreaded most might not happen. Midsummer 2007: Another angry phone call from his wife makes it clear. She's gone. *I am never coming back, ever.* The marriage is done in everything but name. Twenty-four years. Gone. He calls Todd Clem, a syndicated radio host who had become his best friend. I will not bother you here with the backstory of the type of person who legally changes his name to "Bubba the Love Sponge," or becomes a shock jock known for killing a live pig on the radio, for having porn stars use sex toys on each other for his listeners' benefit, and for calling the 2010 Haiti earthquake "a cleanse." What matters is that Hulk and Bubba lived in the Tampa area and had become best friends. Not best friends like you and I have best friends, the kind of best friends that a man who has been in the public eye for decades, a man whose personal life is falling apart, can have—a brother. Bubba had been with Bollea while Bollea's father died. Each held one of the man's hands as he went.

Terry calls Bubba, he tells him the news about his marriage, he breaks down. All of it. It's too much. His friend insists he couldn't possibly let him be alone at a moment like this. A few minutes later, he's at Bollea's house. Soon they're in Bubba's car—*you're coming with me*. "Heather," Bubba says excitedly to his wife on the phone as he drives, "we're on our way."

On the other coast, at the same time as Linda Hogan is ending their marriage, *Valleywag* is terrorizing the sheltered nerds of Silicon Valley. Peter was giving an interview to a newspaper in Frankfurt, Germany, admitting to his interest in and mounting concern over *Valleywag* and his place on its radar screen. "If I'm honest, I look at it quite often, even if it's hard or embarrassing for me," he tells them. Little did he realize it was only going to get harder. The clock was ticking down the weeks until the words *Peter Thiel Is Totally Gay, People* would become a headline in a world very far away from Pinellas County, Florida.

As they pull into Bubba's home in St. Petersburg, Terry nearly collapses as he makes his way up the walk. His guard is down, there is no armor, no outsized persona left. The signature yellow and red bandanas of Hulkamania are not there to cover up his pain. But he doesn't need that in this moment. These are his friends, these are the people who love him, who make him feel like he used to feel, before everything had fallen apart. They hug him as he enters the door. This is good. This is home.

Heather grabs him by the hand and pulls him in the direction of the bedroom. What is this? His giant hand touching hers. It is a surprise. It is not a surprise. The couple had joked with him about this, it was a standing offer—we have an open marriage. *My wife wants to fuck you*. As Bollea's marriage fell apart, the Clems had offered a sympathetic ear. Now, standing on the threshold of the bedroom, of another man's bedroom, they are offering something else. Bollea feels the first throb of an erection. He has a good sense of what to expect. She motions from the bed. But Bollea stops. There's something in the pit of his stomach. He wants this—after months of rejection, loneliness without his wife, here's a beautiful woman who wants him, who has been begging for it, but this is so weird. Being offered a man's wife. No strings. There has to be a catch. "Bubba, you're not filming this, are you?" Bubba recoils. *What is wrong with you? I am your fucking best friend,* he says. *Your best friend, how could you even ask me that?* Perhaps this was what convinced him. Perhaps the beautiful woman a few feet away was enough to overwhelm any reservations. It doesn't matter. Bollea continues into the bedroom. Bubba hands him a condom and walks out of the room.

Not a word is said about how, the summer before, the husband and wife had paid a handyman to install a small camera on the wall over the wet bar in the bedroom. They didn't tell him that, at some point in the evening, one of them had walked to the closet where the camera was hardwired, inserted a DVD, and pressed the record button. Hogan did not know, as he began to undress and approach the naked woman, another man's woman, on the bed, that the red light flashing in what looked like a smoke alarm, or possibly a motion detector, on the left wall of the room was capturing every move he made and every word he said. A vulnerable moment had brought him into the room for the first time, and that camera would be recording on the many other nights when he visited, the other nights he returned with permission for that illicit thrill, doing the thing that no amount of consent could make right.

Like all flings, it would run hot and then dissipate and he would move on, though for a time he would actually *move in* with the Clems, as if their relationship wasn't sordid and strange enough. And when he did move on, he would do so in ignorance for nearly five full years of that one critical, life-changing detail, living his life without any idea that footage of multiple encounters of him having sex with his best friend's wife existed.

He had plenty to occupy his thoughts anyway. His troubled son would crash his car and nearly kill a friend a month after that summer night in that bedroom in 2007. His wife would file for divorce three months after it. Both events would send his life into chaos. They would put his boy in solitary confinement. He would go every day to see his son, to keep him sane, and then their conversations recorded in the jail visiting room are leaked to the media. He would pay millions to the victim's family to make the whole thing go away. He had hung on with his wife, he had thought his marriage might be fixable. He would get the news that she had finally filed for divorce from a reporter while he is driving, and still, knowing what he knew—knowing what he had done—it shocks him enough that he has to pull over. It is a long dream, a nightmare that won't end. Should he end it? Could he?

He would find himself in the bathroom, gun in hand, finger on the trigger, bottle on the counter, family gone, wondering how much pressure it would take to release a round that would finish all this. He tells a reporter not long after that things were bad enough that he can empathize with O. J. Simpson, who also saw his wife with a much younger man spending his money. He could see himself turning his home into that bloody crime scene. He does no such thing, thankfully, but this was a man who peered over the edge for a half second too long, who in that half second thought about how freeing it would be to go over. Something like that changes a man's soul, stays with him no matter what good may come later.

But with time, he began to rebuild his life. He found religion again. He read *The Secret* and practiced positive affirmations. He got married for a second time. He kept working. He would say it was as if he were breathing "clean air" again. He was mostly out of wrestling. He was happy.

In those intervening years, the things he hoped he could pretend had never happened had secretly metastasized, eating away, unknowingly, at the foundations of his new life like a cancer. He had no idea that his best friend had taken these tapes and hidden them in a drawer in his desk, that they'd come up as a piece of property in his friend's divorce, or that they'd later be stolen out of that desk when it was left unattended during a move in late 2011 from one Tampa Bay office to another, allegedly by a scheming employee and aspiring DJ who wanted his own show. He was enough in ignorance of these tapes that he'd confidently lied to Howard Stern a year before they leaked that he'd never have sex with someone married to a friend of his, citing "man law," saying he wouldn't even do it if Bubba and Heather had been divorced for a decade.

The cocoon of his new life is first pierced at 1:00 a.m. on March 7, 2012, when the first rumors of a Hulk Hogan sex tape surface on TMZ.com. The story doesn't say who Hogan is with or when the tape was recorded. Does it hit Bollea instantly what that tape could be? Or has he blocked it out? The wishful thinking keeps him hoping it's just a rumor, or that it was with someone else. By 8:00 a.m., Hogan has already replied, telling TMZ he has no idea who could be in the tape with him, that there were a lot of women in that dark period of his life. He gets a letter from Vivid Entertainment and one from Sex.com offering to buy the tape. One letter reads, "We understand that you believe this tape was made without your permission . . ." but they want to buy it anyway. Hogan and his lawyer, David Houston, go on TMZ to discuss the tapes, to do some damage control. He tries to make light of it. The hosts tease him for wearing a thong in the video; he and his lawyer joke that at least it's not him with a man.

Then blurry images from the tapes appear online. This saps the humor out of the situation for him. It's clear to him when he sees these photos, just as it is clear to Bubba, what tapes these are, though it does not explain how they got there. His new wife confronts him one afternoon as Hogan napped: "Did you do this? Did you sleep with Heather?" He can just barely see himself in that bedroom he has tried to forget, one of those nights he must so badly wish he had never spent there. He can't deny it, not to his wife, anyway. But perhaps he can keep it from ever being made more public than it is. Perhaps he can prevent it from humiliating him and his wife more than it already has. "If anyone goes forward with this thing," his lawyer tells TMZ, "we're going to find them and prosecute them."

It is here, for the first time, in March 2012, that all our characters begin to intersect in the way that will move this conspiracy from planning toward action. Casey Carver, the publicist for TMZ, emails links to TMZ's coverage of Hogan to tips@Gawker.com, an email address which is forwarded to the editors and writers of every Gawker site. She wants the traffic that Gawker can send to a scandal like this, and she knows this story is right up their alley. Just two days earlier Gawker had published the hacked naked photos of Christina Hendricks and Olivia Munn. The day after, Denton would agree with the assessment of an NBC News correspondent doing a profile on him for *Rock Center with Brian Williams* that his website is "snarky . . . sexual . . . shameless . . . mean (occasionally)." But for now, news that there *might* be a sex tape of a professional wrestler isn't enough to get Gawker's editors interested.

Nick and Peter would subsequently have very different summers from Hulk Hogan's, the last summer before their proxy war would go from cold to hot. Thiel watches Facebook go public, and though the IPO has its technological issues at market, Peter sees his net worth become liquid with unimaginable amounts of money. He cashes out more than $1 billion worth of shares for himself and his partners. Denton, too, is riding high: Gawker's revenues are on track to be more than $25 million that year, a long way from those days in his living room, blogging around the big table, and yet he is dealing with his own technological issues, though of a more personal nature. He loses his iPhone and spends a sleepless night worrying his own risqué photos might end up on the internet.

Then, in late September, a talent manager named Tony Burton, whose agency represents radio stars like Howard Stern and Mike Calta, reaches out to A. J. Daulerio, the editor of Gawker, with a tip of his own:

> I have a client that has a very significant DVD they want to send you. But they are asking to mail it to you for anonymity purposes. Can you provide me with an address or PO Box?

A phone call hints to A.J. what's on this DVD—proof of that story TMZ has been running all summer. It would be the kind of unsolicited scoop that changes the course of a life, but was also the culmination of a reputation that A.J. has been building for some time. He knew what to do with the stuff that no one else would touch. Naked photos of Brett Favre? Embarrassing pictures of an athlete out at a club? Topless photos of someone who *looks like* a coach's daughter? The Erin Andrews peephole video? Send them to A.J. He doesn't care. He'll run it. He'll make it work, and if he can't, he'll link to it. That's his job. The year before, *GQ* published a profile of him with a photo showing him standing on a toilet, holding spy equipment, underneath the headline: "A. J. Daulerio: The Worldwide Leader in Dong Shots."

"A.J. can be disarmingly tender," a close friend and colleague would write, but "A.J. is also sadistic and takes distinct pleasure in watching people humiliate themselves. If I'm being optimistic, I think that mostly what he loves is viewing humanity and he has a particular affinity for the rawest of raw moments. Maybe he's just a dickhead deep down." He was the bad boy, he loved to be the heel. "All the bad stuff Gawker did, *that's* why I wanted to work for it," he said. In the fall of 2012, he is thirty-seven but looks younger. He's driven himself hard—work, late nights, parties, drugs—but it doesn't yet show. He has black hair, and scruff, the disheveled feel of a mischievous sidekick or the neighborhood rascal. Yet behind the eyes—one brown, one blue—where there are often flashes of energy and lightness, there was then also a kind of emptiness.

An envelope arrives at Gawker while Daulerio is on vacation. It has no return address. An email follows a couple days later from the source who had first teased it: "Did you get your package?" Inside that envelope is everything Hogan might have feared and everything that a leader in dong shots would have hoped for: an unedited thirty-minute DVD of Hulk Hogan having sex, one of at least three tapes stolen from Bubba Clem's desk. Daulerio instructs his video editor to shorten the clip to what he would later call a one-minute, forty-one-second "highlight reel." He would run it just seven days after the initial unsolicited tip had arrived.

Gawker, October 4, 2012:

Even for a Minute, Watching Hulk Hogan Have Sex in a Canopy Bed Is Not Safe for Work but Watch It Anyway

We can try to imagine what Daulerio and Gawker know here, as they rush to publish this scoop: They know that the tape was likely recorded without consent. TMZ had spammed their tip line with a half dozen stories about this fact. The headline on one of them reads: "Hulk Hogan—I'm the VICTIM of Sex Tape Setup." Every editor had gotten it. They know other outlets have not run the tape. They know that Hogan's lawyer had threatened to go after anyone who ran it. Daulerio and Gawker know that they themselves had been sued in the past for running sex tapes—at least twice, once for $80 million by Durst, and in another case which they'd had to settle for the low six figures. They know, as they would later admit in legal filings, that it would be relatively easy to pixelate out the genitals of Terry Bollea and Heather Clem, and that this was easy enough to do since they'd done it before on other videos. They know that writing *about* a sex tape is protected in a way that the actual footage itself might not be. They know they could ask Hogan for a comment. They knew they could have done some basic reporting after receiving the tape. But they didn't want to or feel they needed to. These are not speculations, but admissions, extracted piece by piece, reluctantly, under the penalty of perjury, in the course of hundreds of legal motions and depositions.

But the page views. But this is an exclusive. This isn't just rumors of tape, this is the tape that the rest of the internet could only chatter about. Can we sit on something we know that so many people will want to see? We should sit on it because it embarrasses some rich guy who is already ridiculous?

"Gawker is not in the business of holding back information," Gawker's managing editor Emma Carmichael would later say in her deposition. If they got it, they ran it. A Gawker writer would defend a similar story a few years later by saying, "Stories don't need an upside. Not everyone has to feel good about the truth. If it's true, you publish." These people had come to believe that "truth" was the governing criterion, and that the right to publish these stories was absolute. As far as their experience was concerned, they were correct: There had never been serious consequences. They had called every bluff. They had published what every other media outlet would have deemed unpublishable and not only got away with it—the audience *loved* them for it.

Of course they knew that running stolen footage of a naked person was not exactly right. *Jezebel*, a Gawker site, had made a name for itself defending women against every kind of slight, defending their rights to privacy, defending them against men who tried to victimize or bully them online. *Jezebel* would define its views more clearly in outrage when a rival blog published a controversial story about someone's sexuality: "Don't out someone who doesn't want to be out. The end. Everyone has a right to privacy. . . ." Except Peter Thiel, and now Terry Bollea, apparently.

Less than two months before the Hogan piece, a Gawker writer who would later become the site's editor writes a piece condemning the rise of "fusking"—the practice of stealing photos from online accounts and posting them. In it, he rejects any attempt to blame the victim, or any excuses made for the "behavior of thieves and creeps" when they steal people's private things. Gawker had seen the anger and outrage about Hunter Moore when it had written about him and his media site built around so-called revenge porn. Commenters even cheered when Gawker reported that the FBI was investigating Moore. Yet when that tape arrived to its SoHo offices, Gawker would whittle it down to a highlight reel and run that naked video of Hulk Hogan in front of an audience that numbers in the millions—a video not just of Hogan, but also of the woman he was filmed having sex with, who also had not consented to its publication. Gawker would promote it to their Facebook fans: "It's probably time you watched this snippet from the Hulk Hogan sex tape with a woman some claim is Bubba the Love Sponge's wife. Work's over. You're fine."

Gawker had the air of a wildly overconfident champion. They had bested every opponent, rejected every convention and condescending person who said it was wrong. Its writers and editors had felt the satisfaction of proving a jeering crowd wrong, and drank to the dregs an elixir that made them think they were both unbeatable *and* the underdog at the same time.

"Because the internet has made it easier for all of us to be shameless voyeurs and deviants, we love to watch famous people have sex," A.J. wrote in the opening to his piece. "We watch this footage because it's something we're not supposed to see (sometimes) but we come away satisfied that when famous people have sex it's closer to the sex we as civilians have from time to time." It is a classic Gawker mix of humor and salacious detail. Knowing how the readers loved the glimpses of the story behind the story, in narrating the tape, A.J. explains how the tape came into his possession. "Last week, a burned DVD copy of Hulk having sex with the woman rumored to be Heather Clem (Bubba's ex-wife) was delivered to us through an anonymous source. They wanted no payment. They wanted no credit. Their only request was that we watch it. So I did—all 30:17 of it—and hyperbole aside, it's a goddamn masterpiece."

Gawker would later say this writing they posted with the video was important context, that the tape was secondary to the point they were trying to make as journalists. Perhaps it cannot be said for certain what ultimately drove the more than seven million views to the page: was it the cultural analysis, or the one minute, forty-one seconds showing Hogan erect and naked, Clem naked and sucking, naked and fucking from the hidden angle of the blinking smoke detector on the wall above the bed? Or perhaps it can be.

Still, one must credit the writer: "He stands on the side of the bed and the woman scoots up from the pillows and resumes giving the former WWE heavyweight champion of the universe a blowjob," A.J. writes. "It is a slow, dutiful blowjob and Hulk is thrusting himself into her mouth to speed up the process. This goes on for a few minutes and at one point Hulk examines the canopy bed curtains in a way that suggests he'd like to purchase this particular style for his own canopy bed some day. She takes a break. She spits loudly. She resumes for a few seconds, but it appears the spit has worked because Hulk mutters something in a growly sex voice. The woman removes him from her mouth and spins around on the bed like an excited puppy. She stands. They grope each other and stare at each other." Gawker would call it, when they promoted the story online, "the heavyweight champion of sex tapes."

David Houston, then acting as Hogan's criminal attorney, rushes to send a cease and desist letter that officially informs Gawker Media the tapes were recorded without consent and that Bollea would pursue anyone who published them. It says quite bluntly, "Any attempt to hide behind the veil of the 'newsworthiness privilege' will fail and cannot possibly save anyone from making unauthorized use of the video from liability." Houston takes time to dictate a second letter, this one to go out over email, to Nick Denton personally. It arrives at 11:16 a.m. the morning after the post runs. There is no monetary demand, or legal saber rattling. It is another approach entirely, a last-ditch attempt: "I'm sure you understand as a human being . . ."

Imagine if Nick had. This story would end here. There would be no conspiracy—not one involving Hulk Hogan anyway. But Denton did not care to understand as a human being. He had hardened, too, it seemed, or grown indifferent or incautious. Was it financial? A few days after the post, he would write a memo to his staff titled "Phew." Their traffic slump of several months was over. "Phew: We've had a great run of stories. Gizmodo's iPhone coverage was exceptional. Gawker scored with royal breasts and Hulk sex." The page view bonus for writers on the site that month is maxed out—a kicker of 20 percent of the editorial budget is split among the writers who contributed to it. He is riding the high of several million page views, and the rush of the headlines ensures once again that Gawker is the rebel of the media set.

Daulerio, too, did not seem to relate to Hogan as a human being. He wrote in a follow-up post a few days later, "Hulk Hogan's all mad, but I do hope he takes a moment to appreciate how much worse the coverage of his half-hour sex rodeo would be if it had been acquired by another outlet desperate to score another Exclusive to keep their dim lights shining. . . . In the meantime, we'll just wait for whatever happens next and focus on other things because this all fades away more quickly when you try to move on."

Nick would dismiss both of Houston's cease and desist letters and leave it to his lawyers to respond. His litigation counsel, Cameron Stracher, sent a letter on October 9 not to acknowledge the fundamental awkwardness or unpleasantness of a difficult situation, not to explain that the post would come down or be adjusted to reflect this new information, but to dismiss and antagonize, to pick, unknowingly, one more fight with one more enemy, that would eventually bring conspiracy and destruction to Gawker's door.

"The video depicts Mr. Bollea having sex with a married woman in the woman's home under circumstances and in a place where he has no reasonable expectation of privacy," the lawyer wrote, apparently taking the position that a private home does not entitle people to privacy. The video *barely* has any sex in it, he says, and besides, the public is interested in Hogan's private life and that makes this fair game. Gawker will give on one thing, the lawyer said, no doubt aware of the meaninglessness of the gesture Denton had offered many pissed-off powerful people before: If you'd like to make a statement about the video, we'll happily post it at the bottom of the story. Otherwise, they are telling him, get lost.

Bollea's shoes are heavy in the moment. It's difficult to envision oneself inside them. He had rebuilt his life. He had refused, at first, to entertain the possibility that his best friend could have been responsible for this. He had held on to that idea even after the tape had leaked. Now he is struggling through his prescheduled media tour for a wrestling special, making an appearance on the fourth hour of the *Today* show with Kathie Lee Gifford and Hoda Kotb. Off air he breaks down crying with Kathie Lee. He drags his enormous, aching body into the bathroom to compose himself and then moves on to the next interview. It's TMZ again. TMZ has seen the full tape—they don't tell him that they paid close to $10,000 for the opportunity, but they will tell him this: there is definitive proof that Bubba Clem knew it was being recorded. Terry Bollea begins to lose control of his limbs. There is pain in his chest and it radiates outward to the rest of the body. Is this the heart attack that finally gets him, retribution for years of steroids? The wave of a panic attack consumes him. He is shaking. He is no longer Hulk Hogan the professional wrestler, the world champion. He is a broken man again.

Machiavelli's warning once again rings prophetic: "Anyone who is threatened and is forced by necessity either to act or to suffer becomes a very dangerous man to the prince."

Bollea decides he must act—to protect himself, to protect his career. Not just against the people who taped him and leaked it but against the people who published it, too. He won't be sending Nick Denton flowers. What he'd like to do is send him all the fury and rage and despair that has accumulated in his life. This is a man who had just given 70 percent of his community property to his ex-wife, who had been kicked around, who had nothing to lose. He was desperate, and he proceeded without a thought as to how he might actually win or whether he could even afford to try. But in telling reporters that he planned to sue, Hulk Hogan catches the luckiest break of his life. He makes his case and intentions known to Charles Harder and Mr. A, two men currently enjoying the beginnings of their retainer and the backing of Peter Thiel, two men looking for precisely this kind of opportunity.

For months, Harder had simply been watching Gawker, studying it as he had been asked to do, billing by the hour as he looked for an opportunity to validate Peter's proposed strategy. He had looked backward, mostly, at old stories, at exchanges where people had threatened Gawker with legal action, yet none of this had gone anywhere. Then suddenly, that week in October, the opportunity had arrived: Gawker had not just published a leaked celebrity sex tape—which itself is often illegal—it had run one where the celebrity had said very loudly and publicly that it had been recorded without consent.

Harder thinks on it, reads what he can, and then picks up the phone and dials David Houston: I represent a wealthy client who is willing to support fights like yours, do you need any help? The voice on the other end of the phone is incredulous. Is this a joke? Things like this don't happen. Houston has no time to consider who the benefactor is, what his motivations are, what Gawker might have done to this person. *Did they go after his children? Is he in this for fun? How much is he willing to spend? Are we the only people he is helping?* None of this can be considered for more than a few hours. His client is desperate. The longer this tape exists on the internet, the more it will work itself into the corners of the web's underworld, the harder it will be to ever remove. The longer they wait, the more it looks like Hogan was in on it, or that he's benefiting from the publicity.

The boss is called by Mr. A. *I think we have our case.* An opportunity Thiel had been looking for since that evening in December when he had first had his own privacy rudely intruded on, the kind Mr. A had suggested at their dinner. Could this be it? Has Gawker finally put themselves in a place where he might be able to get at them? Thiel gives the green light—he'll fund Terry Bollea's case as far as the man is willing to take it. The conspiracy will proceed.

The team works late over that weekend, pulling citations and reviewing briefs, rushing to build a case from scratch. Nearly forty pages of claims are assembled, beginning as they must with "Defendants have engaged in intentional, outrageous, irresponsible and despicable conduct. . . ." Hogan's publicist is apprised of what will be coming, a press release is hastily written. All this is done in secret, joining the parties fully together for the first time, Peter Thiel, Charles Harder, Mr. A, and Hulk Hogan, in compartmentalized collaboration spread out over the globe.

We could say that the planning phase of this conspiracy ended on October 15, 2012, just seven days between the first contact between Harder and David Houston, just ten days since Gawker plunged ahead with publication. The beginning of the next phase would be marked by Hulk Hogan and a tweet: "Now my actions will speak louder than my words. HH."

A few hours later, Charles Harder walks up the steps of the Sixth Judicial Circuit Court of Pinellas County, Florida, with one client next to him, the other ensconced in his offices at Thiel Capital on an otherwise ordinary Monday conducting business as if a press conference in Florida is the farthest thing from his mind. Runners have been dispersed to file lawsuits in state and district court against Gawker and Bubba and Heather Clem, each for their role in the creation and publication of the tapes. The press release is on its way to every major media outlet. Harder is dressed in a black suit and silver tie. Hulk Hogan stands behind him, his white mustache stark against his tanned face, surrounded by the clear stubble and scruff of many recent rough weeks. Wearing all black to emphasize the menace of his six-foot-seven-inch frame, he looks on from behind sunglasses that hide the pain in his eyes, while Harder addresses the camera.

"Terry Bollea never consented to any aspect of that video. After he and his legal counsel demanded repeatedly that Gawker remove that video from its website, Gawker refused to do so. And it continued to post that video. The acts of Gawker Media are illegal, outrageous, and exceed the bounds of human decency. The lawsuit against Gawker seeks damages in the amount of $100 million. . . . The actions of the defendants cannot be tolerated by a civil society. Hulk Hogan will take all reasonable steps necessary to ensure that all persons and entities who were involved in this are punished to the fullest extent of the law."

Few know who this lawyer is, why he's come in from California for this case, nor would they suspect it is the first press conference he has ever given. Most suspect that Hogan is simply posturing, running the same tired playbook that every celebrity breaks out when they release a sex tape to boost their career. But they are wrong. A real challenger had entered the ring. He was oiled and dusted and ready to fight. And hidden from both the crowd and the opponent are the teammates he can tag in when he needs them.

Gawker claimed that it was ready, too, and had been for a long time. A *Valleywag* editor had, in 2006, complained in an interview that for all the traffic he'd snagged and media attention they'd gotten, what was really missing was a legitimate legal challenge. "We haven't gotten a serious legal threat so far," he said. "We're still waiting for a good solid cease-and-desist and a good lawsuit." They fired him for saying it . . . but they rehired him a few months later.

Deep down, Denton had always shared the same swaggering belief—he was just smart enough not to say it so uncouthly. He and his writers had longed for a worthy challenger. They had dared the powerful to come after them. They joked that you were nobody until somebody sued you. Now they had a good lawsuit—*a nine-figure lawsuit*—in state and federal court. They were confident they would knock this opponent down as they had every other powerful person who had challenged them. A professional wrestler? That was Gawker's game, too. This would be fun.

This would be easy—and good for business. Besides, it could always be made to go away if it wasn't.

And so they sleepwalked on.

PART II

The Doing

CHAPTER 8

Prepare for Setbacks

Take two steps forward. Take one step back. There is often very little visible forward momentum in a conspiracy. It is, rather, as the poet Lucretius described life, "one long struggle in the dark."

This one is no different. Despite the fanfare on the courthouse steps, Harder's two lawsuits are almost immediately dealt a string of setbacks in both federal and state courts. On October 22, just seven days after filing, Hogan's temporary restraining order—a short-term, stopgap measure to remove the tape—is denied by U.S. District Court judge James D. Whittemore in Tampa. A hearing for Hogan's request for a preliminary injunction, his second attempt to get the tape taken down before the two parties battle it out at trial, is scheduled for November 8.

In a rush to strengthen his cases after the first legal setback, Harder scrambles to add a copyright claim to the federal suit. In a way, this is in line with Thiel's strategy as he has first outlined it, looking for opportunities outside the First Amendment. Since Gawker doesn't have the broadcast rights or a license to the copyright of the video of Hogan and Clem having sex (just as it wouldn't have rights to music or photography created by someone else), Harder is hoping he can at least use this as an opportunity to get the tape off the internet before he fights the longer case on the privacy claims. It's not a great opportunity, by any means, but it is an opportunity nonetheless. Except there is a problem: Hogan doesn't actually own the copyright, either. Bubba would, since he recorded it—the same Bubba they are also suing in Florida *state* court for doing precisely that. To proceed against Gawker in federal court, Hogan will need to get it from him.

In the final days of October, a series of moves are made. Hogan offers terms to Bubba, the world's worst best friend. For just $5,000 and an apology from the man who put all this in motion, the person who, since the announcement of the lawsuits, has called Hogan the "ultimate lying showman" on the radio and claimed that Hogan knew he was being filmed the entire time, Hogan will agree to drop the case against Bubba Clem. Hogan and his team tell themselves it will be worth it if the copyright will give them leverage against Gawker in court and the settlement keeps Bubba from turning the case into a spectacle with more contradictory statements.

No sooner do they settle with Clem and get their needed copyright than another discouraging blow lands upon them. On November 14, Judge Whittemore rules on Hogan's motion for injunctive relief against the tape. The motion is denied. The tape can stay up on Gawker's site until the case is settled, and those page view numbers can continue to turn over on the big board in Gawker's offices up in Manhattan.

This is the nature of the American legal system, and of conspiracy as well. It's slow, adversarial. Moral quandaries and personal issues are reduced to brief moments and decided on small points of law. Even a winning case will likely see as many setbacks as it does victories, and it falls upon the constitution of the players to weather the former to get to the latter. And this isn't even the real legal battle—these are just arguments over the attempts to obtain what is called "prior restraint" of speech. The conspirators were trying to get the tape taken down before—*until*—they'd won their case. Harder's thinking was that a sex tape recorded without consent was so egregious that a judge would be sympathetic. Gawker's lawyers enjoy disabusing their opponent of this notion. So does the judge.

Most of the team can take these bumps in stride, particularly since the motions don't necessarily affect the main issue of their case. Peter has waited five years for an opportunity for a Gawker lawsuit. Mr. A has been at it for more than a year. Charles Harder, well, this is his job. But Hulk Hogan? His situation is far more personal. Every day, he wakes up to a world in which anyone with an internet connection can access video footage of him having sex with his best friend's wife. Hogan would complain in one filing, via his lawyers, that a Google search for "Hulk Hogan" autocompleted to "Hulk Hogan sex tape." One Gawker headline ten days after the tape was excerpted on its site explains the predicament well: "Many People Asked This Hulk Hogan Cosplayer About His Sex Tape This Weekend." Even Hulk Hogan *impersonators* were feeling the embarrassment.

It's enough to make a sane man question: Am I sure I want to do this?

Hogan had decided to fight Gawker in the belief that his "couple million bucks" and being *right* were sufficient. Hogan had sued people before—the makers of Cocoa Pebbles, a car dealership, even his own ex-wife for defamation. But those had been typical lawsuits, against typical opponents. He would learn quickly, as Peter had already come to see, that Gawker was a different sort of opponent.

In the meantime, there is pressing business to keep them all, particularly Hulk Hogan, occupied. In the days after the tape had been published on Gawker, but before he'd filed suit against it, Hogan's personal lawyer, David Houston, received a cryptic email:

Subject: Hulk Hogan Tape

Please call regarding above.

It was from a lawyer named Keith Davidson, who claimed to represent the parties who had the tapes and knew who shopped them to the media. Davidson would inform Hogan and Houston that the clips that had run on Gawker could be just the beginning, that the leak was simply a "shot across the bow" to get his attention. There were more tapes, "one that's more inflammatory than the others . . . that carries the lion share of the value." Would Hogan like to prevent anything from happening to them?

Negotiations start at $1 million

Under the direction of the FBI, which was called in to investigate what looks like a clear attempt at criminal extortion, Bollea and Houston are asked to participate in an elaborate sting. It's a conspiracy within a conspiracy—negotiating to meet, purchase, and transfer ownership of the materials at the heart of the Gawker lawsuit. If the sting is successful, not only will Hogan finally possess the full tapes that TMZ had teased and Gawker had sampled, but he may learn more about how they came into A.J.'s hands in the first place.

In December 2012, Houston and Hogan find themselves in a suite in the Sandpearl Resort hotel looking out over Clearwater Beach, less than a block from the small memorabilia and fan store Hogan had celebrated opening a few innocent weeks before. In the adjoining room are a half dozen FBI agents. Both Houston and Hogan are wearing wires, and the clock in the room is not a clock but a camera. Another camera is hidden in a flowerpot on the counter. Houston has a $150,000 check on him, a dummy check for the 50 percent down payment on the tapes, and a $600 real check to pay for the polygrapher whom they are planning to subject the owner of the tapes to. Keith Davidson enters the suite at precisely 11:00 a.m. Like Denton, he has a large round head with hair cropped close to de-emphasize a receding hairline. He wears conspicuously European cut and tailored suits to cover his growing pudge. In 2008, he'd formed a law firm "focused on integrity, enthusiasm, and creativity." His presence in the room is a testament to the latter two, less so of the first.

The men shake hands, and a pink-faced Davidson begins to describe what is on his client's DVDs. It is straight to business, and not pleasant business. The first item of which is confirmation of a fear that remained in the back of Hogan's mind since the first moment he heard about the existence of these tapes. It's something he hoped against hope never made it to tape. Because in that private bedroom, he'd not only had sex with Heather Clem on multiple occasions, but he'd gotten high and he'd *vented*. He'd vented about banal things, like the men who had harassed him at a strip club, and what he'd eaten that evening, and as the nights wore on his venting would gradually grow deeper and darker. He had vented about more serious things, ranting about his future ex-wife, and about who his daughter was dating and what he thought of her boyfriend. He'd let out all the nastiness and anger and frustration pent up in his life. He'd bared what was in his heart and that heart was broken, bitter, and black. He had said things as bad as he had ever said in his life, that he'd want no one else to ever hear, and he'd said them in a house he didn't know had walls that could talk.

It's all there, Davidson says, at the forty-nine-minute mark of one of the DVDs.

Worse, he tells him, there is also Bubba on tape, entering the room shortly after Hogan had left and saying to his wife, "If we ever did want to retire, all we have to do is use that fucking footage."

It is here, as Davidson casually dangles the biggest betrayal of the man's life, as Hogan considers the prospect of however many other career-ending moments were unknowingly captured on film, that we might forgive Hogan if his hand drops briefly to rest on his trademark fanny pack. In that fanny pack is a nine-millimeter handgun. He is licensed to carry it in Florida, but here, in this situation, he shouldn't be. A part of him must be hoping for an excuse, any excuse to go after the person whose perversion had created the tape, the writer who had so joyously broadcast it, the greedy unknown individual attempting to profit from it, and the lawyer who enabled them all to do so. This man is the source of his trouble, actively extorting him, and unlike Bubba or A. J. Daulerio, he's standing right in front of him. Yet he also knows, for certain this time, that there are cameras, and those cameras are recording everything he does for the voyeurs in the next room, who will be charged with taking this case to court if it goes that far.

Davidson asks if he can speak to Houston privately, and the two lawyers—one who represents celebrities, the other who represents the exploitation of their most embarrassing moments—head into the bathroom. Davidson drops the pretense: He tells Houston that he has not brought his actual client with him, but a representative. He admits that his client is an ex-employee of Bubba Clem's and explains, in a semantic dance around plausible deniability afforded only to lawyers, how the tapes were acquired. "I don't know if they were stolen," he says, "and quite frankly, I don't want to know if they were stolen." *But I have them and you want them.* Then he leaves the bathroom and promises to return with his client's representative.

In a few minutes, Davidson is back in the room trailed by a worn and nervous associate with brown hair and dark, empty eyes that speak to the confusing mess that has brought her here and the cold determination of her own to get what was promised to her. Davidson walks her to the polygrapher, secretly hired by the FBI, and then suggests that the three of them—Houston, Hogan, and Davidson—head down to the lobby to wait for her to finish. What ensues must have been the most awkward lunch of all time, Hogan and Houston sitting there with the man who treats shaking them down for hundreds of thousands of dollars no differently from selling a set of golf clubs on Craigslist, while they try desperately to stay in character and avoid revealing the fact that the FBI is recording all of it. At some point, Davidson suggests they go to his hotel room—which the FBI has explicitly asked them not to do—to watch the tapes.

Alone in this room, without the cameras, unsure whether the wireless microphones can even work at this distance, Hogan's fantasies return. Davidson excuses himself to use the restroom, leaving the tapes unguarded on the bed. How easily Hogan could grab them and break them in half, then kick in the bathroom door and do the same to the man who had been so stupid as to give him the opportunity. He resists, he resists all of it. *This is what the law is for,* he tells himself. This isn't even real. We've set a trap and he's walked right into it. We're getting the FBI the evidence they need. So the government can do their job—enforce justice. No civil society would allow something like this to go unpunished.

Hogan can barely glance at the computer screen as he stands across the room, as far as he can get from it, going through the motions of verifying the tapes with the lawyer for the purposes of the sting. He sees his silhouette and that is the verification he needs. He doesn't know that his microphone is picking up the audio of all of it, that he is creating another tape that will haunt him just like the first one. All the while, Davidson is talking. Talking like they are all friends. He tells of the other people supposedly caught in the Clems' bedroom, passing along that there is a rumored tape of Heather Clem and General David Petraeus together. Davidson tells him that his client was the one who gave the tape of Hogan to Gawker.

"So wait a minute, so what you're saying is that the person you're representing . . . released this to Gawker then?"

"Yes."

"You know that for sure?"

"Yes."

"And to TMZ?"

"Yes."

His client's representative would be telling the polygrapher the same thing just a few floors away. That they'd held back the most damaging DVD to sell it, and they'd leaked the other to Gawker to drum up interest for it, to get Terry's attention, to make it worth his while to pay for the rest of them.

The pieces come together then. The tapes had been stolen. TMZ had seen one, reported on it, and confirmed its existence, but didn't actually publish the video. Gawker had come next, its lust for anything salacious and its indifference to who might be embarrassed along the way making the site the perfect unwitting agent for this plan, and now, here Hogan was, in the hotel room, paying $300,000 for what the lawyer claimed were the only remaining copies.

After three and a half hours of this charade, all that is left is the awkward formality of the exchange itself. They discuss what kind of pen to use to sign the document; Hogan asks if a marker will work. They joke about whether the laptop bag the DVDs were brought in comes with the six-figure purchase. Terry signs, struggling to keep his hand from shaking as he does it. Davidson signs, indifferent to putting his name on a piece of straightforward extortion.

Ending this humiliating, maddening trip through those nights in that house where Terry Bollea never should have gone, Houston hands over the check. This is the cue. Crouched and waiting, the FBI agents just a few feet away kick the door in and swarm inside the room, filling it with guns and shouting. As they detain Davidson and his representative, Davidson texts his client, who is casually shopping with his wife at a nearby mall, "Raided, need legal representation."

It could not have gone better. How much more incriminating could Davidson have been? Yet Terry Bollea is deeply shaken. He leaves the hotel in a daze. It's his wedding anniversary, but he doesn't want to go home. The adrenaline hasn't exhilarated him, it's turned sour in his system. He feels sick. Scared. There is hope, though; a room full of officers of the federal government heard proof that he didn't leak these tapes himself, that he was being shaken down. They saw evidence that he hadn't known he was being recorded. He tells himself that this is going to work out. That he's done everything he can. Then he proceeds to drive around Florida, hoping to lose himself in traffic.

As Terry Bollea traveled up the Courtney Campbell Causeway, he couldn't have known that back in the hotel room things were already unraveling. The first words out of Davidson's mystery woman's mouth were to deny what she had just said on tape: *The most important thing is that we were not responsible for the Gawker sex tape leak. Davidson told me to say that in order to complete the negotiations.*

And there were still those legal troubles. In the week after the sting, Hogan and Harder expected to hear if their preliminary injunction on the copyright claim of the tape would be approved—now the third try to get the tape taken down pending the outcome of the trial. A legal analyst would note that Hogan was dangerously "close to a three count where the bell will ring." And on December 20, the bell did ring—injunction *denied*.

Hearing the message clearly from the rulings that it is not the right venue for his case, Harder is essentially forced to withdraw the complaint from federal court. It's a desperate move, but Harder amends the existing complaint against Heather Clem in Florida to add Gawker as a defendant to that case. He had tried repeatedly to get an injunction to get the tape removed in anticipation of what would likely be a lengthy legal battle and was rebuffed each time by Judge Whittemore. Instead of keeping two fronts open (one of them clearly a losing front), Harder was attempting to consolidate them into one case, and there was only one avenue for that: Florida state court.

Critics would call this forum shopping, and in a sense it was—but it really only mattered whether that strategy worked or not. Gawker immediately appealed to Judge Whittemore to block this move, calling it egregious and fraudulent. Considering their run of success, Gawker's team naturally assumed they would prevail again. If they were right, not only would Hogan's hopes of getting at Gawker be crushed, but Thiel's first case would be over before it ever really began.

It's been setback after setback. The same judge telling them repeatedly: No, I'm not going to take down this sex tape of your client. Sorry, Terry, I don't care that this is humiliating you. Telling Peter Thiel, hidden off in the shadows, I don't care how well you thought this through, it's going to be harder than you thought.

Of course. Gawker has phenomenal First Amendment lawyers, a firm named Levine Sullivan Koch & Schulz. This is the firm that had beaten back lawsuits against the *Washington City Paper* by the billionaire owner of the Washington Redskins, against Condé Nast, and against the Hearst Corporation. For the time being, Gawker has insurance to pay them, too. These are the kinds of lawyers who have boilerplate briefs written for these types of lawsuits before they're even filed, just ready to go, itching for someone to challenge centuries of precedent when it comes to the rights of the press. This setup allows publishers to sleep at night, and enables the lawyers to spring into action at a moment's notice. And frankly, it's a good thing that the American judicial system favors defendants in these matters. What that meant for Terry Bollea, however, and for Peter Thiel, was that their odds did not look good early on. *The Hollywood Reporter* would lay it out frankly, saying that if Hulk Hogan still wanted to win, his only chance was to "say his prayers, eat his vitamins, and hope for one of those out-of-body moments that he once experienced during his professional wrestling days when he suddenly gains a new source of strength and makes a miraculous comeback."

Hogan would say he never doubted himself, but after all that there is no way he couldn't have. The federal judge had said plainly that Gawker's publication of the sex tape was "in conjunction with the news reporting function" and that the "factual finding supports a colorable fair use defense." He had rejected Hogan and his lawyers on every single attempt except the one they made to flee his courtroom. And an appellate court had done its own rejection of his case. The headlines weren't any kinder. The media not only thought he would lose, they were rooting for him to.

Meanwhile, Gawker had simply carried on doing what it did, much to the delight of millions of viewers. In February, it had received video of a tech entrepreneur, drunk, running around naked on a beach in India, and ran it. A few weeks later, it was forwarded an embarrassing email from a sorority girl at the University of Maryland, ran it, and watched the piece go on to nearly six *million* views (and lead to the girl's resignation from the sorority). On April 18, one of Gawker's writers would publish a screed against the editor of the *New York Post* in the aftermath of the Boston Marathon bombing, which called the editor in an enormous headline and graphic a "bigoted drunk who fucks pigs." And in lighter news, A. J. Daulerio's instituted practice of what he called "traffic whoring," where specific days and specific writers were assigned the duty of shamelessly chasing page views—mostly via viral pieces designed for Facebook—had been an incredible success. Revenues in 2013 were up more than a third over the year before and profit was doubling.

So when on March 27 the conspirators finally get good news, Gawker is hardly fazed by it. Judge Whittemore rules that Hogan's case can proceed in state court, acknowledging that Harder's new amended complaints no longer address any federal issues, thus making it a proper matter for Florida's state court. Then another piece of good news: three weeks later in Florida state court, Judge Pamela Campbell grants the temporary injunction that Harder and Houston had wanted for so long. The video *and* the post have to come down pending a trial verdict.*

Perhaps it had been the rising sense of its own power that gave Gawker the confidence to make the decision in April 2013 in response to Campbell's granting of the injunction that Hogan had sought. Gawker's editors decided they would simply not honor her decision. It was *obviously wrong,* they believed, an aberration in a record of repeated rulings in their favor. John Cook, Gawker's then-editor, writes a post titled "A Judge Told Us to Take Down Our Hulk Hogan Sex Tape Post. We Won't." Cook would admit later in his deposition that he hadn't even watched the full tape until the judge had ordered it removed, but in that moment, because someone had told Gawker they couldn't run it—now he would fight for it and care about his right to do so intensely. He would reject the order as unconstitutional and commit Gawker to fight any attempt to make them follow it. And in Gawker style, he's not just going to resist a judge's order, he's going to do it with flair and petulance—throwing a link to the sex tape in the post and immediately sending the article to a number of reporters, to make sure Gawker's refusal to comply gets attention.

Harder would plead with Gawker to follow the order and threaten contempt motions but to no avail. We asked earlier who the underdog was in the dynamic. It is probably not the party that can defy an order from a judge and get away with it.

Setback after setback after setback.

* Eight months later, this ruling would be overturned by an appellate court. Another setback.

And before 2013 is through, there will be one more. After very little communication from the U.S. attorney's office after the sting, Harder and Hogan and Houston would finally hear from them: no charges will be filed nor will explanation ever be given for why. Not even "Sorry you put your life at risk in this hotel room for nothing," just a big *no*. Meaning that everything that happened in that room had been for nothing—or worse. In July 2013, seven months after the sting, Hogan is told by the Department of Justice that it will not be pursuing the case. Worse, they find out in September that the attorney general will be holding on to the DVDs from Keith Davidson pending the outcome of the trial, and only then give it to whomever is deemed the "rightful possessor."

It's the drive where you hit every red light. The project where everything seems to go wrong, at the same time. When you ask yourself, "Why can I not just catch a *fucking* break?" It is the nature of conspiracy. If it was easy, everyone would do it. Fate rarely conspired to help conspirators—and if it was on their side, why were they forced to do all this sneaking around then? No, fate sends to the conspirators of the world the best of its Murphy's Law and entropy and crises of confidence.

The essayist and investor Paul Graham, a peer and rival of Peter Thiel's, has charted the trajectory of a start-up, with all its ups and downs. After the initial bump of media attention, the rush of excitement from the unexpected success, Graham says that the founders enter a phase where the novelty begins to wear off, and they quickly descend from their early euphoria into what he calls the "trough of sorrow." A start-up launches with its investments, gets a few press hits, and then smacks right into reality. Many companies never make it out of this ditch. "The problem with the Silicon Valley," as Jim Barksdale, the former CEO and president of Netscape, once put it, "is that we tend to confuse a clear view with a short distance."

Here, too, like the founders of a start-up, the conspirators have smacked into reality. The reality of the legal system. The defensive bulwark of the First Amendment. The reality of the odds. They have discovered the difference between a good plan and how far they'll need to travel to fulfill it. They have trouble even serving Denton with papers. Harder has to request a 120-day extension just to wrap his head around Gawker's financial and corporate structure. This is going to be harder than they thought.

It always is.

To say that in 2013 all the rush and excitement present on those courthouse steps several months earlier had dissipated would be a preposterous understatement. If a conspiracy, by its inherent desperation and disadvantaged position, is that long struggle in a dark hallway, here is the point where one considers simply sitting down and sobbing in despair, not even sure what direction to go. Is this even possible? Are we wrong?

Machiavelli wrote that fortune—misfortune in fact—aims herself where "dikes and dams have not been made to contain her." Clausewitz said that battle plans were great but ultimately subject to "friction"—delays, confusion, mistakes, and complications. What is friction? Friction is when you're Pericles and you lay out a brilliant plan to defend Athens against Sparta and then your city is hit by the plague. Friction is when your trusted research tells you one thing but you come to find the situation on the ground is completely different, that the data had it all wrong. Friction is the Russian *rasputitsa*, the endless mud that makes quick work of brilliant plans and bigger armies. And so the essential trait of the successful man is not only perseverance but almost a perverse expectation of how difficult it is going to be. It is having redundancies on top of redundancies, so you can absorb the losses you eventually incur. One must not just steel one's heart but also one's spirit so that there is no such thing as an obstacle—just information. The earlier you spot and anticipate setbacks, the less demoralizing they will be.

We want things to be easy. We want them to be clean. They rarely are.

Napoleon's dictum for the general-in-chief is that he "must not allow himself to be elated by good news or depressed by bad." In the course of any campaign there will be plenty of both. A conspiracy meets with more setbacks than successes. It's rolling the dice—making a decision, knowing that unforeseen issues will come up. Lots of them.

By the time of their second string of setbacks in 2013, Peter Thiel was already six-odd years into this dance with Gawker. Mr. A was two years in. Harder himself was nearly a year in. It was well into the end of its beginning and it had not begun well. If there was anything they had to be thankful for, it would be something they could not appreciate until later, and that would be that they were mercifully in the dark about all that remained ahead of them, all three long years of struggle and difficulty that were still to come.

Fortunately, Hogan's excitement and despair were tempered by more realistic expectations from Thiel and Mr. A. The last time Gawker had settled a lawsuit related to a sex tape, the participants—three of them—walked away with roughly $100,000. Total. The celebrities involved in it had almost certainly lost money fighting for its removal. Mr. A would point out to Peter that there was very little precedent of sex tape cases going to trial and pegged their chances of winning at even odds at best. Despite the $100 million damages claim, the conspiracy was aware that the Hogan case might not be progressing toward some final deathblow. It could be tossed out of court (as it nearly was), it could settle for some small but survivable amount, a jury could award only token damages. Knowing that this might be only one of many cases they would have to pursue, Thiel and Harder and Mr. A had perspective that Hogan would never be able to have. *Bollea v.*

Gawker had a *chance* of being a great case, but they were very much prepared for it not to be. Then again, they also didn't have their asses on the line—or *online*—so they could afford to meet these setbacks with a greater degree of equanimity.

"If you think of what you're doing too probabilistically where you have all these different steps, and there's a chance that all these steps fail, then the conspiracy is very complicated, like a Rube Goldberg contraption, where something is just going to break down for one reason or another," Peter explains. "What Mr. A convinced me of in 2011 was that this is not a statistical concatenation of probabilities—it was that if we simply executed on a few of these things correctly you would win."

So for all the setbacks, there was actually a sense of progress, momentum even. As long as those few big things were still aligned correctly, all was not yet lost. With this criterion, the situation was not quite as bad as it looked: The conspirators were battling it out with Gawker in public and yet Gawker had no idea that there was a conspiracy. They had gotten a case to stick in state court, and they were about to begin the discovery phase of the trial, a place Gawker had never been taken to before. Yes, it had not occurred exactly as expected, but that's how it goes. "You take two steps forward and one backwards but as long as you're progressing that's what matters," said Mr. A.

And there was a big, concrete step forward for the conspirators, one giant setback for Gawker. One that neither side would fully understand at the time. Gawker's lawyers were still focused on the immediate prior restraint motions in front of them, and it would be some time before Harder and Mr. A would see the huge advantage they had gained. In being forced to drop the case in federal court and limit their case entirely to state court, the conspirators were given a lucky break. Gawker's legal strategy, still then backed by that subsidy of $750,000 in insurance money, would be one of attrition, fighting until its opponent ran out of money, or until the policy went dry and Gawker had to decide if it wanted to keep going. But in Florida, where Gawker had driven Harder to in retreat after so many federal court victories, this strategy was not so favorable. A quirk of Florida law held that in order to appeal a civil verdict, petitioners have to post *supersedeas bond* equal to the amount of the verdict—essentially proving they could pay what they would owe if their appeal was not successful. A 2006 Florida statute had limited those bonds, but still, the cap was $50 million. If Hogan could actually get to a trial, if he could get this case in front of a jury, and if that jury sided with him in any substantive way, Gawker would be finished.

While Gawker's revenues would be strong that year, approaching $35 million, it was still an independent media company without deep-pocketed investors. Gawker and, least of all, Nick Denton did not have $100 million to give to Hulk Hogan, and Denton's insurance was not such that it would likely cover damages. Gawker didn't have $50 million on hand, either, which would be the amount it would have to put in escrow with the state of Florida if it was to lose and seek to appeal to a higher court. Yet perhaps it was because of the company's growth, or perhaps because a trial seemed far away and the news had thus far been entirely in his favor, that for years Nick Denton would be talking about how many "rounds" he could go with Hogan, that his worst-case scenario would be ultimately winning the case "on appeal."

"We weren't so omnipotent that we knew every nuance of Florida law," Mr. A would say of the conspirators' understanding about the potential strength of this position that they almost had fallen into. In 2013, they were still reeling too much from most of the setbacks to see much good in anything. Just trying to maintain equanimity in the face of that had been enough—to be elated or even optimistic was too much just yet. Indeed, had they known how favorable their legal position in state court would be, they might never have bothered with federal court in the first place. Still, fully aware of it or not, confident or filled with doubts, the conspirators had in fact gained a strategic position that could potentially give them everything Peter Thiel and Mr. A had hoped for when they began to plot Gawker's destruction in that restaurant in Berlin. The decision by Charles Harder to attach a $100 million number to Hogan's lawsuit had been in part to get headlines, but now, if they were to get anything close to it from a jury, it would be an immediate knockout blow to Gawker. No chance for appeal. A bankruptcy event. Better, Gawker didn't even seem to be aware of its glass jaw.

There were other subtle advantages, too, which were there now but would only come to reveal themselves as time passed. The district court judge would be far better disposed to a local plaintiff than federal judges might have been. The early setbacks, coming one right after another, would also contribute to the growing confidence of their opponent. Judge Whittemore's repeated rulings had given Gawker the sense that the law was overwhelmingly on its side. Gawker's confidence, as it had been since its beginnings as a company, tended to bleed over into contempt. Its early belief that Judge Campbell had no power over them, that they could disregard her rulings, would undoubtedly make Gawker less sympathetic to her in the years of motions to come. Finally, it was no small thing that the media coverage had been favorable to Gawker and its chances. Far away from Florida, Nick Denton would be surrounded by peers, even competitors, who were convinced that this case was open and shut, that it was only a matter of time before it resolved in his favor, and that in the meantime it didn't need to be taken seriously.

And so it is that even setbacks can contain opportunities within them, if conspirators are patient and resourceful enough. Few ever make it out of the trough of sorrow—in business, in life, in conspiracy. Certainly, not a single opponent of Gawker's ever had. Deterred by the obstacles Gawker had placed in their way, they settled or they quit, or they decided it was better to make nice and apologize.

But this operation had planned for those obstacles and had survived the first onslaught of them. And now the conspirators would have to make *good* out of the opportunities they presented.

CHAPTER 9

Know Thy Enemy

The great Sun Tzu said that you must know your enemy as well as yourself. To not know yourself is dangerous, but to not know your enemy is reckless or worse. Because without this knowledge, you are unaware of the opportunities your enemy is presenting to you, and worse, you are ignorant of the opportunities you present to those who wish to do you harm.

Gawker's editors and principals did not know the enemy they had made. They did not know what motivated Peter Thiel, what kept them a going concern on his daily to-do list. It was a mistake that would cost them, but one that can be forgiven since it is difficult, if not impossible, to study and know an enemy you do not even know exists. And the Gawker team, on a very literal level, had no idea that in the shadows, scheming against them, was the quixotic, contrarian, billionaire genius they'd so thoughtlessly outed five years earlier and then casually taunted ever since.

They did, however, know that Hulk Hogan—Terry Bollea—existed as an enemy. Even if they did not *know* him, either. He had, via interviews, told anyone thinking about publishing the tapes what his intentions were and articles had been sent directly to Gawker's editors by the outlets that ran them. When they had proceeded with the tape anyway, his lawyers sent Gawker cease and desist letters within hours. They had not listened. Instead, Gawker's writers laughed and made fun of him in some thirty pages of group chats, joking about his "silky pubes" and whether his penis had a matching do-rag. If Gawker had in 2012—or in the years to follow—properly sized up what was in front of them, perhaps they might have found a way to apologize and see the matter quickly fade away.

But that was all in the distant past—water under a bridge too far and too many preliminary legal victories away—by the time the first round of depositions in the matter of *Bollea v. Gawker* took place. A deposition is a simple but obligatory part of the discovery process in legal proceedings. In it, the lawyers for both the plaintiff (Bollea) and the defendant (Gawker) are able to ask witnesses a number of questions related to the case, in search of information they can use against the other in court. They are expansive, fact-finding interviews where almost nothing is off limits—attorneys can object but answers are preserved for the record—where many important issues are explored and questioned by each side. Although depositions do not occur in a courtroom, witnesses are under oath—they must swear to tell the truth—and often these depositions are videotaped so that they may later be shown to a jury.

Gawker did not seem bothered by the fact that this case had proceeded this far. We know this because we can see video of them, A.J. in his white button-up, Denton in his sweater, both unshaven, casual, not interested in being there. We can see just how little they could be bothered by this pesky lawsuit they were facing—how deeply they underestimated the fight they had picked and the legal quagmire they had entered.

On September 30, 2013, in New York City, A. J. Daulerio appeared for the first of the major depositions in the lawsuit, something that was, in his words, "basically a nonsense and completely ludicrous formal fucking deposition over something we had already won." It's easy to read contempt into that sentence, but it's something more subtle than that. It's bewilderment, bemusement even. Because Gawker had seen the case against it rejected repeatedly by a federal court, because A.J. believed that these rulings showed that the article was well within the bounds of the First Amendment, he considered the matter essentially over.

To A.J., the deposition was a pesky obligation, and every word of his answers and twitch of his body reflected it. This was not an entirely unreasonable position. Every other case against Gawker had been thrown out or settled over the years, and this one appeared to be heading in the same direction. And he had other reasons to be dismissive. The man had already left Gawker and was on his own. And was this lawsuit even about him? Many other defendants were listed—including the people who, in objective fact and admission, had actually done the vile act of recording this tape. A.J. would later tell a reporter that he might have been hungover during the deposition. The man's life was a mess at the time, he thought the deposition was a formality in a matter that would soon be forgotten, and who could blame him?

Originally, Charles Harder had been scheduled to do the deposition, but a scheduling conflict meant one of his less aggressive attorneys was sent in his place. In one of the many pieces of luck that must occur for a conspiracy to succeed, the personalities of these two individuals could not have matched up better. The casual, plodding patience of the interlocutor seems almost designed to highlight Daulerio's indifference.

"Did you give any consideration prior to October 4, 2012, as to whether publishing the Hulk Hogan sex tape would distress Hulk Hogan?"

"No."

"You didn't care really, did you?"

"No."

"Had you known that Hulk Hogan would be emotionally distressed by this publication you would have still published it, correct?"

"Sure, yes."

"So it's fair to say [that] . . . played no part in your decision about whether and what to publish?"

"Correct . . ."

"If you knew for a fact that he was secretly taped and would not have authorized that, you would still have published the tape, would you not?"

"Yes."

There was no intensity to the deposition. A.J. is as patient as he can be, under hours and hours of questioning. The pace is meandering and calm, and A.J. finds himself lulled into it, the way warm weather lowers inhibitions and brings with it a sense of freedom. School's out, it's summer. *Are we about done?*

For 95 percent of it, he would say, he felt he had been under control—he had reined in his impulses to make a mockery of the entire proceeding. Yet there is one break, after being worn down by the pedantry of the questioning and the unreasonableness of the lawyer's questions. The result was just a joke. A single joke. One about which he would say that, under normal circumstances, every person on the planet would understand where he was coming from. But of course, these are not normal circumstances. This is a $100 million lawsuit.

Joke or not, it would be a remarkable exchange etched into the legal record and the destiny of this case.

"Can you imagine a situation where a celebrity sex tape would not be newsworthy?" the lawyer asks A.J.

"If they were a child."

"Under what age?"

"*Four.*"

"No four-year-old sex tapes, OK."

Perhaps there was no reasonable answer to this question, or perhaps A.J. saw it as the trap that it was and thought a joke would help him escape it. In any case, he liked what he said enough that later in the deposition he would call back to his own line, like a comedian calling back to a good punch line from earlier in the night. *Would you run a sex tape of Miley Cyrus if it came across your desk? "Was she under four at the time of the sex tape?"*

As he left the deposition, an attorney for Gawker told A.J. he'd done great. If this had been said merely as reassurance, so be it, but it does not occur to anyone at the time that the deposition had been a disaster. The joke had been one exchange among many. A few days later A.J. and Gawker's lawyers were sent an errata sheet that would allow him a month to review the transcript and change or clarify anything he might have meant. He picks up a pen to make one alteration—changing the word *post* to *posted*—and signs the rest. He swears it was all fair and accurate.

But the truth is no amount of corrections could have adjusted for his tone, or what was captured on video. The emotionlessness of that answer: What age is too young for you to publish a sex tape of? *Four.* It might have been meant as a joke, but it didn't totally feel like one, and in a case that would hinge so much on video footage, what mattered is that it didn't *look like one*.

Nick Denton's deposition on a cloudy Wednesday morning in early October 2013 is certainly less outwardly stupid, but it takes a similar blasé tone. If Denton wasn't worried, why would his subordinates have been? Yet unlike Daulerio, Denton is calm and wry, and expresses no outward contempt for the proceedings. Nick Denton is an inherently curious person, the kind of person who though he might not seek out such opportunities, when given the chance for a conversation with people who have radically different opinions from his own, he at least likes to take advantage of it. So he does. Several times the lawyers need to push Denton back to the matter at hand and have to decline to answer some of his questions back to them. To him this is not a procedure of legal significance, it's a bizarre function of a Kafka story and he is bemused by it. It is an emotion anchored in his belief that this proceeding, like all the others, will be nicely wrapped up in due time.

When Denton does answer, he is not cold or vicious, nor is he what the public might expect when they consider the stereotype of a brave editor or publisher. He is philosophical, deigning to engage in the absurdity of this discussion—not for his sake but for yours. He is not evasive, he is expansive. He wants to talk, he wants to explain himself, because he knows that he is right and you are a well-intentioned idiot. He admits, for instance, that he has not actually watched the tape he is being sued for $100 million over. Why would he concern himself with such a thing? He'd taken a few minutes to read the story a week before his deposition, but still, he tells the lawyers, he does not quite see why a celebrity would be so upset about it. Denton could only see words, words written by A.J., as "sweet, as sweet as in sympathetic." Besides, this is what Gawker does. This is why people flock to the site. *Of course, we published a tape and an article about an illegally recorded sex tape. Wouldn't everyone have done the same thing?*

As with A.J.'s, there is a certain irony in the fact that the blinking camera sitting across from Denton in that deposition room was recording a video as well, and that what was captured on this recording would be wrenched from context and used against him in a public forum, too. And who wouldn't, if they were trying to embarrass and undermine someone in front of a jury, rush to make use of comments like the ones Denton made in those long hours of questioning in that drab room in front of a camera?

"I believe in *total* freedom and informational transparency. I want everybody to know everything. And I think society, this country that I moved to will be better off if we could talk freely about *everything*. So that's—I'm an *extremist* when it comes to that. That's why I love the U.S. I love the presumption that the expression is free and I want to make fullest use of that liberty that the internet provides," he said calmly to the camera.

There is a story that Herodotus tells in *The Histories* about a war between Sparta and Tegea. In it, the Spartans were "so confident of reducing the men of Tegea to slavery" that they literally brought chains with them. But they lost, having dreadfully underestimated their enemy, and with poetic justice the prisoners were "forced to wear on their own legs the chains they had brought." Gawker's depositions would prove not dissimilar. Both A.J. and Denton would one day be marched into court chained to the words they had spoken in the depositions they had so confidently conducted.

"I think Gawker had a Superman complex: you can shoot me with a gun but it will bounce off my chest. That was their attitude," says Harder. "I knew we had a benefactor who for the moment was paying the bills. But I never believed for a second that we were invulnerable. They just seemed to think that nothing could stop them and nothing could harm them." Why else would Gawker decide in late April not only to ignore Judge Campbell's injunction, but to respond by filing to disqualify her from the case entirely?

There was a simple reason that both Denton and Daulerio might underestimate the significance of the statements they made in their depositions. According to the transcripts of the nine Gawker employees deposed as part of the trial, including its CEO, its COO, its CTO and chief strategy officer, and its editor, not a single one had been deposed previously related to a Gawker matter. Six of them had never been in a deposition before, ever, for any reason.

Over the years, Gawker had been sued at least a dozen times. Fred

Durst in 2005. Dane and Gayheart in 2009. HarperCollins and Sarah Palin in 2010. A flight attendant who worked for Arnold Schwarzenegger in 2011. Dr. Phil in 2013. A *New Yorker* profile on Nick Denton mentions offhandedly that the sites received at least one cease and desist letter nearly every week (if this was true, by 2013 it would have added up to hundreds and hundreds). In one 2013 filing, Gawker's lawyer tells the judge that they have received so many cease and desists over the years that it would take *at least* several days of her time, plus several days of another lawyer's time, just to go through and organize them for the court. She pleads that doing so is essentially an impossible task. There are so many lawsuits and claims against Gawker that in 2010, *years* before Hulk Hogan had entered the picture and before Peter Thiel had even hardened enough to consider hiring Charles Harder, one of Gawker's lawyers would joke to the *Observer* that they had been sued enough times to literally fill a book. "One day," she said, "there will be a book called *The Collected Legal Works of Gawker Media*."

Despite all these letters, after Gawker has been a party in multiple lawsuits and seriously threatened with legal action many more times, not a single case had ever proceeded to even this preliminary stage of discovery. In Daulerio's words, Gawker had "kind of walked through the raindrops for over a decade." They *were* Superman, at least up to that point. They didn't take any legal matter seriously because they never had to. But the past is no indicator of the future—ask the fattened Thanksgiving turkey or the proverbial man stacking straws on a camel's back. It's Rome telling itself that no one could ever cross the Alps. Then one day Hannibal appears in Italy with his elephant. *Shit*, they can do that?

Thiel's team would have had no idea about this fuller context until all the depositions were completed, until they looked at the first answer to the first question by each Gawker employee: "Have you ever been deposed in a Gawker matter before?" "No, I have not." That initial hunch—that secret edge that Thiel had first suspected—that no one had ever truly challenged these people before was confirmed. "At that point," Thiel said, "we knew that we had gotten further than anybody else. It was a sample size of one. If you thought of it as a ten-step secret plan, and the deposition was Step 3, and you could get to Step 3, very deterministically, if you have a halfway decent lawsuit, you can get the person deposed. If it turned out that he was deposed many times before, that would've been a less good fact. When we were the very first person to ever get there it suggests that nobody even tried. We are in terra incognita here. This undiscovered country."

For the first time, Gawker's leadership is out of its own element, no longer in its familiar position of safety or comfort—of being the bully on the block—whether they understood that seriously or not. In a joint interview from 2013, when even the idea of a trial was a faraway impossibility, Denton explained to a reporter how puzzled he was that anyone would bother to pursue this seemingly minor issue with such intensity:

> [Hogan has] pursued every single possible avenue, and I don't really understand the logic of . . . I don't understand what they want. Do you? I find their motivations hard to follow. I don't really understand the relationship between the lawyers and Hogan. I don't understand who is getting what out of this. It must be very expensive for them, and I don't see that they have a particular prospect of some kind of mega-payday. Sometimes it's hard to deal with seemingly irrational antagonists. . . .

And then, in the same interview, Denton casually outed yet another gay celebrity. The reporter would, in a gesture of that journalistic self-censorship Denton had complained about, redact this unsuspecting person's name before publication.

"When we published the Hulk Hogan sex tape, no one cared,"

John Cook would say in an interview. "We've published a lot of stories where people are shocked and outraged and you feel that outrage. . . . Hogan did not have that dynamic at all." Gawker cared about what their readers thought, what their friends in the media thought, and since those audiences were okay with the post, the pesky opinion of a court in Florida didn't seem to matter much. When Gawker's writers looked at Terry Bollea, as they looked at so many of the people they wrote about, they saw not a person but a character in the game of their digital day-to-day existence. They saw the comical, cartoonish professional wrestler, the stupid celebrity who like all celebrities must enjoy all kinds of publicity, good or bad, chosen or otherwise. They did not see a man who'd lost nearly everything and had been pushed to his breaking point. Besides, their lawyers had won all those preliminary motions, and that must have meant something.

There were signs, though, if anyone had wanted to look, that they might have made an enemy who would be difficult to appease. The mansion that Hogan filmed his reality show in had once been worth $25 million. It sold in 2012 for $6 million. The other houses, the friends, the family, the glory days—they were all gone. His wife had taken 70 percent of their marital assets in the divorce settlement and promptly settled in with a younger man. How long and how far had Terry Bollea crawled from the shipyards of Tampa to get to where he got? How many chairs did he take to the head? How many dingy arenas did he perform in to build this character? How much did he love being loved, by children and their parents alike, as the caricature of American excess and goodness in the Cold War? This is the man who got to play the hero for a living and now much of that is gone. And here some New York blog was humiliating him by parading his best friend's betrayal across the *world wide* web and putting his naked, aging, balding body on display in a sex tape he had never asked to be in.

He was a man with little to lose. The kind of person to whom you wouldn't want to give a singular obsession, and the kind of person whose singular obsession you likely do not want to be. I ask Denton repeatedly if he feels like he misjudged Hulk Hogan, but even now I think he cannot admit that he did. Thiel was the one behind the conspiracy, so he gets all the credit and the blame. Yet Hogan deserves some, too. He was the one who charged ahead, who could have accepted any of the settlement offers that would be forthcoming, who didn't *need* to and probably shouldn't have filed the lawsuit in the first place. It probably would have been smarter for him if he hadn't—he might still be in the WWE Hall of Fame if he had walked away when the setbacks started.

It cannot be said that Gawker was not warned. Hogan's personal attorney makes many attempts to explain to Gawker's lawyers who his client is, what motivates him, what kind of man it takes to make it as a professional wrestler, where the act might be fake but two bodies hurling each other down against the mat is real. Do Bollea's many surgeries signify nothing to them? Do they think the injuries were fake, too? This man *fights*.

There was an exchange between Charles Harder, the ambitious lawyer with something to prove, and Seth Berlin, Gawker's lead counsel, after one of Gawker's early legal victories in the case. Once again, Gawker thought that this ruling would finally put the matter to bed. Berlin approaches Harder. "Where's all this going? How long are you guys going to be at this?" He gets his answer: "Until my client is bankrupt or until you guys give up."

This could so easily be something that one lawyer says to leverage a settlement from an opponent. In fact, it is what lawyers often say to get settlements. They claim their client is going to fight to the end, but rarely is this true. Certainly, it was more reasonable to assume that it was just typical posturing, rather than to guess that it was impossible for Hogan to go bankrupt because he had a billionaire backer.

Looking at the facts as they could see them, the Gawker people don't heed the warning or take it as an opportunity to negotiate. Instead, they try to exercise their own leverage.

In March 2014, after the unremarkable depositions of Heather and Bubba Clem in Florida, Hogan's lawyers are working at the Sandpearl, the same hotel that was the site of the disastrous sting operation a year and a half before, when Heather Dietrick, Gawker's general counsel and eventually the company's president, calls to suggest she drive over and talk. Believing that a serious settlement offer might be forthcoming, David Houston agrees to meet and they discuss the case while they walk down the beach. Heather has an offer: Gawker is willing to *let* Hogan dismiss the suit. If he does so now, they will not go after him for attorney's fees. We will let you bend the knee, and we will not hold it against you that it took so long for you to come to your senses.

Harder's warning, then, was dismissed as unbelievable. In part because it was. *Nobody fights to the end.* If they did, a lot more cases would end up at trial and with a verdict. Gawker seemed to believe that Hogan had forgotten that he's not an actual hero—that he just played one in a fake sport. He'll figure it out, they thought. He'll see the futility of resistance soon enough. But Heather had taken the safety of this assumption. She had been so confident in her assumption that right there on the white sand of Clearwater Beach, just a few blocks from Hogan's home and the hotel room where he'd put himself in danger for nothing, she felt she could dictate the terms. In a sense, she helped turn Harder's prophecy true.

"I took it as an insult," Hogan would say. "'*If you drop the lawsuit we won't charge you attorney fees and let you walk away.*' In my opinion she was saying, 'We won't destroy your life like we destroyed everybody else's.'" Now he wanted not just to fight them, but to prove that they had seriously underestimated him, that they had no idea who he was.

Deterrence is an important strategy. The more intimidating you are, the less people conspire against you. Yet the powerful must always be very careful with their threats, with their demonstrations of superior resources. Aimed poorly, they have a nasty habit of backfiring.

The significance does not seem to have registered to Dietrick and others at Gawker that this case, even in 2013, had already gone further than any past lawsuit they'd been forced to defend. The kind of enemy they had made, the way in which they had aggravated him, was not yet clear to them. That they'd actually made an enemy, that this wasn't some theatrical production, did not yet compute.

Thiel had said something to *Wired* magazine not long before this juncture, speaking not about the case but about an investment, that makes it clear how much he relished this kind of ignorance. It's what he exploits, counts on even. "The things that I think I'm right about," Thiel said, "other people are in some sense not even wrong about, because they're not thinking about them." In this sense, it's an oversimplification to say that Gawker was *wrong* about the threat it faced. It was actually much worse. It was totally and utterly unaware of it—unaware of how much harder it was making it for itself with each decision, each misreading, each misjudgment.

At almost every step Thiel avoided making this mistake himself.* He had assembled a team of patient, cautious individuals who were prepared to spend essentially any amount of money and work for any amount of time. He did the job of the commander, of the strategist: to discern what is going on in your opponent's mind. They had not plunged into anything—he had waited multiple years before even making a move, so that the first step together wasn't also right off a cliff. They had taken the time to think not just about what the Gawker

*It is also worth noting that tattooed on Hulk Hogan's right wrist in cursive script is one word: *Awareness*.

people thought, but about what the Gawker people thought about *what other people thought about them.* According to Harder, they had read Gawker as "people who don't settle," and this belief was confirmed through their interactions. "Everyone is a person who settles unless they demonstrate to you over time that they are not a person who wants to settle. They had insurance and they were very stubborn and righteous. They believed so strongly that they were right and that we were wrong in challenging them, because in their mind the First Amendment was so strong and so clear in their favor, that who are we to challenge them? That was their attitude."

In pursuing a strategy of total destruction through the financial support of legal challenges to Gawker, Thiel was acknowledging its strength as an adversary. He wasn't sure specifically what it was capable of—he couldn't have known when he began in 2007 that in 2012 Denton would still be "sick" of him, that Denton would be sending chat messages suggesting to A.J., having taken over as Gawker's editor, that he write a piece on the rumor that Peter Thiel was bad in bed. Nor could any of the conspirators have anticipated at the beginning what would be said in those depositions, or what would be unearthed during document discovery—the chat logs, the emails, and the documents that Gawker would have to turn over. He had spent his time just thinking about, studying, and poking around these people he was going to pursue. He gathered every opinion he could get, pumped people for information, listened to every single warning and whispered legend about how invincible Gawker was as a media outlet. Knowing this doesn't prevent him from proceeding, but it does determine *how* he proceeds. He prepared for an arduous legal battle and patiently waited for the right opportunity to begin one. He found partners who were willing to take on that fight, and he remained, as ever, open to learning more about his opponent as information came in. Gawker might not know Peter Thiel was its enemy, but that enemy had come to understand it even better than it knew itself.

What Thiel learned watching those depositions of Denton and Daulerio was that the men were worse than whatever uncharitable assumptions he had previously held about them. Who says those things in a legal proceeding? Who jokes about publishing child porn while under oath? Who describes an illicitly recorded sex tape and the article that brought it to millions of people as "sweet"? Do these people not understand how they come off?

As surprised as Thiel and Mr. A and Charles Harder are by what they've seen, they are also encouraged. If Denton and Daulerio were delusional enough to say them on the record, reckless enough to make these unforced errors, there was no telling what other missteps they might make on this slow road toward a jury trial. If they had never been deposed, it meant that this was all unfamiliar territory to them, and that the decisions Gawker would be making were going to be tinged with that arrogance. And, flashing forward, if Harder could get them far enough, what would a jury think of those comments? What would it be like to put these two on the stand?

There is something invigorating about taking action, getting away from the planning and toward the doing. But the feeling you get when it seems like real progress is being made, that you could actually win . . . that feeling washes away all doubts. And that is what the conspirators were experiencing for the first time.

CHAPTER 10

The Power of Secrets

Secrecy has always been the essential element in conspiracies. It is, after all, very hard to have a secret plan you've told everyone about. For obvious reasons, it's more difficult to destroy someone or something when they know you're coming for them.

History is, if anything, one long exercise in the triumph of secrets. It could be argued that the entirety of the Second World War hinged on one critical event: the Allied breaking of Enigma, the codes with which the Axis powers communicated their secret plans. And then the conspiracy to keep Ultra—the code name for the Allies' codebreaking method—secret for the entire war, never letting the Germans and Japanese and Italians know that they knew their every move.

Today, we have a complex relationship with secrecy insomuch as we live in a world that no longer values it. Transparency carries now in the modern mind the weight of moral imperative. This two-handed truism sits at the foundation of Gawker's mission and cult-heroism: the full exposure of open (and closed) secrets. It has become a perversion of Nixon's line about the cover-up being worse than the crime where today it's automatically a sin if you keep it a secret.

Thiel's plot against Gawker was wrong, it would be argued, and the obvious proof of this was that he tried to hide what he was doing for so long. Nick Denton would call Thiel a hypocrite for not meeting him in the open. "Wouldn't the libertarian solution," he told me, "have been to make his own counterargument? To meet speech with speech. It's not like Thiel was lacking in outlets, or the money to make new outlets if he felt his voice was not loud enough."

It might be the libertarian *way*, but it certainly wouldn't have been any kind of solution. What would Gawker have done had Peter Thiel taken it on in a war of words instead of secretly plotting its undoing? It would have torn him apart.

When people who don't like what you're doing know that you're trying to do it, they are more likely to be able to stop you. It's that simple.

"We are bred up to feel it is a disgrace to ever succeed by falsehood," read a plaque on the wall of LCS, the secret division of the British government tasked with its covert operations and intelligence. "We will keep hammering along with the conviction that honesty is the best policy and that truth always wins in the long run. These pretty little sentiments do well for a child's copybook, but a man who acts on them had better sheathe his sword forever."

Imagine if halfway through the plot, Nick Denton had discovered that Peter Thiel had been scheming to destroy his company. Not only is this itself a juicy story that would have exploded as it was published and burnished Gawker's outsized reputation, but it would also reveal Thiel's sensitivity. That he had tried and failed to secretly settle his score against Gawker would have been a perennial taunt, and Thiel would have looked stupid for getting caught (to be outed as gay was upsetting, but to be *shown* as bumbling?). Gawker would have been merciless in its coverage of him, and the rest of the media would have followed. Second, it would have shifted Gawker's legal strategy; certainly knowing that its opponent had unlimited resources would have changed how it litigated, and how it managed its own legal bills. Third, exposure assures him an enemy for life: the rest of the media. Failure doesn't put him back at square one—it costs him his private life forever. There is no such thing as an "almost secret" conspiracy of any significance.

Even if Thiel could have avoided those risks, there is no other way, at least not if he wants to set a precedent in court against Gawker. Having his name associated with any of it makes what was intended to be *justice* look like the settling of a petty personal score. Secrecy is not just the best option, it's the only one.

And because of its value, it was by extension difficult to obtain.

In a December 2013 filing, some two years before even the beginning of the trial upon which Thiel's chance of victory would hinge, Gawker's lawyers push back on some document requests from Charles Harder. They complain to the judge that they suspect since Harder now represents at least one other client suing Gawker, he is assembling a "litigation dossier" on Gawker Media—attempting to use the discovery process in this case to amass documents for future cases. "There is only one possible motivation for plaintiff's request," Gregg D. Thomas and Seth Berlin write in the filing, "that plaintiff, and especially his counsel, is attempting to use the discovery process in this case to obtain information for use in other matters."

Gawker's unknowing step toward the truth puts Thiel's conspiracy in peril for the first time. How much longer will it be until they begin to guess what these "other matters" are? Will they get spooked enough to settle and eliminate Thiel and Harder's chance for a knockout blow?

There were many moments in World War II when it looked like Hitler's unshakable faith in Enigma would finally and correctly be shaken. Each time, the Allies must do what they can to keep the ruse alive, to keep the secret safe. How many ships do we allow the U-boats to sink? How many can we save? What kind of defense can we give the city of Coventry, knowing a terrible bombing is coming? What are we willing to sacrifice of ourselves to keep this edge?

How little could Harder divulge or allude to in making a sufficiently vigorous defense of his (and his client's) intentions and not land himself too close to that fuzzy legal line between truth and deception? Much hinges on Harder's response here; indeed, the plan itself is in the balance. By the time he files his motion, 2013 has passed into 2014.

> Gawker's contention that the documents are being amassed for an improper purpose is false. Gawker's intent and the outrageousness of Gawker's underlying conduct are the elements of the tort claims pleaded by Bollea. Gawker's prior conduct and its policies and practices when faced with claims that it violated the rights of the subjects of its stories are relevant to these claims.
>
> Finally, Gawker argues, both in its moving papers and in the Dietrick Affidavit, that Charles Harder, counsel for Bollea, supposedly is seeking this discovery to compile a litigation dossier for use against Gawker in other cases. This argument, which could have been raised in opposition to the motion to compel, is unsupported by any evidence. Gawker has not shown a single instance where Mr. Harder, or any other attorney for Mr. Bollea, has misused confidential information produced in this lawsuit. The fact that Mr. Harder may represent other celebrities, or that Mr. Harder's other clients may have, in the past, made cease and desist requests to Gawker, does not establish that any sort of "dossier on Gawker" is being compiled. Gawker's argument rests on pure speculation, and nothing more.

Is this a lie? It is close. It's threading the eye of the needle of legal logic. Gawker's argument was pure speculation, but it was not incorrect. "Attorneys are allowed to make dossiers of people and companies, including parties to the case, third parties, witnesses," Harder would tell me. "It's what lawyers do. It's part of fact gathering, and being organized." In this case, it was fact gathering not simply for the purposes of Hogan's case but for all the ones Harder was pursuing and would pursue at Peter's direction and with Mr. A's direct involvement. They were not yet sure in 2014 that Hogan would be a knockout blow. Perhaps he was simply the stiff jab that would set it up.

So Harder does his dance to keep the secret alive, the exhilarating, terrifying moment passes, and the mischief continues. The judge denies Gawker's motions and gives Harder the documents he needs. The dossier grows. Emboldened by the near miss, the mischief escalates. Harder will repeatedly complain in arguments that Gawker has "exponentially greater financial resources than Mr. Bollea," leaning over the semantic edge, as he is obligated to do on behalf of his client and in pursuit of this strategy. He can say what he likes. What he could never do would be to say the truth: *We are assembling a legal dossier. We have unlimited resources. We are pursuing as many cases against you as we can. We won't stop until this is over, until you're gone.*

Peter had learned from his early experiences with Gawker and the media that those with unconventional beliefs should probably keep most of what they think to themselves. But a conspiracy is more than just an unusual opinion. Thiel's strategy inherently depends on secrecy. The various coconspirators see only what Peter allows them to see. Harder himself, based in Los Angeles, is in part chosen for the purpose of misdirection. Hiring a law firm in San Francisco might have hinted at the conspiracy's connection to Silicon Valley. Hiring a law firm in New York City (where Gawker is based) or Washington, D.C. (where Gawker's lawyers were based), might have led to an earlier reveal—a chance run-in during a client lunch at Balthazar on Spring Street where Denton regularly dined, or a drinks meeting in the lobby bar of the Mayflower Hotel, two blocks from Gawker's lawyers' offices and where all manner of D.C. political intrigue has occurred.

Thiel hired Mr. A as his operative for similar reasons. He is young, he is foreign, he has no footprint to speak of, there is no discernible connection between him and Peter. He can operate in the shadows because he is one—a shadow—and more, he wants to remain one. The majority of their communication is done over the phone or alone in Peter's home. Emails can be subpoenaed, or can be hacked. Meeting in public, being seen at Thiel's offices or in public only increases their chances of being discovered. When Mr. A communicates with Harder and others, it's through the encryption app Wickr so that his communications are untraceable and delete themselves after a certain number of days. Few know who he is, few are likely to ever find out that he is Thiel's operative, and this allows them to function as a conspiracy.

Secrecy is both a power and a pall. Magellan, a Portuguese citizen sailing for Spain, cannot even tell his own captains where he thinks the straits lie, because the second he does they will mutiny and find them without him. He has but a few loyal men whom he swears to secrecy. Together, they vow to keep their plans "hidden like a poisoned dagger," and thus are also protected from harm since they are the only ones who know where they are going. It is also a distance separating those who know from those who don't, creating contempt and distrust on both sides. The troops can't and shouldn't know everything the general is doing, which means the general stands alone and suffers alone. The less the conspirators know about the leader's plans, the less likely they are to expose them—the less likely they are to undermine or question them. The less likely it is that the enemy will find out and block them.

For this reason, employees at Harder's law firm do not know whose name is on the checks that cover their own payroll each month, but they assume that Hulk Hogan is paying his own bills. The case couldn't have been taken on contingency—there wasn't enough business to support the hours they were putting in, and his small firm, just getting its feet set, would have bankrupted itself trying to carry such a long case so early. Harder retains local counsel in Florida for the purposes of arguing the Hogan trial, and even this firm is not told that there is a benefactor funding the case. Hogan and Houston do not know the name of the person paying their legal bills until after the verdict they had fought for four years to get, and they do not meet Mr. A or know his real name until the trial itself. Charles Harder discovers the name of his mystery benefactor in 2016 when he is in his closet getting dressed for work, well after the verdict been rendered. The phone rings and the reporter is demanding to know whether he will confirm or deny that he had been collaborating with Peter Thiel. The spouses of those involved are kept in the dark until news reports break it to them. And as of this writing, even the *existence* of Mr. A is a fact unknown by the mainstream media.

In every conspiracy, there is temptation to talk, especially as you near your goal. The weight of silence and deceit begins to weigh on the participants. You might be sitting at a dinner with all your friends. Each speaks with such ease about their recent successes, each is able to talk freely and share their opinions. Yet you can say nothing. The conspiracy has consumed countless waking moments, produced a number of successes you want to brag about, and probably even more difficulties that you could desperately use support and reassurance on, but you don't say a word.

Metellus Pius, leading the Roman army in Spain, is asked by one of his soldiers, "Where are we going tomorrow?" He replies, "If my tunic could tell, I would burn it." As tempting as it is to gossip, and Mr. A would say that the pressure was immense and that they craved a release, as validating as it might be, it will only make things harder. How did Uber get itself into trouble in 2014? By discussing hypothetically the *option* of digging up dirt on the journalists it thought were treating it unfairly. Where did Uber's senior executive choose to do this? At a dinner party. He must have told himself that he wasn't really giving anything away, that he was just floating an idea out there. Uber believed the dinner was off the record, and yet, when someone pointed out that a plan like the one he outlined might backfire, the strategist confidently replied, "Nobody would know it was us." Except, of course, for the people he had just told.

"Psychologically, there is this weird thing where you want to brag about these things that you're not supposed to," Thiel would say to me. Freud explained this phenomenon a hundred years ago: "He that has eyes to see and ears to hear may convince himself that no mortal can keep a secret. If his lips are silent, he chatters with his finger-tips; betrayal oozes out of him at every pore." This is how Peter justified the few friends he told and how he suspects he was eventually discovered. Just as rules are meant to be broken, it seems, secrets are meant to be shared.

Even benign conspiracies are revealed this way, through the irresistibility of telling someone, *anyone*. The author J. K. Rowling's pseudonym "Robert Galbraith"—which she conceived of with her publisher and attorney so she might write other fare without the weight of Harry Potter expectations sinking the chances of its success—was revealed when her lawyer told a friend of his wife's who promptly gave the secret away on Twitter. Robert Greene: "The main weakness in any conspiracy is usually human nature: the higher the number of people who are in on the plot, the higher the odds that someone will reveal it, whether deliberately or accidentally." One of the few in Thiel's circle who would later suspect his involvement would find a major clue in a completely innocent Facebook photo posted by Mr. A that was tagged with a location in a small town in Florida.

I do not envy Mr. A's position. He cannot complain to Peter Thiel about anything because Thiel is his boss and a demanding, perfection-obsessed one at that. He cannot complain to Harder about his boss because he must maintain the illusion and image of an ordered house with many chefs in the kitchen. He cannot speak to his parents, to his lovers, to his friends about what he's doing. He can't even brag about the power he has amassed or the surrealness of his life. He must continue to pretend that he is no one and nobody. He must also know that he is the fall guy—the one who will be showered with attention if caught, any chance of the privacy he prefers obliterated.

Even Peter himself was not immune to the temptation to talk. In 2009, he sat down with a reporter named Connie Loizos at PE Hub, a venture capital website, and was asked about coverage he had gotten from *Valleywag*. The conspiracy was just one of many ideas in his mind at that time, not yet fully formed. Which is why he probably felt comfortable talking about it. "It's disturbing to me that there are people who are so angry out there," he said to her. "Maybe I'm wrong and did something terrible to them, but I'm not particularly flattered by being targeted. I actually think it's sort of the psychology of a terrorist, where it's purely destructive and that *Valleywag* is the Silicon Valley equivalent of Al Qaeda." He's asked in response if he really means this, and he explains that he does, cogently laying out the argument behind what seemed at first like a rather extreme thing to say. "It scares everybody. It's terrible for the Valley, which is supposed to be about people who are willing to think out loud and be different. I think they should be described as terrorists, not as writers or reporters. Terrorism is obviously a charged analogy, but it's like terrorism in that you're trying to be gratuitously meaner and more sensational than the next person, like a terrorist who is trying to stand out and shock people."

The stakes weren't high enough yet, so there didn't seem to be many consequences for sharing his thinking. And there was likely a part of him that hoped that if he could just put the right label on it, find just the right words, it might have some impact (as Nick would say, he met speech with speech). This was naïve and not without consequences. The response to those comments made that clear enough. *Valleywag* thanked him for his remarks and considered them a compliment. His comments were a gift (and netted 15,000 page views). Much later on, this record would in part be how the conspiracy was traced back to him. (Who could have funded the lawsuit? Could it be the billionaire who once called Gawker terrorists?) A few dopamine-filled seconds of catharsis turned into fingerprints that ruined his chances of a clean getaway.

And when Thiel looked not for catharsis but for advice? Thiel would occasionally find himself driven, as Freud said, to share and to hint at what he was hiding. At dinner parties or in long leisurely meetings with friends, he would try to brainstorm what he was working on and gauge their opinions or get ideas. Almost to a rule, no one really took it seriously, even those who knew him well. "It sounded like this fantastic megalomaniacal-sounding plan that seemed so incredible that they chose to ignore me," Thiel would say of these conversations. "They probably thought they were dealing with someone who was insane."

Yet secrecy remained the overwhelming rule for all involved because they knew what was at stake. A conspirator cannot tell someone they're coming for them, even if they ask you directly, "Are you coming for me?" The endeavor is already difficult enough, the odds far enough outside one's favor, that to give advance notice would likely be fatal. The fox must outsmart the lion, it must avoid the snare the hunters set for it.

The concealment of intentions is critical to countless worthwhile and perfectly legitimate enterprises, not only in business or defense but also in journalism. In her classic *The Journalist and the Murderer*, Janet Malcolm wrote, "If everybody put his cards on the table, the game would be over. The journalist must do his work in a kind of deliberately induced state of moral anarchy." I don't think anyone thought that a Gawker reporter was obligated, when he or she reached out to the subject of an unflattering article for comment, to tell that person what would be in that piece. I don't recall Gawker putting up a webcam inside its offices so the world could monitor what it was doing. In fact, the journalist's right to secrecy is enshrined in law, and nowhere is it more protected than in New York City. In this very case, John Cook would repeatedly assert New York's State Shield Law in an attempt to avoid being deposed. In the deposition he was eventually forced to give he repeatedly asserted his right to keep the identity of sources secret and to refrain from disclosing stories that might be under way. *Because his job depended on keeping secrets*, he was saying. Even in the course of the trial, both sides, Gawker and Hogan, agree to a privilege log which prevents public release of Hogan's private information as well as Gawker's trade secrets and financial information, which it repeatedly insisted were an issue. Working with a lawyer is inherently secretive—no one can force them to disclose what they have learned from their clients. This, too, is considered an essential privilege.

"What if I told them on day one," Harder asks, "that this is bankrolled by a billionaire and so bring it on?" It certainly would have damaged his credibility in front of the jury and the judge—*these people aren't the little guy*—and Gawker's lawyers would have been thrown in his face at every opportunity. "In terms of how Gawker would've litigated, I would think they would realize they can't bring motion after motion after motion and appeal after appeal after appeal because it's not going to have an impact. When they didn't know who was behind it—they assume it was Terry paying—they thought it was going to come to a point where he couldn't continue anymore and had to raise the white flag." It's easy to miss this now that one side has won and the other lost—that long before that, one side was quite confident they were winning. Gawker's lawyers had sized up their opponent and believed they had an advantage. They were relentlessly exploiting that perceived advantage with each filing, each motion, each appeal and tactic that prolonged the litigation. Harder would play into this perception, repeatedly, in filings. After denying the dossier accusation, he would complain to the judge in another discovery battle that the fight wasn't fair, because again, "Gawker has exponentially greater financial resources than Mr. Bollea." He would file motions to be reimbursed for legal fees, acting as if his resources were stretched beyond Hogan's capacities. He would accuse the other side of procedural gamesmanship, arguing that they were trying to make the lawsuit as expensive as possible. "This ought to have been a straightforward case to litigate. . . . Instead, Gawker used discovery in this case as a means to exponentially increase Mr. Bollea's fees and costs—in an effort to make the case impossible for him to litigate. Gawker also sought to further punish Mr. Bollea for having the temerity to challenge Gawker's publication of the Sex Video in court . . . two years of needless litigation."

"The truest way to be deceived is to think oneself more knowing than others" is La Rochefoucauld's maxim. To Gawker these pleas of financial hardship from Hogan must have read as confirmation of the edge they believed they had—their money, their brinkmanship would be the determining factor. Because it *was* what they were doing. They wanted to hear his complaints, that he was hurting from it. They were so overconfident, so sure that this suit would come to nothing that they could not even conceive of a scenario in which Harder might have an advantage over them, or might be doing something other than being stupid. And who in their right mind so believes in transparency that they would correct their overconfident opponent's fatal miscalculation?

Yet let us not confuse the need for secrecy with a blanket justification of any type of behavior. The conspirators remained committed and seem to have observed their self-imposed limitation of legal behavior—perhaps out of moral goodness or perhaps simply because they wanted a clean victory. There were plenty of illicit or untoward things they could have done secretly, but to what end? At what cost? "I think there's always this question," Thiel would say. "I do think you always want to think about, you know, when this ultimately comes out. Is it defensible? And I think all the things that we did were defensible. And so secrets aren't necessarily forever. You have to live with it coming out at the end."

Secrets are how real work is done. Peter makes no secret about that. There's an entire chapter in his book *Zero to One* called "Secrets." He's transparent about the fact that he keeps them and believes in them. He just won't tell you what they are. He never pretended to be anything other than what he was. Foolishly he had told the world what he thought about Gawker, and they, along with Gawker, had laughed at him. So now he declined to explain what he decided to do about it.

The brief moment of suspicion from Gawker quickly subsides. Why would a random lawyer with a small firm in Los Angeles be collecting a dossier on Gawker? What good would it do anyway—they'd never lost a case. The filing is the last visible evidence that there was any kind of worry that someone was coming for Gawker with all guns blazing. In September 2014, just months after the accusation, Nick would reach out through a friend to see if Thiel would like to get coffee in San Francisco.

From: Nick Denton
Sent: Wednesday, September 17, 2014 11:24 AM
To: Peter Thiel
Subject: Your political agenda

Hey, Peter—

This is a long shot, but I'm going to try. Would you get together for a coffee when I'm next in San Francisco?

We obviously have our differences, primarily over the politics of outing. And some of our coverage on Valleywag and Gawker has been needlessly gleeful.

But your political views—while mockable—are a breath of fresh air. We have more in common than might meet the eye.

I'd like to get some more constructive debate going between the New Left—which is represented rather heavily in a New York editorial operation—and the Valley libertarians.

The enemy is stagnation, and the vested interests that ensure stagnation. (And yes, sometimes also the culture of internet criticism that stymies original thought.)

That's all I got. Let me know if there's a conversation to be had.

Regards

Nick

Another ripple of fear hits Thiel that Wednesday morning as he opens his email. *Is he onto me? What do they know?* "Anyone who has a guilty conscience can easily be led to believe that people are talking about him," Machiavelli warns conspirators. "A word with another meaning is overheard which shakes your courage and makes you think it was said with respect to your plans. The result is that you either reveal the conspiracy yourself by fleeing or you confuse the undertaking by acting at the wrong time."

But this passes, too. Denton truly just wanted to talk. Two years in, not only did Gawker not know who was behind the Hogan suit, *they hardly even knew anything was happening to them*. Thiel notes to himself that Denton has told him to his face that he finds him to be mockable and punts the invitation. The two will not meet. Not until much later.

The strategy can proceed. In secret, where it belongs, where it will be most effective.

CHAPTER 11

Sow Confusion and Disorder

There's an old line that in war the truth is so precious that it must be protected by a bodyguard of lies. A good strategy, for its part, must be flanked by feints and disguises. Otherwise, the counterstrategy becomes too easy to deduce.

The Russians call this *maskirovka*—the art of deception and confusion. It is as old as strategy itself. Undermine your enemy, Sun Tzu advised 2,500 years ago. "Subvert him, attack his morale, strike at his economy, corrupt him. Sow internal discord among his leaders; destroy him without fighting him." Call down the fog of war, he was telling conspirators and generals and swordsmen, let it descend on your opponent until they cannot see what is right before them. Because "all warfare," Sun Tzu reminds us, "is based on deception." Not just keeping secrets—that's the first part, the passive part, a refusal to reveal your true intentions—but active, outwardly focused *deceit* intended to disorient and weaken the enemy.

The long-term strategic drive to a decisive legal action—the hope of taking a case against Gawker to a real jury of normal people outside the Manhattan media bubble—had been set by Peter Thiel early on. By 2012, not only was the ideal case found with which to execute this strategy, but a lawsuit was filed within days of discovery. As the case wound its way through the legal system in 2013, it had seen many setbacks, some expected and others not, but these setbacks were not without their upside. They had, in the end, created a scenario in which the case's final home in Florida district court might spell a bankruptcy-level event for Gawker Media.

Yet agents of conspiracy would be foolish to simply set it and forget it, to close themselves off to other opportunities just because they had already invested in one. Just a few months after filing the Hogan lawsuit, Harder begins to pursue a variety of stratagems to complement and complicate this relatively straightforward legal attack against Gawker. Some are related and funded by Thiel, some aren't. Some are deliberate, some are second-order effects of other initiatives. The first of these occurs while Harder is still at his original law firm, Wolf Rifkin, which represented the actress and writer Lena Dunham. Gawker manages to get its hands on a leaked copy of her book proposal, which it runs in full about a month after the Hulk Hogan tape, and snags close to 400,000 page views from it. Harder's firm immediately sends a cease and desist letter on her behalf. Gawker's response is typical, which is to say aggressive and obnoxious, providing half-hearted commentary to try to justify its copyright infringement.

One such update:

> *Every ice pop I ate, every movie I watched, every poem I wrote was tinged with a fearful loss.*
>
> Lena Dunham's personal litigation counsel Charles Harder has contacted Gawker to relay a demand from his client, Lena Dunham, that we remove the above quote from our web site. In order to clarify our intent in quoting the above matter from Dunham's proposal, we have decided to append the following commentary: The quoted sentence is preposterously hackneyed

and demonstrates an "I workshopped it at Oberlin" level of quality that permeates the proposal.

Twelve times the Gawker writer does this to defend a leaked document he does not own. But it is not enough. Eventually the post is appended with a final note, "Following the intervention of Harder, we have removed the proposal." (John Cook, who wrote it, never seems to realize that the copyright claim he conceded to here is indistinguishable from the one Harder had made on behalf of Hogan a few weeks earlier after obtaining it from Bubba Clem.)

Call it a reconnaissance in force. Harder had eked out a small victory in the skirmish and learned something valuable. Harder has seen again that Gawker fights pointlessly over trivial matters, even when it eventually turns out to be wrong, often doubling down in the process—that Nick gives his writers great leeway to do this. He also witnesses clearly the pattern that Gawker had come to accept as fact: cross the legal line, get challenged, fight back, and then watch as its opponent decides it has better things to do than fight beyond a symbolic victory. But mostly, the case is convenient cover for cases Harder might take on later. In fighting for Dunham, he managed to tangle with Gawker on behalf of a client totally unrelated to Thiel or Mr. A, on a very different end of the celebrity spectrum, without making Gawker feel like it was being singled out or the target of any larger campaign. He's opened up a second front, however briefly.

Emboldened as he is preparing for discovery and his depositions in the Hogan case, Harder's office gets in touch with several former Gawker employees. Thiel tells me they hire investigative reporters to interview ex-employees as well. They pump these contacts for information: What is it like to work there? How does Gawker operate? What is Denton like? What kind of person is A. J. Daulerio? What does it take to get hired at Gawker? In these discussions Harder learns that Gawker has long used unpaid internships as a part of its business model, and this might be an opportunity for a *third* front. "I was talking to some former employees of Gawker and one of them mentioned that Gawker had hundreds of interns and none of them were paid," Harder says. "Gawker was basically getting free labor. And I had talked to an employment lawyer about this in New York and they said it's one hundred percent against the law."

A number of other media companies, including 21st Century Fox and Condé Nast and Warner Music, had been subject to similar actions; in fact, all had been sued less than one week before Gawker would be. "I had said to the lawyer, are you interested in being a part of this and helping out the interns on a contingency-fee basis? I honestly felt bad for those interns. They were entitled to minimum wage plus statutory damages plus their attorney fees and costs under state and federal law. And I thought it's a win-win if the interns want to be a part of that, if the law firm wants to take that on and get a percentage, then let them do it."

A. J. Daulerio would later speculate to me that Harder was simply pushing this case forward to pump Gawker for information, and in a way he is right. But there was another advantage. Without having to personally do much of anything, Harder was able to bloody and embarrass his opponent without its realizing that he was the one throwing the punches. In 2013, the employment attorney he contacted files suit, alleging that the interns "worked a substantial number of hours, at least 15 hours a week, for Gawker and were not paid a single cent for their work." News of the lawsuit is picked up in multiple outlets including *The Atlantic*, *The Huffington Post*, *New York Post,* and *The Hollywood Reporter.* In the court of public opinion, Gawker is clearly guilty of hypocrisy, having savaged other media outlets for the exact practice it was caught engaging in. "Putting aside the question of whether Gawker had the legal right to keep blog slaves—a question the court will answer soon," one critic would write, "the company's 60-plus pages of excuses are in stark contrast to Gawker's editorial condemnation of other companies who use unpaid interns." *Adweek*'s headline: "Gawker's Unpaid Intern Saga: Do as I Say, Not as I Do."

It's a simple transaction, passing this along, but it spawns a case that drags on for nearly three years. Gawker emerges victorious ultimately, but certainly not better for it. "It is shocking that Gawker would rather spend a million dollars on lawyers to fight its interns than to simply pay money to the interns," Harder would later tell *Forbes*. For the first time, the public saw Gawker as something other than the guiltless underdog—it is an exploiter, too, with its own secrets. The money Gawker spent is money it won't have to fight Hogan, but most important, it's time Nick Denton and Heather Dietrick didn't spend thinking about their case in Florida. And yes, for Harder, it's not only a confidence builder, it's an intelligence builder. It was court-sanctioned spying that, as spying ought to, remained undetected until the end.

In 2014, another opportunity presents itself. In what the *New York Times* would describe as a "strange, rambling attack," a game developer named Zoe Quinn was accused in a post by an ex-boyfriend of having a romantic relationship with a game journalist who wrote for the Gawker-owned site *Kotaku*. What might have seemed like inconsequential relationship drama becomes a flash point, a sudden outpouring of online anger from a typically nonpolitical and insular community. Rallying under the hashtag #Gamergate, supporters of the movement aim to position themselves as standing for "ethics in journalism," "rooting out corruption," and other problems in the video game industry. In practice, they are aiming the brunt of their anger at Gawker because they are mad at the online media conglomerate for years of real and imagined abuses in video game journalism, for political correctness, for the rise of female influence in the industry, and for any other slip-up or mistake they can use to vent their rage. The Hogan case becomes one of the criticisms, too.

Mr. A claims that the conspirators had nothing to do with starting Gamergate, but they undoubtedly fanned the flames. His description of Gamergate to me as "largely autonomous but very helpful" is perfectly typical of the lawyerly gymnastics I've come to expect from him. Peter, too, declines to discuss it on the record. Many of the same figures who would eventually lead the alt-right campaign for Donald Trump—trolls like Milo Yiannopoulos and Mike Cernovich—are active in Gamergate and publicly attack Gawker. While Thiel might not be funding and coordinating these attacks directly, his campaign in the shadows certainly benefits from them, because the enemy of his enemy has created a crisis that cannot be ignored.

Gawker's instinct in responding to things was always defiance and scorn. Why would this situation be any different? One of its writers, Sam Biddle, formerly of *Valleywag*, tweets: "Ultimately #GamerGate is reaffirming what we've known to be true for decades: nerds should be constantly shamed and degraded into submission," and jokes that the solution is to "Bring Back Bullying." It is another joke in the worst possible moment. Given that he himself is a nerd, it's not an actual endorsement of bullying, but the words are there and they can be exploited. What he did not see, once again, and what Max Read, his editor who would defend him, did not see, nor Nick Denton above them, was that the room for jokes, for anything other than coordinated, strategic responses, had been gone for some time.

Almost immediately, Gamergate followers begin an email campaign to Gawker's advertisers demanding that they cease advertising on the site. Thousands of templatized emails are sent to Gawker's biggest clients that say with various degrees of personalization, "Your company is listed as an advertising affiliate with Gawker. In light of

Mr. Biddle's comments, and Mr. Read's support of said comments, I urge you to withdraw said advertising support from Gawker and all its affiliates. This is National Bullying Awareness Month, and these comments are unacceptable in a society where several thousand people commit suicide each year due to bullying. Thank you for your time. If this has been sent to the wrong department, please forward it for me." Advertisers like Mercedes-Benz quickly pull out. Max, the editor in chief, would reply by both calling the advertisers who relented to this pressure a group of "craven idiots" and asking Gawker's writers to be more careful in the future. And yes, he had to go on record to say that, no, the company did not endorse bullying. Gawker would estimate the loss in revenue to be in the hundreds of thousands to *millions* of dollars—money the company needed as its legal bills mounted.

Was there fertilizer beneath this "grassroots uprising"? Funding or manpower from the conspiracy? Is it more than coincidence that Gamergate's target was the same one that Thiel had in his sights? I suspect yes. Max Read would write, in retrospect, "Of all the enemies Gawker had made over the years—in New York media, in Silicon Valley, in Hollywood—none were more effective than the Gamergaters." He just didn't yet think that his employer's enemy in Silicon Valley and in Gamergate was, at least in part, the same. He couldn't have. Which must have made it all the more bewildering. "If this seems bizarre to you, you're not alone," Read would tell his writers and readers. "I feel like I went to sleep in the regular world and woke up in an insane new one."

And in this insane new one there was a new sense of doubt inside Gawker: *Are we not bulletproof anymore?*

"Gawker was antiestablishment and distilled the general sense that the system was hollow and corrupt into specific stories about powerful people," Denton would tell me of the site's original intention.

But over time, in part because of Thiel's efforts, but also because of the natural trajectory of the forces Denton had built upon, "it got diverted into attacks on the Right, fear and contempt of the Heartland, distilled into mockery of Florida Man and the hypocrisy of redneck celebrities. Overconfidence, leading to a war on two fronts."

Really it was a war on a half dozen fronts, from Dunham to interns to angry nerds online, though Nick might not see that even now. It's like the United States waking up one day and realizing that it isn't at peace but in fact fighting in nine different regions at the same time. But what can the country do about it? It sleepwalked into these fights, and it doesn't have the willpower or the clarity to extricate itself from them. There is no victory that can wrap them up, either, only the executive power to admit defeat. So, too, is Gawker beginning to feel the cumulative drag of all the fights it is in, or has been tricked into. Denton has the power to stop them, but he can't quite do it. None of them on its own seems that drastic anyway.

Like a man on the savannah persistence hunting an animal from the herd, Thiel has begun the process of wearing Gawker down, chasing it every chance he has, confusing and exhausting it. "We thought our strategies couldn't be seen as attacks," Peter Thiel explains. "We did not want them to be attacks on reputable media." This is what made the Hogan sex tape such an ideal vehicle for attack. It was not a typical, head-on First Amendment challenge like most media outlets are used to. "This was not a libel thing, this was Fourth Amendment privacy," Peter continues. When people think of the media they want to protect, they don't think of sex tapes and exploited interns. They don't think of people on the other side of ethics complaints and advertiser boycotts by angry mobs. "Nobody is going to defend Gawker on that basis," Thiel would say.

Nobody is going to defend anybody on that basis. Gawker was being separated from its media counterparts, made to seem different, flawed, repugnant—but slowly enough that it couldn't tell the degree to which it was happening. Lawrence Freedman had said in his defining work *Strategy* that combining with others was an important strategic move, and so it was for the conspirators early on. The other side of his sentence is that "for the same reason, preventing others from doing the same can be as valuable." Methodically, Thiel was trying to strip Gawker of its allies, and with the fog settling in thick and heavy around them, they didn't even know it was happening.

The Gawker group may have had a vague sense that they had enemies, sure. They knew in 2014, for instance, that Gamergate's specific goal was to put them out of business. But they are not able to connect the dots, and it's unlikely that Gamergate could by itself succeed in anything remotely close to that goal. They are responding, responding, responding to each individual attack, but are unable to see the strings running between them. The bad boxer rushes to defend against one punch and opens himself up to another. And another, and another.

This is not a pretty image, relentlessly pursuing an adversary until he begins to stumble from exhaustion. But it must be this way. The enemy is weaker when plunged into what the statesman Demosthenes described as a "welter of confusion and folly." A single attack allows resistance to be concentrated, but two or three or four put the enemy between the horns of a dilemma, choosing between equally subpar options. Or, blindly hoping to avoid one attack, he falls headfirst into the other without even knowing. Nero poisoned a suspicious, paranoid rival not by putting poison in his food, because each dish was tested by an attendant. Instead, he arranged for the man to be served a harmless but very hot bowl of soup. It was in the cold water, requested and poured in by the man himself, that deadly poison was delivered. Without this suppressive cover, the countermove is too obvious: when you know where the enemy is going, you go there and block them.

In World War II, the British kept the Germans in a state of

perpetual defense along the French coast for nearly three years through a series of false intelligence, covert operations, and deliberate starts and stops. The Americans believed that overwhelming force would be enough, that the operation could simply be punched through. The British knew better. Having cracked Enigma three years earlier, they understood just how strong the Germans were. Having fought so many times on so many continents, the British knew that war was never simply a matter of overwhelming force. To succeed, the landing at Normandy would need to be not only covered by incredible secrecy, but compounded by an elaborate dummy operation to make the Axis powers believe the troops would land somewhere else. George Patton, arguably one of the Allies' greatest generals, is chosen for the feint at Calais, the obvious landing point, precisely for his fearsome reputation—because he was too dangerous for the Germans to ignore. It was through this deception that D-Day was made possible, prompting Hitler to keep many divisions in reserve, believing that the "real invasion" was still to come, even as the Allied forces were making their way up the French beaches. And it could be argued, as the Russians do, that the invasion itself was merely a feint to keep the Germans busy and distracted from the real strategy, which was what the Red Army was doing in the East, grinding the Germans down, man by man.

Britain's "secret means" prior to D-Day was a grab bag of unrelated, independent tricks and moves. It was about creating an impression, about keeping the Nazis off balance and defensive on a second front for as long as possible. Some of their ruses and commando operations worked, some didn't—but they had a cumulative effect, like the bullfighter harassing the bull, letting the adrenaline course through the animal's veins, exhausting it until the opportune moment when the sword can be slid into the spine.

It would be fitting then that almost everything the conspirators would do would align with the British historian Liddell Hart's maxims for strategy: "Keep your object always in mind, while adapting your plan to circumstances." "Take a line of operation which offers alternative objectives." "Ensure that both plans and dispositions are flexible—adaptable to circumstances." "Do not throw your weight into a stroke whilst your opponent is on guard—whilst he is well placed to parry or evade it." Liddell Hart would compare a strategic plan to a tree, saying that a healthy one has multiple branches, and that a plan with a single branch is but a barren pole. A tree with a single branch is not a tree at all, it's a gallows.

"Hogan was one iron in the fire at that time. We were constantly looking. We were looking for other options and strategies" is how Mr. A puts it. Adding these options was easy. "The project that I was working on was helping people if they felt they had a meritorious claim against Gawker. And if they were going to not be able to afford it, then to offer services. There wasn't a whole lot of that that actually happened other than just reaching out," according to Harder. As the Hogan case edged its way toward trial, additional potential plaintiffs began to make themselves known to Charles Harder as he made himself known to them. A black journalist and commenter for ESPN named Jason Whitlock is savaged in a number of articles on *Deadspin* and suddenly he gets a call from Harder's firm—would he be interested in doing something about it? They meet with him, his agent, and his lawyer to convince him he has a strong case and should pursue it (Whitlock declines but seriously considers it). When Gawker outs a prominent fashion media executive in 2015, his suit against the company is quietly helped along by Thiel and Harder. As late as January 2016, just three months before the Hogan trial, new cases are still being added and filed. Some would be filed even after the verdict. Not all these cases are public, some of their financial arrangements are different, but they are all part of the same grand strategy.

Denton might have also noticed someone trying to buy small

amounts of Gawker shares on the private market. As part of Hogan's suit, his personal finances are being subpoenaed, and motions are granted ordering relatives to turn over information about his family trusts. One website puts out a bounty offering to pay $50,000 for any proof of criminal behavior by Nick Denton ("another tactic borrowed from Gawker and taken to its insane conclusion," Denton would say). Other people sue Gawker, too—people who have nothing to do with Peter Thiel. Quentin Tarantino sues it in January 2014 for publishing a leaked script of *The Hateful Eight*. In September, a baseball broadcaster files a suit against Gawker and MLB Network. In June 2015, the right-wing troll Charles "Chuck" Johnson files a defamation suit. The *Daily Mail* sues Gawker for defamation in September 2015. In October, Charles Johnson follows up his lawsuit with a prediction on Facebook: "I want to make you a promise: Gawker will cease to exist in a year's time. I can't tell you how I know because that would break my word but I promise you it. Either Hulk Hogan or I will triumph over Gawker. It's going to happen." The following year, he would fly to Hungary and start asking questions about the company's finances: "Did Gawker really employ the people they said they did? Were their taxes in order?"

In July 2014, Gawker had also been sued by their second insurance company, Nautilus, the one who had been paying the tab on Gawker's legal bills after the first policy had been exhausted. This policy covered physical injury, like slips and falls, and possibly emotional distress, like what Hogan was claiming. Harder, seeing that Gawker and its insurance carrier were in dispute, sees an opportunity. In Florida, the law states that plaintiffs can't recover damages for unintentional emotional distress in cases without physical injury. So Harder calls the insurance company and lets them know he'll be dropping the claim, clearing the path for the insurance company to exit the conflict by 2015. While it seemed odd to Gawker at the time that Hogan would voluntarily give up one of his claims and willingly eliminate the potential liability of a deep-pocketed insurance company in future settlement talks, it was in fact a brilliant and ruthless move. Now Gawker was on the hook by themselves. Now their war chest was depleted—they'd have to defend their story to that jury in Florida on their own.

Pressure. Pressure. Remorseless pressure.

Aren't these the kinds of tactics that the conspirators had initially avoided—because they weren't decisive, because they weren't exactly ethical? Yes. Yet here they were, using them not as their main strategy but as a kind of hassling maneuver. "A good entrepreneur could deal with a couple of these things," Mr. A would say of the position they had put Denton in, "but five or six is too much." That is the idea. To push them beyond their capacities so they would begin to make mistakes, begin to question even their own judgment.

The timing couldn't have been worse for Nick. His head was elsewhere. As he would tell his staff at the time, "for a good twelve months from the summer of 2013, I was variously betrothed, distracted, obsessed by Kinja (his technology platform), off on honeymoon, off on sabbatical." He called it drift. It had been ten years dancing with the "octopus" that was Gawker and he had put other priorities in front of it. But he was back, he told them. "The drift this year: it will never happen again." The future was hidden from Nick, though; he did not realize how little time was left.

By 2015, as the case wound its way toward trial, what was clear to many for the first time was that Gawker wasn't invincible. The average Gawker writer might not have thought so, but its enemies did. Nick knew. To Harder and Mr. A, Gawker's endless fighting on every motion, its chest pounding in the media, was no longer as intimidating as it had once seemed. It had a shade of desperation to it now. Like someone who didn't want to go to trial, who might have suspected his case wasn't as strong as it looked. Gawker was staggering under the legal fees alone. It's obvious to me that the other cases were weaker, and had they carried the sole weight of the conspiracy, they likely would not have held it. But this is impossible to say for sure. At one point, every legal mind in the country thought the Hogan case was weak—only in pursuing it, only in persevering through discovery did it begin to come together. If pursued rigorously, if Gawker had been given a chance to make more unforced errors, perhaps one of the other cases might have become viable. In the meantime, their role was to add pressure.

Because under attack, sustained and comprehensive attacks, organizations and opponents begin to buckle. The psychological element of warfare accentuates the physical.

Some of the results are unexpected. In 2015, Gawker's writers announce their intention to unionize. Another straw on the camel's back: the introduction of contention between management and employees. I ask Peter if he is responsible for this, too. Was he sowing tension between employee and employer? Was he agitating from within? Apparently, the answer is no. "You know that is the one thing that we actually had nothing to do with. Maybe the business model was under enough stress that it pushed people to unionize. Denton maybe allowed them to unionize because he was sort of pessimistic where the case was going. I don't know. We certainly had nothing to do with the specifics of that," he said. But that's sort of the point. A coach who ordered a full-court press didn't necessarily know for sure whether it would result in a traveling call or an offensive foul or a bad pass, but she certainly hoped it would. Police who are sweating a criminal organization from all sides can't count on catching them throwing out evidence or making an unforced confession, but they know that does happen. No one can be certain of the effects of what Thiel describes as “long-term strategic pressure,” but very few people, organizations, or teams can withstand it.

What is the Gawker team doing while all this is happening, while this seemingly infinite but unrelated parade of shit is hitting the fan? Besides squabbling over collective bargaining and writing long blog posts about unionizing, it’s more important what they are *not* doing, what they don’t have time to do as they deal with all of it: Gawker is not preparing for trial. Nick Denton is not sniffing around for the source of all this pressure, not realizing who is responsible for all these new pains.

Confusum est, quidquid usque in pulverem sectum est—cut anything into tiny pieces and it all becomes a mass of confusion.

There is enough on the public relations front alone to keep them busy. Gawker had long exploited a number of tax loopholes to run its business. It was not particularly secret about these strategies. But as the legal proceedings dragged on, as the effect of the repeated pinpricks began to show, suddenly these narratives start receiving steady coverage in the media. *PandoDaily*: Gawker is no longer even trying to pretend it’s not grotesquely hypocritical on taxes. Disgruntled former Gawker exec: Nick Denton is a coward, here are the company’s financials. CNN: Hulk Hogan sex tape trial could destroy Gawker. *New York Times*: “Gawker’s Moment of Truth.”

This is the problem with making enemies, with generally treating everyone with contempt and creating a culture of fear. They despair of revenge until you are weak and vulnerable. They look forward to the day when the tables are turned. They will descend on you like a pack as soon as they think they can, and in Gawker’s case, they give no quarter because Gawker never would have, either. It’s said that gangsters look good up until their last fifteen minutes, when it turns really ugly and sad. This is where we are in this story, right before the turning point where it suddenly stops looking so good.

Being feared, Machiavelli says, is an important protection against a conspiracy. The ultimate protection, he says, however, is to be well liked. Not simply because people who love you are less likely to want to take you down, but because they are less likely to tolerate anyone else trying to, either. If a prince guards himself against that hatred, Machiavelli writes, "simple particular offenses will make less trouble for him . . . because if they were even of spirit and had the power to do it, they are held back by the universal benevolence that they see the prince has."

Not that people had ever refrained from criticizing Gawker in the past, or were hesitant to sue, but the tenor is different now. One alt-right participant would tell me that Gamergate was like the scene in the movie *300*, where the Spartans hurl a spear and it grazes Xerxes's cheek, just barely drawing blood. It's the moment when the Greeks confirmed that he was not invincible, it's what gave them proof that they could fight and possibly win. Something had always deterred the pack from descending on Gawker in the past and now that was changing. Which meant that Peter Thiel was no longer fully in charge of what was happening. Events were to be driven by the conditions of the conflict both sides had created.

Yet it would be the destiny of most of these cases to amount to little in the end. But that was because their purpose was never to amount to much by themselves, only to contribute to a ratcheting up of the tensions inside Gawker. Once that happened, once there were enough of them, the stratagems could be allowed to dissipate on their own.

In World War II the British had been inclined to continue their campaigns of disinformation and confusion indefinitely; it was Churchill's nature, he loved the sport of it. The Americans finally intervened.

They knew that while the cause could be advanced with these tricks, a war couldn't be won by pinpricks. Once the enemy is weakened, the beaches have been softened, the morale dispirited, now one can resume the main thrust. It is easy to lose track, in the tit for tat, back and forth, of feints and moves and countermoves, of what is real and what isn't. This is where strategy matters. "It was really Bollea, by far, the biggest focus and the biggest amount of money and the biggest everything," Harder said. "At the end of the day you had to go all in on the things that were most likely to work," Thiel said. The Hogan case was it. "At some point the word 'strategy' becomes a euphemism for procrastination. A lot of different plans, a lot of different plans, and they will take a long time and you never—" and there he cut himself off as he so often does. So I'll finish it for him.

You would never end up getting to the *trial*. You'd never end up facing Gawker down in front of a jury. The Hogan case was the one that, through 2014, Gawker, lulled and distracted by everything that was happening to it, had half forgotten about and convinced itself was an open and shut matter. The Gawker team believed the law was on their side and that they were still winning in the court of public opinion.

"Do we have enough here? Or not?" Peter would eventually ask. And they did. It was time to begin the windup for the knockout punch.

CHAPTER 12

The Ties That Bind

Most conspiracies are not found out. They are betrayed. Or they collapse from within, a betrayal of the cause itself.

In ancient Rome, slaves who revealed conspiracies were often given their freedom in exchange. The conspiracy against Nero collapsed when a plotter named Scaevinus asked his servant to sharpen his dagger and hosted a generous dinner where he gave away most of his fortune. The servant took news of this strange behavior to the emperor. An insider to the Gunpowder Plot to assassinate King James I would write an anonymous letter that exposed Guy Fawkes's involvement in 1605 and earned Fawkes a one-way trip to the gallows. François Picaud, the man who inspired the story that became *The Count of Monte Cristo*, found his revenge plot partly thwarted when he was betrayed by a collaborator who attempted to blackmail him. In the end, this blackmailer murders Picaud himself and relays the whole story on his own deathbed a few decades later, turning the most famous revenge plot in the history of literature into a meta-warning to every would-be conspirator today: beware your allies.

The secrecy of a conspiracy and its execution, then, is not purely a matter of planning and discipline, but also a matter of the bonds that bind the conspirators together. Once you get everyone on the bus, how do you keep them onboard? How do you reward them for loyalty? How do you get the best out of them? How do you trust them, knowing as you do the lengths to which they're willing to go and secrets they're willing to keep?

Terry Bollea had been an eager recruit in 2012 because he had no other options. He was desperate. He wanted to get a tape off the internet. Thiel wanted to destroy Gawker. These goals overlap, but only insofar as Peter's target is one of the parties responsible for the Bollea tape's being on the internet. By 2015, it turns out, Hogan is getting tired. Gawker's legal strategy of attrition—delay at every step, challenge at every issue, appeal at every defeat—is nearly, clearly, barely, almost working. Because Thiel is tired, too. So is Mr. A. Harder isn't tired, but he's a lawyer, and their game is played by the hour. How are these men going to fight through the exhaustion that comes with attrition?

The line attributed to the management guru Peter Drucker is that *culture eats strategy*. It's a truism that applies as much to conspiracies as it does to businesses. It doesn't matter how great your plan is, it doesn't matter who your people are, if what binds them all together is weak or toxic, so, too, will be the outcome—if you even get that far. But if the ties that bind you together are strong, if you have a sense of purpose and mission, you can withstand great trials.

Gawker once had a strong mission, an animating force that brought everyone together in a similar fashion and moved them forward. It was them against the world. It was, as Nietzsche put it, a war of knives against the present age. Hypocrites, liars, petty tyrants, smug assholes—all found themselves in Gawker's crosshairs when it launched in 2002. A ragtag army of amateur writers found a great equalizer in writing on the internet, in telling unvarnished truths and not giving a damn about the consequences. Denton's operation channels the energy of the disaffected and the angry. He is paying them relatively little. He is working them hard. He is empowering them—making them arbiters of culture, of acceptability, of cool. They might not be rich, but if they can bring the rich and powerful to their knees with their writing, it might feel like the same thing. Is this enough for loyalty, though? Is this enough to bring them together in adversity?

Over time, culture can sour. "Creeds, like streams, gather strength as they narrow, thriving on bigotry," the biographer William Manchester observed. Gawker's creed might not have been carved in stone in the building but it was clear: If you think it's true, publish it. If they complain, laugh and then hit 'em again. The problem with approaching the world from this cynical, antagonistic stance, though, is that eventually you can't help but become that which you rail against. Over time, punching up turns into punching, period—at everyone and everything. Gawker's growth would make it precisely what it criticized: powerful, unaccountable, unaware.

Operationally, it was full of contradictions. Denton owned the vast majority of the company. Its writers participated in a fraction of the value they created. Denton paid himself a $500,000 salary. The growing profits of the site were squirreled away in foreign accounts. Daulerio, by way of contrast, worked at Gawker for five years and had nine thousand shares by the end of his time there, a 0.0059 percent ownership interest in the company. Bonuses for a post that might do five million page views could be just a few hundred dollars after it was divvied up among the editors and the writers. Waiters at an average busy restaurant make more than that on a Thursday after tipping out the kitchen, the bar, the runners, and the host. But money had never been a large part of the animating force for the writers. Instead they were frustrated at a company they felt was becoming more corporate, and they disliked that Denton carried himself like he had something to lose. That this was a natural and unavoidable outcome of success did not matter. There was no publisher on earth that would be able to knock on the door of $50 million a year in gross revenue, as Gawker had in 2014 and was poised to do in 2015, without accompanying change or inner conflict. As the owner of this company, as the one responsible for those changes, Denton disliked that his writers could not appreciate what they had, that they weren't grateful for what he had created. Denton was no longer in the same world as his writers. Nor was he an outsider like his writers, not anymore.

To me there is no greater embodiment of this tension than John Cook, who joined Gawker in 2009 as a reporter. After a year, he left to take what must have seemed like a better job at Yahoo!. Just five months later, Cook was back at Gawker, having been unable to fit into the culture at Yahoo!, his former bosses saying that he left because "he prefers the license Gawker gave him to add his opinions into his reporting to the scale and credibility Yahoo! News could offer." He is back at Gawker in 2013 with his "license," the opportunity to challenge a circuit court judge and be patted on the back for it. He is promoted internally, until he tries to leave for a better job at *The Intercept*. And yet again this doesn't work out, and within nine months he is back at Gawker. Because it couldn't work out anywhere else, he was as pure a model of Gawker's best and worst qualities: he was courageous and unflinchingly honest, as well as, in the words of his own colleagues, "a colossal asshole" and a "broken shitheart."

As a boss, Nick Denton gives writers exactly what they want: freedom, power, backing. He encourages them. He doesn't meddle. He doesn't intervene if an important friend is upset about a story that Gawker publishes. But by giving his writers what they want, Denton doesn't necessarily give them what they need. Most would leave to take better jobs at other outlets: the *New York Times*, *Observer*, ESPN, and *The New Yorker*. A.J. would himself leave what he had called his dream job to go run Spin.com and then to start his own platform. It's the writers who stayed, year after year, then, who defined the culture. The effect of this over time was that Gawker was staffed by the kind of impolite, impolitic people who could not work at your average company. This was their home, the island where they were not misfits. It was, as one longtime Gawker writer would say, a "fellowship of the weird and surly and otherwise unemployable, the culture of writers who couldn't quite imagine being anywhere else, with anyone else."

These writers, some young, some old, of all genders and backgrounds, had one thing in common: they had accepted the freedom Nick gave them and taken a maximalist interpretation of it, believing that, as Nick would realize with regret, "freedom is the freedom to do whatever the fuck you want." Freedom is rarely appreciated. Look at how Nick was rewarded for giving it. Not with loyalty. Not with good decisions. Not with respect. Denton would famously, and one could say hypocritically, enforce a strict no photography, no cell phones policy at his wedding. It was his one private moment, the one day he did not want to be interrupted by the technology and publicity that ruled his life. By the 250 guests, it was observed to the letter, with one exception: a Gawker writer named Rich Juzwiak, one of Nick's best men, would sneak a phone in and get caught taking photos.

The people at Gawker, even the ones making important decisions which the company would have to answer for—it was John Cook who wrote Gawker's response to the first injunction in the Hogan case—had trouble observing the basic rules of society. They had trouble thinking about the consequences of their actions and the optics of how they would be perceived. So when someone like Cook wrote a blog post, essentially telling the judge to go to hell in 2013, he was drawing a line in the sand that everyone else at Gawker had to toe, to their eternal public relations regret, and creating a headwind the lawyers had to struggle against. Denton had encouraged this reckless energy because it made for good stories, but now, in the fight for his company's life, it was working against him and not for him.

Culture eats strategy.

Denton can feel the legal screws tightening, but he can only pass the pressure on to those beneath him. They can only respond by acting out, by resisting, by making poor decisions they're not qualified to make. It didn't matter how good Gawker's First Amendment arguments might have been—the brattiness with which they asserted them did not help their cause, either. In the court of public opinion, it was growing worse, too. Gawker was a mess of contradictions and falling apart because of it.

"From an economically rational perspective Denton was very misaligned with everybody else by 2015," Peter would say. "It was like a textbook example of a Marxist exploitation. He had the most equity in it and he had a lot to lose, whereas the slave wages they were paying their writers meant that the writers had nothing to lose."

Denton was as misaligned culturally as he was financially. He has gotten married. His husband is friendly, spiritual, empathetic, an artist from Houston, not New York. It becomes almost a running joke among his friends, *Nick is happy*. His heart has grown and it's changed him. Among his employees, this is almost taken as a sign that something is wrong with him. It's made him soft. That tinge of nihilism has been passed on to the organization like a baton of dissatisfaction.

"The worst thing about running Gawker," he tells me, "was feeling stretched. Pulled in different directions. And it got worse. I felt the polarization. You try to explain to your people how the world works, but it isn't their world, not their bubble." At an all-hands meeting about the site's editorial future in 2015, Denton would say he had come to believe that the Hogan case was on the line of acceptability. One of his writers would live-tweet Denton's comments, laughing to her followers that Denton had expressed a "hulk of regret" about the sex tape. She said it like these comments wouldn't be used in the lawsuit that would determine the fate of the company she worked for. Like this was all a joke.

Except Denton knew that it wasn't. He had begun to despair of convincing his writers, the misfit toys he had made a home for, of their apocalyptic reality. He knew that a loss in court could likely be the end of the company he'd built, the end of meetings for that writer to live-tweet, the end of a carefree environment that would tolerate that kind of insubordination. "It's a $100 million lawsuit," he would tell the *New York Times* when asked if he had begun to worry about the case in June 2015. "We don't keep $100 million in the bank, no."

Few do. Which is the devastating opportunity that conspiracies take advantage of: what is the thing they have not planned for?

If Thiel is Melville's Ahab, manically chasing a white whale wherever it takes him, then Denton is Melville's Benito Cereno, a prisoner on his own ship, unable to communicate the terror of his position, being driven slowly insane by the sound of the sharpening hatchets of his crew. He can't sell the company with a lawsuit hanging over it, he can't settle the case without going back on much of his rhetoric to the writers and in the press. He would try to push the writers to be nicer, to ask them when they would be gratuitously mean or reckless, "What's your purpose here? What are you hoping to do with this post?" He thought he could manage the energy. He tried new editors, wrote long memos, held long meetings about his editorial vision. But the incentives were built into the core of the company. The writers had no stake in the business, only in the notoriety. They were measured in page views, and they knew the best way to get them was to say and do the things that no one else could—or would. And yet Denton also knew that he could not afford for them to be too much nicer anyway. He needed the traffic to show the growth to lure in new investors to pay the legal bills he was now drowning in. He needed to keep the audience entertained, too. They were fickle, they did not appreciate his predicament. They have their own problems, and don't care about his.

And what of Gawker's audience? In the beginning they had been there with Gawker, sending in their comments, cheering and jeering at every rich, famous hypocrite whose scalp Gawker was able to nail on its big board of traffic. Nick and the writers assumed these masses, these statistics on his website were fans—loyal, self-aware followers—who knew they were complicit in what was happening. He forgot what Kierkegaard had said about the public and how the gossip press was like a mean dog that could be watched with amusement from afar. The papers could be set upon some superior, and everyone got to watch and never feel bad. If someone ever got hurt and the police came, the public could say: *I wasn't the one who bit you. That's not my dog, I am merely a subscriber.* Nobody would ever have to admit that they had enjoyed the story in 2007 when Gawker had outed Thiel, or that they were one of the seven million plus people who had watched the Hulk Hogan video.

So Nick had begun to do what any normal person would do: look for an escape hatch, even if he wouldn't describe it that way. "Nick already had one foot out the door," A.J. would say of Denton's mindset from late 2014 on. "He was already thinking of his next act." Denton spent a good chunk of that year investing in and retooling the technology that underpinned Gawker, as if he were trying to transition away from gossip journalism and return to his love of technology, the love that had preceded Gawker and never caused him this kind of trouble. He had long ago split Gawker into multiple companies: Kinja, which owned the underlying software and infrastructure of the sites, and Gawker Media, which owned the articles, with the profits of the latter mostly going into the Hungarian-based former. Denton thus had sent millions away overseas. He had designed a corporate structure that minimized its tax burdens, that potentially shielded it from government authorities and legal repercussions (another operational contradiction, since Gawker had itself written big articles criticizing other rich people for hiding assets in the Cayman Islands).

It wasn't simple greed, as many claimed. Denton's mother had escaped the Holocaust and lost everything. As a child, he caught her hiding household items that might be easily converted to currency in a crisis. His grandmother, who by Nick's count had rebuilt her life from nothing on four occasions, carried her money on her and was skeptical of his internet business because it wasn't real money if he couldn't touch it. He believes the world is precarious—he's been told of its instability too many times by people who could vividly describe losing everything. Perhaps deep down he knew that Gawker could never last, which was a perfectly rational belief, but it's hardly a vote of confidence in the business. Perhaps he didn't quite want it to last anymore.

So who is the captain of the ship? The guy with an exit strategy? Or the rabble impressed from raucous ports now resembling a crew? Whoever it was, Gawker lacked strong adult supervision. "There are no outside investors to make us compromise our goals," Denton would write in a memo to his staff. It's an inspiring, clarion call to all those whose first instinct is to speak the truth and consider politics later—but it also means nobody there is responsible for urging a middle course, so that they might live and fight another day. A rare mutual friend of Thiel's and Denton's would tell me that this was Gawker's main weakness, one that was inevitably going to cause a fatal problem, if not from Thiel then from someone, eventually. There were no competent managers or operators in the company. And why would there be? Denton had never raised outside money, had never expressed serious interest in selling the company or taking on partners—which meant there was little upside to attract these executive types to the company. Which is how A. J. Daulerio, a rebellious, self-destructive thirty-something with a drug problem and hardly a penny to his name (even before the verdict he would have a net worth of -$27,000), had ended up as the editor of a company worth hundreds of millions of dollars.

Was A.J. thinking about the long-term health of his employer when he rushed to publish the Hogan sex tape? Was he thinking about protecting the brand when he tossed up the clip of that girl on the bathroom floor or linked to a site that was hosting the peephole video of ESPN reporter Erin Andrews, which the rest of the media had banded together not to cover? By the time the bill would come due for these things he didn't even work at Gawker anymore. Were the writers who rattled their sabers and marched perfectly into Thiel's traps ever thinking beyond the argument in front of them? Did they ever consider whether the company they worked for had $100 million to gamble on this case? This did not occur to them. The ties that made them bound and determined to defend their publication of the Hogan sex tape did not also bind them to the welfare of the outlet that published it.

Somehow, it was on A.J. that the role of Cassandra would fall. After he left Gawker and its insular culture he could see the situation unfolding more clearly than his former colleagues. As their codefendant, he would grow alarmed enough to write an email to the editors who took over and ran the company after him, attempting to wake them up, to stave off the disaster that might be coming to everyone involved. As the bad publicity had piled up from the pinpricks of Thiel's campaigns, Nick had asked Daulerio if a writer named Ben Wallace at *New York* magazine might be a good candidate to open up to about the case, to get Gawker's defense narrative out to the world. A.J. is aghast: *Gawker is one of the biggest media platforms in the world*. What does it say that they cannot write their own story? That they have no ability to explain to the world where they stand?

From: A. J. Daulerio
Sent: Wednesday, June 3, 2015
To: Lacey, John, Tommy, Tom

Seriously, you guys, take control over this situation. Think about the fact that you now have a fucking PR squad trying to place this story. You're telling me you don't have someone on your staff of geniuses who can do a better job talking about this than Ben Wallace??? I mean, FUCK Ben Wallace and then FUCK him again.

Your editorial operation has spent two fucking weeks worth of radical transparency devoted to whether or not your staff should unionize but, Christ, the whole company is facing a $100 million lawsuit that could render all that "dick-twirling" pretty irrelevant. (And shit's gonna change, when that verdict comes down. That truth is well established.)

I absolutely have no personal stake in this lawsuit whatsoever. NONE. You guys, however, do. And the guy you need the most to care about it is being a real fucking pussy at the expense of your operation.

This shit is happening in less than a month. Internally, you're underprepared. And most of you know that.

Stop having fucking meetings and take charge.

Love you all. Fix it.

Over the course of several conversations, including another one that day over chat, A.J. begins to share his serious doubts: *The trial is a month away and we are not prepared.* They had spent all their energy pressuring Hogan, fighting him off, but it hadn't worked. He tells Gawker's managing editor that Gawker "should settle. And push for a settlement more aggressively. Because we're gonna get smoked."

"A wound to the reputation not only does not heal, but grows deeper every day which goes by," E. L. Godkin wrote in *Scribner's Magazine* more than 125 years ago. He wrote this about the rise of the mass newspaper, in an article that would inform Justice

Brandeis's "Right to Privacy" argument. Godkin would say there was one way to heal those wounds: a "formal and public refutation of the slander." That is, *an apology*.

It never occurs to anyone at Gawker how easily such a gesture would have frayed the bonds that tied its enemies together. An apology would have sapped the conspiracy of its power and put Thiel's and Hogan's goals in conflict. It would have put Gawker in a position to be the good guys again in front of a jury: *We said we were sorry. This guy who screwed his friend's wife just won't let it go.* But to apologize they would have had to see themselves from another perspective, an unbiased and human one that was capable of wrongdoing and meanness, and they couldn't. Instead, their intransigence only serves to bind Hogan and Harder and Thiel closer together. *These people will never be held accountable unless we do it. These people think they are above any wrongdoing.*

Denton would later say that there was a hard-line faction inside Gawker who came to believe that "truth itself is the only necessary defense." These are the true believers who would never have allowed Denton to apologize for anything that Gawker did, ever. The outing of semiprivate individuals—okay, because it was true. Posting naked photos of celebrities—it might be gross, but it was allowed because the photos were real. Bullying, attacking, criticizing, all of it permissible under the limitless scope of the First Amendment.

This kind of purity is childish, the domain of people who live in the realm of theory and words and recoil from the real world where someone can punch you in the face if you say the wrong words to the wrong person. There is always a defense necessary; discretion is the responsibility of freedom, the obligation that comes along with rights. If not in court, then in life. If not to other people, then to yourself. But that's only part of it—Nick was the leader. He had allowed that to happen. He had allowed them to proceed closer and closer to trial without really bothering to think through these hard issues, without facing the hard truths about his company. Even the hard truths about how *other people would see his company.*

A.J. would tell him directly in one of those emails that it was "time to wake the fuck up," that the company—the one that A.J. had left two years before but was tied to as long as this case dragged on—was "turning into a bloated, arrogant, self-absorbed mess." How had Gawker been so embarrassingly outmaneuvered by Gamergaters and let itself be savaged in the press over a couple of exploited interns? He might have also done well to ask, where was Heather Dietrick in all this? Wasn't she supposed to be part of the adult supervision—not one of the untrained puppies but a leader? In 2013 she had joined Gawker as its chief counsel. She had been there when the article was published. Since 2014 she had been the company's president. Yet she has not convinced her boss, or her coworkers, that this lawsuit is unlike the other cases they have faced, that Hogan is going to go all the way. (She had been told this directly, after all.) Or perhaps she has fallen in with the hard-line faction, too—leaving Nick without the perspective and the advice he so desperately needed.

Still united in principle, in common cause against an evil enemy, Peter's side is not without its problems. It, too, could have been torn apart by its own contradictions and systemic issues. Rich donors are notoriously easy marks. They fund boondoggles as often as they fund the efficient, ruthless machines that people fear are running the world. It's a real-life luxury tax. Limitless resources are corruptive. They make people lazy. Take Mr. A. In 2011, Thiel's net worth was roughly $1.5 billion, and conservatively the interest on a billion dollars is hundreds of thousands of dollars *a day*. Having hooked Peter's interest in the project, finagling himself into a role as the man on the ground, essentially anything he could have asked for would have been his, had he run back the playbook he used in Berlin. Instead of asking to be paid from the beginning—which he could have—he waits. "You prove what you can do and you get paid even more," he says. Though he would come to draw a $25,000-a-month retainer plus expenses from Peter, it was proving himself indispensable to Peter that was the real payday. The people he would meet while orbiting Thiel's world, the things he would learn in the course of this conspiracy, made the paycheck almost secondary. The $300,000 man is not necessarily the one who will tell you honestly, "Hey, this isn't working. I think it's time for you to shut this thing down and let me go."

If Mr. A is the professional son, the ambitious young man who worms his way into the life and the heart of the successful power broker, the distinction remains in the word *professional*. He started this when he was twenty-six, his first big job. He's thirty now. A grown-up by any standard. How much does he still enjoy calls at 2:00 a.m. from a billionaire with high standards? He is liable to jump to another project at any moment, and the question always remains how willing he is to endure the setbacks and the down moments, if there are other offers on the table, if his own projects begin to succeed. Professional sons often go from father to father, trading in their last one for a better one if they can. Had Peter himself not surprised the partners when he had gotten up one day and walked out of Sullivan & Cromwell because he was ready for something different?

The potential for misaligned incentives extends to Harder as well, who is paid at rack rate—north of $500 an hour—and is paid monthly without fail. He was growing rich off this conspiracy regardless of the outcome. His law firm is built around this client. Which is precisely the problem. A lawyer at the wheel of a gravy train with what appears to be endless runway tends not to be the best, most conscientious lawyer and can easily derail things due to his own recklessness. The question is whether Harder is one of those attorneys. "I never believed that I had a blank check," he tells me. "I was never told

I had a blank check. I try to be efficient in all my cases, but I was really trying to be efficient in this one." It's partly fear that the well might suddenly go dry, that the mandate could change with little notice, that keeps him diligently working toward a victory. His desire to keep the train on track means a constant need for good news, for little victories, for signs of progress. And in turn, Mr. A also allows him to feel that Harder does have access to substantial resources, that he will not be nickeled and dimed, that they want him to be aggressive, and want more than anything to *win*.

If Denton is a prisoner on his own ship, then Thiel, too, in his capacity as Ahab, is a prisoner of momentum. He has to keep everyone interested in the hunt. Can he keep it together long enough to get to a trial? Can he keep Hogan on board and through to the end? Can he keep the lawyers from advising Hogan to settle? Can Mr. A, the person he has depended on now for so long, stay the dutiful servant that he needs him to be? How many years can you expect a kid to put in a half million airline miles? If the exhausting level of secrecy doesn't crack any of his coconspirators, could it crack Thiel? How long will he want to keep spending hundreds of thousands of dollars a month? But to quit now, would that solve anything? Or would it be more embarrassing to have tried and failed than to push forward and let them all howl at the end?

"Men often deceive themselves about the love that you judge a man bears to you," Machiavelli says about conspiracies. To maintain loyalty and faith among conspirators, he says, "it must be indeed that the hatred is great or that your authority is very great." Without a blinding hatred for the enemy as motivating fuel or without the absolute power of a leader, conspiracies fall apart under the pressures of the long journey. Machiavelli tells the story of one brilliant conspirator, Nelematus, who upon explaining his plan to his potential conspirators, locked them inside his house and demanded they swear to participate on the spot or else he would turn them in for the very conspiracy they wavered on committing to.

Since that is not exactly an option for Peter Thiel, what ties them together really is Gawker and what they'd come to feel about it. Gawker had not only incited a conspiracy, but in the course of the trial, its actions, its tone, its arrogance had fused its unknown, unnamed opponents together. "We were not all perfectly aligned by any means," Thiel explains about the setup between him and Hogan, between Mr. A and the lawyers, between the lawyers and everyone else, "but it was the evil nature of our enemy that was somehow super galvanizing. Even as it got to be this bigger, more complicated thing, we were able to achieve a certain unity of purpose over time." This was a sense that grew as each day passed. Seeing Gawker as evil became easier the longer it went on. Mr. A had said the more they studied Gawker, the more they interacted with this organization, the harder it was to see any redeeming qualities: because of what Gawker's writers would say, how its lawyers acted, and everyone's inability to show even a slight understanding of what Terry Bollea was so upset about.

Culture transcends strategy.

Most conspiracies fail and most fail from the inside, not the outside. The bonds are frayed internally rather than cut by some external source. Will that happen here, will Gawker have lasted long enough, sowed just enough tension, been just prickly enough to escape once again? Or will it have finally met an opponent it can't demoralize?

CHAPTER 13

The Testing of Faith

It always takes longer than expected, per Hofstadter's Law, even when—and this is the critical part—one takes Hofstadter's Law into account.

By 2015, Gawker had deposed more than twenty-five people in connection with the case. Harder had deposed almost as many. There were countless flights from L.A. to Tampa, San Francisco to L.A., L.A. to D.C., L.A. to New York, D.C. to New York, New York to Tampa, Reno to Tampa to L.A to New York. There has been an FBI investigation, a Tampa Police Department investigation, countless hearings. Nearly a million dollars have been spent on a special magistrate solely to sort through evidentiary disputes. It had come to be that Harder needed his own boutique law firm solely to support this endeavor. Legal filings alone amounted to some 25,000 pages. So many papers were filed in this case that it overwhelmed the underbudgeted Pinellas County court system, leaving the judge to sheepishly ask that the lawyers print an extra copy of each document and provide her with one.

They had been at this not for months, as Gawker might have expected, but *years*.

The issues were driven in a feedback loop of tit-for-tat intensity: Gawker wants access to Hogan's medical records. Harder wants access to Gawker's financials. Gawker wants to know about Hogan's history of marital infidelity. Harder wants access to information about Denton's wedding and his prenuptial agreement. Why hadn't Gawker turned over these emails? Why had Hogan blacked out certain phone numbers on his cell phone records? No issue was too small, nothing had been left unexplored. They fought over whether lawyers should be able to take vacations. Whether depositions should be filmed. What day they should happen on. Whether this expert or that expert was truly qualified, whether this part or that part of the other side's expert testimony should be admissible. Though it had almost no bearing on whether Gawker was legally allowed to publish clips of a sex tape of this nature, for more than a year they fought for access to the confidential FBI reports, transcripts, and tapes of the sting from 2012. Harder in turn had fought equally hard to prevent these tapes from being turned over, fearing they would immediately be leaked to the public.

Each of these disputes, played out in hundreds of motions and responses and motions in response to responses to motions, was litigated by people who had to be paid and who were happy to keep earning their fees. The result is billing that almost boggles the imagination. One Gawker motion contains sixty-two exhibits, and from the seemingly endless coffers of Peter Thiel some $70,000 is drawn with which to respond and defend against that motion. Harder would complain on many occasions, "Your Honor, this is an incredibly simple case," yet he practiced his own excesses and attrition tactics, too. A single set of filings for motions related to a discovery issue, which we know of only because Harder attempted to get a judge to order that Gawker reimburse Hogan for them, cost a staggering $427,665.46. Nick is spending, too. By one estimate, there were at least fifty in-person hearings from 2012 until the trial, and teams of lawyers for both sides attended each one, with Gawker bringing as many as four attorneys to relatively perfunctory hearings. Charles Harder says he believes there was perhaps only a single hearing in which lawyers paid for by Peter Thiel outnumbered lawyers paid for by Nick Denton. Mr. A had been right when he had first estimated for Peter Thiel in 2011 how many years it would take and millions of dollars it would cost to take on this insane venture.

But it was at long last nearly at the finish line. Two steps forward, one step back had added up, slowly, surely until here, now, in July 2015, they were on the verge of trial. Their case had survived summary judgment attempts, it had survived motions to dismiss, it had survived being knocked out of one court and into another one. And now after all that fighting, a trial date was set: July 6. The docket was locked. No one had taken Gawker to trial before, no one had even gotten close. Everyone else had been stymied or intimidated—including some of the most powerful people in the world. Potential jury instructions are discussed.

Getting in front of real jurors is no easy feat in the American legal system. Most cases don't even get in sight of them—it was, Charles Harder thought early on in the process, more likely that the case would be thrown out of court than make it to trial. Those were simply the odds. But the conspiracy had defied them. The moment, that decisive judgment, that decisive blow that Peter Thiel had been cocking back, was nearly ready to be released.

Except it won't be.

Because despite all the preparations, all the setbacks that Thiel's team had prepared for, Denton's lawyers had one last delay tactic to play and they played it quite well. For on July 2, 2015, responding to an emergency motion, the Second District Court of Appeal rules that the trial will not happen on July 6 as planned. A legal technicality meant Gawker would be given more time to prepare for trial and to sift through the evidence from the FBI sting—the one that had happened months *after* it had published its article—and to delve deeper into Hogan's life and investigate the provenance of the tapes it had cared little about in October 2012.

Mr. A is in New York in 2015 as the eve of trial approaches. He is confident enough in his chances of victory that he has set up operations close to the bankruptcy attorneys who would be necessary if Gawker lost catastrophically. *Don't count your chickens before they hatch*, but he has. He has the large television in the room hooked up to his computer so that he might stream the trial live when it begins. Harder has kept him informed of these last-minute legal wranglings from the ground in Florida. He reaches Mr. A in a suite in the Park Hyatt hotel via email: "The trial has been continued." Only in the legal system would the term *continued* actually mean *discontinued*.

The call to the benefactor: we couldn't get it done. The new trial won't be for another nine months. Just as conspiracies are rushed forward by events, they can be interminably delayed and disrupted by them.

Harder and his team were already in Florida, practicing their final arguments. Even the media had been certain enough of the dates that they'd made dozens of travel accommodations for hotels, restaurants, and parking lots which, when they were suddenly and abruptly canceled, rippled through the economy of Pinellas County. Mostly the setback ripples through the morale of the conspirators. It is a discouraging thing to have fixed the noose, to have made your preparations, to have mentally told yourself that today is the day, only to have the person slip out of it at the final second. Do you doubt your hunches here? Do you reconsider all the calculations that you've made? Do you give in? The critical question then is how you respond to this setback, a setback far more serious and demoralizing than the trough of sorrow which happens earlier—for this is when you felt like you could taste victory, that it was within your grasp.

Churchill once compared an offensive force to throwing a bucket of water over the floor: “It rushes forward, then soaks forward, and finally stops altogether until another bucket can be brought.” It’s the moment in between those buckets when a conspiracy is most vulnerable, because the combination of stasis and exposure begins to evaporate those ties that bind. But even more than that, it is here that one has the brief time to reflect and consider: *Is it worth another try? Do I have it in me?* Perhaps the judge had known that both sides would soon be reaching such a moment, that they would be asking themselves this fundamental question of will, because a few days before her ruling, she had warned them, “This is way too early in the game to be getting tired.”

“There was real second guessing,” Peter explains. “Are we totally wrong about everything here? And were our timelines wrong? Maybe none of our cases are going to work and maybe this whole plan doesn’t make sense.”

Gawker’s legal strategy had been designed to create these kinds of doubts. To make its opponents think: *Maybe we can’t afford to beat them*. Because if someone did beat Gawker, there would be a land rush of enemies coming to pile on after the precedent was set. “The conversation in early 2015 was ‘We are going to bankrupt you. We are going to destroy you, we will run out the clock. Doesn’t matter if you have a good or bad case. You’re going to run out of money.’ They made that argument against Hulk Hogan,” Thiel says. “‘You will get no justice because you have no money.’” The problem is that Hulk Hogan and Charles Harder were in a position to defer that message to someone not well deposed to heed it. Peter Thiel had at first despaired of a fight with Gawker because he felt a certain powerlessness, that it was a media outlet, that it had the First Amendment to hide behind and there was nothing he could do about it. Now here, at least in this specific instance, seeing Gawker’s legal strategy laid bare, that power imbalance is flipped. There is something about the arrogance of Nick Denton's position that grates on Thiel, that drives him to continue almost out of spite, to spend whatever it takes to win. Mr. A is asking Peter Thiel if he's willing to still fight it out, to go another nine months. It would fall on Thiel here, would they continue? and the answer coming from the other end of the line is "Yes."

And so the next bucket of water is brought and the water rushes forward. Right to the next crisis.

On July 16 in the evening, a Gawker writer named Jordan Sargent, filling his quota of posts and page views, and not thinking a single thought about the lawsuit that had been hanging over his employer for years, writes a post that outs the married CFO of Condé Nast—the brother of a well-known and well-liked cabinet member of the Obama administration, a man with three children, who was being extorted by a male escort. In a previous era, it would have been the type of story that Gawker insiders would have loved—a salacious personal story that exposes the hypocrisy or shame of a competitor. But this time the public response was swift and decisive: they were appalled. No one enjoyed gawking at this. It is branded "gay-shaming," and the writer is accused of ruining the man's life. A well-known journalist would describe the article as "reprehensible beyond belief," calling Gawker "deranged" to even consider publishing it. Lena Dunham, who had tangled with Gawker as one of Harder's last clients at Wolf Rifkin, would tweet, "How many cruel and unnecessary stories must Gawker publish before people realize this isn't a fun site to browse over their cereal?" Calls for advertiser boycotts would begin anew, this time with more than just video game nerds cheering them on.

The world had not stood still in the years since Gawker launched, and readers were far less inclined to look at being gay as a secret to expose, as they had been when it had been done to Peter Thiel. Denton himself, the man who had complained about the misplaced sense of decency, is horrified, too. "This is the very, very worst version of the company. I don't want some guy blowing his brains out and that being on our hands," he would say to his staff. He's also smart enough to be horrified by how it *looks*: this is not what he wants, but more important, it's exactly what he doesn't need right now. He has spent millions of dollars in court trying to prove that Gawker is a reputable website that does good, important, and ethical work; that exists well within the outer limitations of the First Amendment protections afforded to publishers and people alike. Now, when the strategy could not be more precious, one of his own writers not only undermines it, but obliterates the notion.

To Nick's credit, he moves quickly. He pulls the story with a short explanation: "I believe this public mood reflects a growing recognition that we all have secrets and they are not all equally worthy of exposure. The point of this story was not in my view sufficient to offset the embarrassment to the subject and his family." The staff at Gawker mutinies and several resign, strongly believing that this is *exactly* the kind of article that Gawker was built to publish, that they had come to the site to be given the ability to publish. Denton writes a post to the editorial staff:

> This is the company I built. I was ashamed to have my name and Gawker's associated with a story on the private life of a closeted gay man who some felt had done nothing to warrant the attention. We believe we were within our legal right to publish, but it defied the 2015 editorial mandate to do stories that inspire pride, and made impossible the jobs of those most committed to defending such journalism.

The irony of this position is not lost on the conspirators. It's an opportunity for Denton to check his assumptions, too, to reexamine the stand he has taken here with Hogan about running the surreptitiously recorded sex tape of a famous man and an unfamous woman, but he can't. Or at least he doesn't. He's put too much into this case. He's fought it publicly for too long to give in now. His rhetoric had boxed him in.

But any enjoyment of Denton's predicament, watching him squirm and seeing his hypocrisy laid out in undeniable publicness, would not last long for Harder or Thiel. Within a few days, the conspirators would be reeling from their own self-inflicted blow.

It would be rooted in their own dark hypocrisy: the audio from the sex tapes which would finally expose to the public what Hulk Hogan had vented about in that bedroom, what he'd hoped would never come out. The thing that Bubba Clem had said he could retire off, the venomously awful, sickening things that Hogan had said when he thought he was in private. When he'd been unguarded enough to repeatedly use the word "nigger" to describe his daughter's boyfriend, who he deeply disliked. "I mean, I am a racist, to a point," he says, and then punctuates it with "fucking niggers." "I guess we're all a little racist," he says, ending again with "*Fucking nigger*" like it's a perfectly normal way to wrap up a thought.

How do these tapes get out? How does the transcript make its way to the press? No one is sure. Rumors of their existence had been floating around since Keith Davidson's client shopped them to websites. The client could have leaked them, or he could have been sloppy with his sharing at some point over the last few years. Davidson himself could have leaked them. We do know that Gawker had maneuvered for some time to get access to them, had warned repeatedly in mediation and in hearings that these comments might someday get out. Denton had alluded to them in a blog post right before the trial, promising the reveal of a "third act" in the case. Gawker would finally get confirmation of these rumors and access to the tapes when the FBI handed over their evidence of the sting, which included the audio of Hogan's and Houston's microphones as they sat in that hotel room with the extortionist, forced to listen to those racist comments played back to them. We know that just a few days after Gawker got those tapes, just as Gawker was imploding around a press crisis of its own making, Hogan's comments are made public, and now the story changes.

Who leaked them matters only so much. The impact is enormous. Hogan is indisputably the bad guy again. And Gawker moves to take advantage of it, finally telling a compelling story of the case as A.J. had demanded. Its story about Hogan's comments after the leak does 750,000 views.

A friend said that it wasn't that Denton was without ethics, just that sometimes he lost sight of them. Literally minutes (fourteen minutes to be exact) after the *National Enquirer* broke the story that exposed Hogan's comments, A. J. Daulerio's blog, *Ratter*, which had received a $500,000 investment from Nick Denton, tweeted "XOXOXO" to Hogan and shared the link to the story. We know from a later admission that A.J. had long considered leaking them himself. We know that he *could* have done it. We just don't know if he did. There is video you can watch of Nick Denton, recorded after the trial, speaking about the tape of Hogan's comments. In it, a year of expert public relations falls away, and the darker, vicious side of Denton appears if only in a gesture. "The irony is that it probably would have never come out," he says of the tapes. "Would it have come out?" Denton asks rhetorically. The implication hangs there. Would it have come out if Hogan had not pushed him toward trial, if Hogan had walked away when he and Heather Dietrick had said they would let him walk away? Denton pauses. Shrugs. "I don't know. I don't think it would have come out." Yet even if Gawker is responsible, if Denton had launched his V1 rocket in a final attempt to break the will of his opponent, even if these tapes were irrelevant to the trial at hand, it doesn't change the fact that Hogan said those words—that he had laid this trap for himself years ago already and now he had fallen in it.

Hogan's family is mortified. He is kicked out of the WWE Hall of Fame. He loses the rest of his endorsements. People had been disappointed in the sex tape, but here—here they were disgusted. The shoes Gawker had walked a thousand miles in were now on other feet, and their wearer was just as disgusted with himself as everyone else was—because he knew they were right to be. It was the worst thing he'd ever done, ever said. There was nothing he could do to take back those words.

Harder had warned Hogan that these comments might come out. Hogan had proceeded anyway, telling himself that it didn't matter. "I knew it was coming. I knew what would happen if I kept pushing, but no, I just couldn't walk away." He wanted to win so badly he thought it worth the risk. But that had been theoretical. Now he had run the risk and the dice didn't go his way.

It should be said that Gawker's legal team had always and reasonably held a basic assumption, and it's one that undergirds the litigation system: people will act in their rational self-interest. Hogan, disowned by all his allies and friends, losing his remaining income, exposed and vulnerable for a second time, should have had to quit. The rational thing would be to drop the case. This is what Gawker thought. At some point, the other side gets tired of being hit and lacks the energy to keep hitting back. This is what its highly paid legal advisers had been telling them and were telling them now.

Except it didn't quite go that way. Not only because Peter Thiel is funding the case in the shadows. There is one upside to losing it all. What is it? At least for a conspirator, now you have nothing left to lose.

There is the famous story sometimes told of Aeneas, sometimes of Cortés, sometimes of Xiang Yu, who ordered their ships burned or sunk so the men have nowhere to go but forward, so there was no chance of returning home the way they had come. Thiel and Harder had done nothing so deliberate as far as keeping Terry Bollea committed. Nick Denton, or whoever had leaked those tapes, had done it for them.

Hogan can't walk away anymore. I'll quote it again from Machiavelli: "Anyone who is threatened and is forced by necessity either to act or to suffer becomes a very dangerous man to the prince." He was dangerous before, when he had been humiliated and exposed. But there was a chance that reason might win out. That an apology might take the sting out of his shame and a reasonable settlement offer might salve the remaining wounds. Whatever it was, Gawker counted on his giving up at some point. Even his backers had to consider the contingency that he might eventually settle and leave them without a client. That had always been the risk in an arrangement where the client got to make shots. Hogan could have made the call to walk away while he was ahead. Now, that's gone. There is nothing left for him. To borrow a phrase from Robert Frost, there is no way out but *through* Gawker.

Denton, too, thought that Gawker could afford to beat the risks it was taking. "We have a higher tolerance for risk than most organizations," he would say, to himself and to the media as they approached the trial. Gawker had always been willing to face the odds that other companies wouldn't. It would write stories that others wouldn't. It would fight cases other companies would settle, go to war with entities others were afraid to touch. But with this case, Gawker's team was facing the reality of that risk, and the backlash of the scrutiny it had brought upon them. Now, here they were feeling that pressure, feeling the real cost of the odds. Thiel, too, had always been the man who made contrarian bets, who sought out the uncrowded trades, who was willing to be mocked and scorned if he thought he was right.

His bet here isn't public, but he can see what the public thinks of his horse.

It's not even a matter of winning anymore. Both sides have spent several million dollars thus far. Both have made huge wagers on their public reputations. Peter can't walk away. What if Gawker eventually discovered he was behind it and was still around to do something in retaliation? What if the media found out, some ten years in the future, that he'd launched a conspiracy, only to bungle it and fail? He'd look terrible. There is another not so small consideration: Thiel had persuaded Hogan and other people to come this far; he couldn't simply quit on them.

Gawker's reputation is on the line. Nick, A.J., John Cook, Max Read, and now Jordan Sargent had put it there. They'd all said publicly, either explicitly or implicitly, that Gawker would win. This was a First Amendment issue, they'd said a thousand times, as much to convince themselves probably as to sway public perception, and they were the only ones brave enough to fight it. They couldn't walk back that kind of rhetoric. And perhaps they had also begun to sense—if not consciously—that this is not just an ordinary opponent they are fighting against, that this isn't going to stop unless Gawker wins decisively.

At Shiloh, Ulysses S. Grant had been caught by surprise. Flush off two victories, convinced he had superior resources and tactics, he was confident he would win. Yet he had thrown everything he had at the Confederates and been thrown back. It had begun to pour rain on the troops as they attempted to settle in for the night. Grant had seriously injured his leg in a fall a few weeks before. He is desperately short of reinforcements. Sherman finds him and begins to politely discuss plans for retreat. He says to him, "Well, Grant, we've had the devil's own day, haven't we?" Grant, backlit by the camp lantern, squints as he clamps down on the stub of his cigar, "Yes. *Yes*. Lick 'em tomorrow, though." And this is precisely what happens. Napoleon, too, describes warfare in that simple way: Two armies are hurled at each other and both are thrown into confusion and disarray by the force of the collision. Victory is simple. It goes to whoever reassembles and redoubles first. If either party thinks this would be a chance to rest, they are wrong.

All are scrambling now—Gawker, Thiel, Hogan—not to try to get an advantage but for their very survival. They have collided with great force and are thrown into disarray. Publicly reviled, any could be down for the count. Is it stubbornness that keeps them going? Foolhardiness? Determination? Boldness? A death wish? What remains is simple: who will get to their feet fastest, confidently tell themselves "Lick 'em tomorrow" . . . and mean it?

CHAPTER 14

Who Wants It More?

Every conspiracy, every campaign, is a battle of wills. Of the conspirators, of the defense, of the laws of nature. All these forces are intersecting, interacting with one another.

And though we'd like to think that planning and resources—or righteousness and worthiness—determine who wins and who loses, they don't. So often these things come down to a simple factor: Who wants it more?

Hillary Clinton spent her whole life trying to become president. She began her final campaign nearly two years before the election, cutting off at the pass anyone within her party who might seriously challenge her. She raised more money than you could ever possibly need. Donald Trump was underprepared, erratic, constantly in his own way. But it cannot be said that he did not want to win very badly. He wanted to win even more than Hillary. The last few weeks of the election made that fact indisputable. She had already won in her mind, she felt she deserved it. Trump, on the other hand, was willing to do anything, go anywhere, bear any shame, tell any lie, ally with any group if it meant he could take it from her.

And he did.

Gawker, too, might be seen as the overconfident favorite, the politician with the polls predicting victory, the team with the heavy lead in the fourth quarter, but dogged by that same persistent unlikability. In early 2015, Gawker's chief strategy officer was deposed as part of the lawsuit and asked, as a matter of course, if she was familiar with the particulars of the case being made by Terry Bollea. "I am somewhat familiar that there is a lawsuit," she answers. "I wasn't familiar with the actual name of the person." She doesn't have any personal knowledge about the case, she tells the lawyers. "My understanding is there is a post at issue and that there's been some sort of legal—" She cuts herself off. "I'm unfamiliar with the claims." The chief *strategy* officer of a company is only somewhat familiar with a nine-figure lawsuit hurtling toward a trial; she doesn't even know the *name* of the person suing them. She didn't think she needed to. A.J., for all his earlier warnings to Gawker's leadership, would tweet that his trip to Florida was going to be a summer vacation. Nick Denton estimated publicly that his chances of facing a disaster in the courtroom were only one in ten.

Gawker was protected by the First Amendment. Everyone said so. *Didn't you read the piece in the* New York Times? *Hogan doesn't have a chance.*

Nine months would elapse between the delayed trial and the one that would ultimately render the verdict on the conspirators and the conspiracy. What will they do with this time? What will they do with this opportunity to reflect on their cases? On the terrain on which the two armies will clash into each other for a final time? How seriously would they take this? Who wants it more?

There is a story about a young John D. Rockefeller who found himself stuck with bullying, corrupt business partners. He wants to break with them, but he can't, because they control the votes. They are squeezing his business to death. They abuse him, talk about forcing him out. What is he to do? Quietly, Rockefeller lines up financing from another oilman and waits. Finally there is a confrontation; one of them tries to threaten him: "You really want to break it up?" *Yes.*

He calls their bluff. They go along, knowing that the firm's assets will have to go to auction. They're sure they'll win—Rockefeller doesn't have that kind of money. He bids, they bid, he bids, they bid. Rockefeller wins the auction. A few weeks later, the newspapers announce his new partnership—revealing who had backed his bid—and the news that Rockefeller is, at twenty-five, an owner of one of the largest refineries in the world. On that day his partners "woke up and saw for the first time that my mind had not been idle while they were talking so big and loud," he would say later. They were shocked. They'd seen their empire dismantled and taken from them by the young man they had dismissed. Rockefeller had wanted it more.

The story of this conspiracy, too, is the story of one person working while the other talked big and loud. One side confident in its power and the self-evident inarguability of its position—believing until the very moment of the trial that it would likely be tossed out, that even if it wasn't, the verdict would be overturned by a higher court—and the other side, painfully aware of its own vulnerabilities, and with growing certainty of the evilness of its enemy, willing to put in the work and the money it would take to win.

Gawker did, however, make a number of settlement offers. There had been confidential mediations, first in February 2015, then again in September, and finally on January 28, 2016, roughly a month before trial. The offers began at $4 million and crept up, by the time Gawker had taken on its first outside investment—from a Russian oligarch, no less—to more than $10 million. There had been many hard blows with the stick from Gawker to Hogan by this point—endless motions, the reveal of his darkest shame and secret—but now, tired and partly ready to be done, Nick was offering the carrot. A very big one.

The Gawker team had spent the last three years at least partly convinced that victory was more or less theirs and that it would come easily. That there was only one heart and mind they needed to win:

Hogan's. That if they could just be difficult enough and slow enough, that if they could convince him they would never back down and he could never win, things would never get this far. That if they made themselves a bitter enough poison pill he would leave them alone. They had gone to great depths to intimidate, demoralize, and deter him. They'd spent hundreds of thousands of dollars doing it. When Bollea's lawyers said he wouldn't quit until he was bankrupt, Gawker responded with a strategy that said, "Well, I guess we can do that for you." They had slowly consumed his life, embarrassed him, pressured him, dragged him through a hundred motions, and eventually in the course of the litigation, exposed his racist secret to the world—a scandal that in truth had next to nothing to do with whether Gawker should have been allowed to publicly post a sex tape of a celebrity but effectively ended his career as a result. Will it work? Will he give in? Maybe he won't, they thought, but his lawyers will. No attorney lets his or her client walk away from an eight-figure settlement, not with this much baggage weighing him down. It would practically be a breach of their fiduciary duty. This was not only a test of faith, this was a test of mettle.

Though the other offers had been legitimately made and it appeared that Hogan was tempted by them, $10 million was money of another kind. If only they knew just how close Hogan was to accepting it. "It's a game of spouses, too," Mr. A would say of conspiracies. "We think it's about the principal figures, but if the spouses at home say we should settle, things could be over." Lying there stewing night after night, as the numbers go higher and they get closer to trial, Bollea's wife extracts a promise: if they offer you $20 million, *you have to take it*. She has no dog in this fight—she didn't sign up to be humiliated, to watch her husband have sex with another man's wife on video in a courtroom, to hear it as the lead story on every news channel in the country. All that could end now. He would be spared the media attention and end up a very rich man again. He has no legal fees, after all. That's been seen to. He can just walk away.

Even long after the conspiracy had ended, Gawker seemed to be unaware of what it must have taken from the conspirators to keep Hogan in the game. Another lawyer I spoke to, one who had worked on another famous and particularly egregious violation of celebrity privacy, would speculate that there must have been some intervention here by Thiel. That no attorney could, in good faith, allow their client to pass on large settlement offers for the uncertainty of a jury verdict unless they knew their client was protected in some way. "You take eight figures if it's offered. End of story," he said. Certainly many people have settled better cases for less, even people who had come to hate their opponent as much as Hogan and Harder did. So perhaps there was some convincing from above to keep Hogan invested and committed, incentives that allowed him to proceed to trial confident in his position. Had Hogan been more willing to settle, or had the number been astronomically higher, perhaps the case would have become another legal footnote in Gawker's triumphant history, killing the conspiracy along with it—delaying Thiel until he could find another case or another Gawker mistake, one not so dependent on a single individual taking it all the way to trial.

Although the number would creep upward in informal talks, it was never going to happen. At the end of the day, Bollea tells himself he *just can't take the money*. After they had threatened, after they had been party to the destruction of his career, there really was no number, he admits to me, no matter what his wife said. "Not only were they trying to make me quit, talk me into quitting before trial, they were trying to reward me for quitting," Hogan would say. Gawker's heavy persuasion from beginning to end had had the opposite effect. It only increased Hogan's anger and hardened his resolve. He'd always been aggressive; he wouldn't have gotten where he was in life if he wasn't.

Now this trait has fused with the intense hate that had developed over the last four years, the hate born from blog posts and refusals to follow judicial orders and depositions and obnoxious offers given over long walks on the beach. His desire to punish and to prevent is too great. Wrapping his own case up in a larger, vaguer cause of justice for everyone written about by Gawker, he couldn't just stop. Well, he could—he called the shots here and not Peter—but he *wouldn't*. Besides, Gawker still hadn't apologized. Hadn't offered removal of the post or an apology. There was no way to feel like this was a win, no way a confidential out-of-court settlement would look like a win to his fans, either. Terry Bollea turns down at least $10 million, quite possibly much more, and smiles to Harder and Houston as he does it.

He is in it to the end, and now hopeful, too. Because something was made clear with that enormous offer: *Gawker didn't want to go to trial*. Were they not the ones who had fought repeatedly for delays? Were they not the ones who, despite claiming they were undeniably in the right, had offered him eight figures to walk away? He could smell fear through the posturing. He could see it.

Peter had known that if he could get over this hurdle, eventually Gawker would be exhausted. "It's going to be a marathon," he would say to his team, "we just can't conk out. There are all these psychological things Gawker is going to try to do to get us to not fight as hard and we can't let them influence us. I'm not going to try to reach a compromise. I'm not going to try to talk to them." Not just to not fight as hard, but to ultimately deter them from going to trial. Because anything can happen in a trial, because very few companies would ever want to put their fate in the hands of a few average citizens in Florida.

That hardness in Thiel, what he'd committed to earlier, never seemed to have wavered. He could have quit when Hogan was exposed. He could have let Hogan off the hook now, let the momentum naturally peter itself out and know that he had cost Gawker more than anyone ever had. That he'd landed more blows than anyone else and that Gawker would be forever humbled and changed for it. Walking away, accepting the settlement would have also all but guaranteed the secrecy of his involvement, too, allaying the reputational fears that exposure brought with it. But the will to continue is stronger. The push for the knockout blow persists.

Yet unlike Denton, Thiel wasn't content to simply ballpark his odds. He wanted proof that the case had the legs to go the distance. *What can we know that they don't know? Where's our edge?* He spent nearly $100,000 for his lawyers to conduct not one but two mock trials in Florida. Gather up a bunch of prospective jurors, pay them by the hour, and run the case in front of them. Judge every reaction, learn everything they like and don't like. No self-serving assumptions, no generous assessment of our strengths. The purpose? As Harder presents their case to these jurors in a nondescript hotel conference room—he wants the hard facts. *What's our worst case and how does it stack up against their best case? Where is Gawker strong and where are we weak? What do we have to do to beat them?* What they find is that even ceding certain advantages to Gawker, Hogan's case plays very well. As far as I know, Gawker conducted no mock trials—at least it couldn't in the Tampa Bay region. Because Mr. A claims he hired the only two firms in the area to conflict them out of being able to work with Gawker. His simple move had kept the fog of war thick around them. No chance for last-minute clarity or perspective.

The verdicts in that conference room in Tampa are stunning: $120 million and $149 million.

Not that there wasn't still time for a reversal. Either side could lose based on a mistake or a miscalculation or a surprise new development.

Nick Denton and some reporters later claimed there were strong rumors that a billionaire was funding the case long before trial.

Some reporters said Denton himself had mentioned these rumors to them. How much of this is retconning—revisionist history based on hindsight—can't be known, but if it is true, why hadn't Gawker's strategy changed? And how much differently might things have turned out had Denton pushed harder to uncover the source? Why hadn't his lawyers made an issue of it in their motions? In 2013, Heather Dietrick had signed an affidavit with her suspicions of a "litigation dossier," but she had left it at that. Denton claimed that Thiel's friends had threatened him with reprisals in 2007 over that initial *Valleywag* article, but he didn't stop to put the pieces together. Just a week into the trial, a legal blog would speculate, "Might a Gawker Hater Be Covering Hulk Hogan's Legal Bills?," but it would get twenty Facebook shares and be mostly ignored, even by Gawker. It was too insane. "Nick understood how crazy it would sound and how desperate everyone at Gawker would sound if they started floating these ideas out there," A.J. said. But that assumes Nick knew it and just didn't want to verbalize it. The truth is probably simpler. "Nick refused to believe it because he did not want to get wrapped in any kind of conspiracy theories," John Cook, then Gawker's executive editor, explained. But is it really *conspiracy theory*? Why is it crazy if that's actually what's happening? It's not paranoia if someone is actually trying to get you.

"The polemical way to say this is that, what sort of investigative journalism outlet can't even aggressively investigate the conspiracy directed against it?" Peter would say. Gawker's mission had been to say the things that other people were afraid to say, it was a site that was dedicated to the idea of showing how the world *really* worked, yet with its life on the line it was silent and it was blind.

Thiel is spending tens of thousands of dollars on a battery of market research as the trial approaches. Telephone surveys. In-person surveys. Dossiers of social media comments about the trial.

Analysis of media reporting. Jury consultants. Bankruptcy attorneys to prepare for the chance that Gawker might try to escape a catastrophic verdict. All this money, all these avenues, spent and pursued in order to leave nothing to chance and to find every edge, every opportunity to land the decisive blow. For nearly a year he had called Mr. A almost weekly to press one key issue: "Are you sure Gawker won't be able to squirrel out of the supersedeas bond if they lose?" His team has been poring over case law to figure it out, to be sure they aren't missing anything, to put themselves in a position not just to win, but to win decisively.

Denton? He is winging it, hoping simply not to lose instead of trying to win. He is riding on the illusion of momentum he does not possess. He is making unforced errors and leaving opportunities open for his opponent. Perhaps he's simply struggling under the cumulative pressure, the mental burden of having a $100 million lawsuit hanging over his head for so long. Perhaps he's missing the insights he needs, having been led astray with bad legal advice. Or he could just be tired. Because here, when it matters, Denton doesn't seem to have much fight left in him.

It's not as if Hogan's case was without its flaws. Not only had he been filmed cheating on his wife with his best friend's wife, it was indisputable that he was capable of the kind of racism that punctuates sentences with "*Fucking niggers!*" Gawker had a point, too—Hogan had talked about his sex life in public many times. He was not necessarily easy to like here. Had the Gawker legal team arrived in Florida early and laid a groundwork of public support, they might have had a chance. They might also have seen earlier—when there was still time to adjust their strategy—just what obstacles they faced in that ordinary county in Florida, which worshipped its hometown heroes despite their flaws, and which looked at the New York media suspiciously and bitterly. The joke about Florida is that the farther north you go, the deeper South you are. Pinellas County is not Miami. It's west of Tampa. It faces the Gulf Coast. It's not the target market for a website of metropolitan elites. There is a moment, when questioning the potential jury pool, where Michael Sullivan, Gawker's lawyer, asks if anyone in the room had heard of A.J. or Nick before. No one answers. He jokes that Gawker is going to need to speak to their PR people about it. In a courtroom ratcheted tight with tension, the laughter is explosive and immediate, even among the defendants. A prospective juror, catching the wave of laughter, replies, "Or they should open an office in the South." This kills, too, but it's less funny in retrospect.

Both sides would know in advance that the small courtroom they would soon be calling home for two weeks has notorious sound and presentation issues. Mr. A and Harder spend tens of thousands of dollars on large printed displays and on sophisticated audiovisual equipment and technicians to run it. If Harder is going to argue that Gawker is hypocritical, Mr. A wants him to show, not tell it. In Gawker's own headlines: "That Type of Girl Deserves It." "At Last, This Revenge Porn Kingpin Has Been Stopped." They will show the jury that 4,439,425 minutes of the video were watched; *3,082 days watched*. They will show the jury the hidden camera. They will show the internal chats between Gawker writers. They will do this on a large flat-screen television and speakers and well-designed foam board. If Gawker was already unfavorable to the jury, it will find it impossible to recover from this kind of branding.

Gawker's presentation will rely on AV and will invest in it, but with disappointing results. At crucial points in their argument, one of their attorneys will have to say, when a headline suddenly disappears from the screen, "This is more difficult than I thought." "It was not my desire to create confusion for you," he says after playing the wrong clip. You never want to waste the time of the jury, one of

Gawker's lawyers would say to me, but that's what they ended up doing in moments that counted.

One side lays the groundwork to present their narrative in word, in image, and in digital—the other, cutting corners, finds themselves mostly lecturing. And doing it to an audience that had already begun to tune out the condescending lecturing from cosmopolitan media types in their life generally, not just in a courtroom. Pinellas County is a perennial swing county and it had already begun to swing away from the message that those D.C. lawyers were trying to sell. Gawker had always been a leader in design and presentation. Part of the reason that Denton's sites were so popular was that they were so easy to use and so fun to read. Big graphics were splashed across the top, videos accompanied many posts, comments were addictive to post. The reason they had edited Hogan's sex tape and posted it alongside the story—when the text alone likely would have been protected speech—was that Gawker felt pressure by the standards they had helped set online: You can't just say what you know, you have to *show it, too*. Where was that standard now? As A.J. had asked a year before, where was their storytelling ability?

They had millions to offer in settlement talks, Nick had taken on his first-ever outside investment in January 2016 when he raised money from a Russian billionaire to keep the site going through the lawsuit, but they didn't invest their time and ability into a good presentation? They had $75 million for a fifteen-year lease on three floors of new office space on Fifth Avenue, one with a special entrance just for its employees so they wouldn't have to interact with the rest of the rabble, but no money to tell the story of their lives?

Maybe they were so convinced they deserved to win that they couldn't bring themselves to really *try*. Of course, Gawker went through the motions of trying to settle because it was what you were supposed to do. They wanted it to go away, but they never thought they would actually lose. Perhaps that's why they didn't push a little bit further, never realizing their opportunity to split the fragile bond between Hogan and his then-unknown backer, and the leverage they might have had there. They assumed Hogan would settle because everyone settles. This was never an unreasonable position—and certainly they had done everything they could to push him in that direction. But that wasn't the problem. The problem was that they took this assumption as a reality. They took hypothesis as fact. *This case will settle.*

Heather Dietrick would explain beliefs about the jury to reporters at the time: "I think as a common-sense matter, they're going to see that, see what he's talked about in the past," she would say. "He's talked about really, really graphic details of his sex life, again and again and again, including on the shock jock's show. These are practical people. I think they're going to see through him and say, 'Give me a break. Take responsibility for what you did here.'"

Oh, Heather. How could you? She should have been telling her boss to settle, rectifying before it was too late the error Denton and the legal department had made in not seeing Hogan's perspective "as a human being" when that cease and desist first came in. Instead she was needling the victim in the media. She was lying to herself and to the people who worked at Gawker. She had it all wrong.

"The external positioning for a year and a half leading up to trial," Thiel says of Gawker, "was that Hogan's case was terrible, and if he won it would be a small amount that would get reversed on appeal. If you have a propaganda line that you keep telling people, there's some point at which you have to start believing it."

Denton had done a lot of talking before the trial. He had expressed his confidence in Gawker's case, perhaps to intimidate Hogan, perhaps to keep the faithful at Gawker happy. They wouldn't have let Nick be anything else. They wanted their leaders to be brash and cocky, as they were. They needed him to be that. And for a while it had worked, well enough that in 2015, Mr. A had begun to seriously consider hiring his own public relations team to fight back in the war of words. But Thiel had resisted. Let them talk themselves into a stupor, he thought, let them convince the troops that this is in the bag. Let them make us look stupid, let them think they are winning. Let them use all that oxygen for bluster that they are going to need if they want to gather themselves enough to confidently say, "Lick 'em tomorrow!" Another maxim from Napoleon: "Never interrupt an enemy making a mistake."

"Nobody ever wanted to go to trial," A. J. Daulerio told me. "That was said multiple times. What were we actually preparing for, I don't know. Nobody wanted their day in court. Why were we acting like we wanted our day in court?"

Lulled by his own propaganda, by the confidence of his legal experts, Nick drifted toward the trial he was ill prepared for. That's one explanation. Another is that he didn't want to win badly enough to prepare, that it felt beneath him to need to defend something he clearly believed was protected. Thiel later speculated that perhaps it wasn't that Denton didn't want to win badly, it was that he actually wanted to lose. Perhaps he had begun to see, the way we all occasionally do when we glance at the rush of oncoming traffic or peer over a high ledge, the sweet possibility of release.

In retrospect, Denton can see the inevitability of it, the way he was being encircled. "If it had not been Hogan," he says with resignation, "it would have been another case. Harder reached out to dozens, maybe hundreds, of potential plaintiffs. Backed or instigated half a dozen cases. He had an open checkbook. This was in the stars from 2010 on." It was in the stars but Denton couldn't see them, not in Manhattan, anyway.

That understanding came later. In the moment, it was just a

sense, a sense that meant after the settlement was rejected, Gawker had no backup plan, no line on the true perspective of a jury, and in fact would soon find that the tactics and hard-line negotiations of the intervening years would be held up as evidence against them. *Who are these people*, a jury would think, *why haven't they shown an ounce of regret about what they did to this man?* Gawker's headlines, Denton's interviews, would all look terrible at trial. Only after it was too late did they realize this. In pretrial motions, Gawker's lawyers would seek to block Denton's comments from being used at trial. They would manage to keep some out, but not all of them. It's as if they simply hadn't thought this far in advance, they never thought about anything but being so difficult and so obnoxious that eventually Hogan would quit. They were so convinced *they* were the underdog that it didn't occur to them that they might appear to be the bully. Or maybe, at some point, they had begun to realize how far off course they had gotten and that, as A.J. had come to believe, settling on the courthouse steps was Gawker's only chance. When that didn't happen, all that was left was hope.

Hope is rarely enough. Especially against an opponent who has come to be consumed by their cause, who can see and taste victory now, and will do everything they can to seal it.

It is with a kind of nasty glee, more characteristic of Gawker than anyone else, that Thiel's team would recount to me, several times, a discovery which they would exploit, which very well might have been the deciding factor in the entire case. In those expensive mock juries, they had discovered that their case played exceedingly well to a very specific type of person. "It became very clear that the kind of jurors we wanted were overweight women. Most people can't empathize with a sex tape, but overweight women are sensitive about their bodies and feel like they have been bullied on the internet. Men don't have that problem. Attractive women don't have that problem. They haven't been body shamed," Mr. A tells me proudly. Hypothetical Juror #3 might not have been a victim of revenge porn. She might not care about celebrity privacy. Hypothetical Juror #3 might not have known what it feels like to be Hulk Hogan, but she knows what it's like to have an unflattering picture of herself on the internet. She knows what it feels like to be embarrassed or ashamed. Which is why they would choose her.

I don't think Mr. A or Terry Bollea or Charles Harder or Peter Thiel, when they first convened in 2011 and 2012, convinced of the moral righteousness of their cause, would have expected to find themselves here. I don't know, had you asked them then, how comfortable they might have been using peremptory jury strikes to exploit the most private body image issues of a very specific type of juror.

But here they were now, telling themselves it was what they needed to do. Or they didn't even need to think about it—because they'd torn out parts of their heart already. It would be like the scene in *Sweet Smell of Success* where the baby-faced challenger stands up to the terrible and powerful gossip columnist who treats people like playthings: "The terrible thing about people like you is that decent people have to become so much like you in order to stop you—in order to survive."

On the lawn of the crinkle-cut Pinellas County Courthouse is a series of large red chairs of various sizes and shapes designed by the artist Douglas Kornfeld. The smallest sits on the corner of Fifty-first and Second Avenue and is adorned with a small plaque stating that the chairs symbolize the diversity of Pinellas County and "those who sit and render judgment on its juries." It is on March 3, 2016, that a few hundred of those citizens are called to serve in the jury pool for this trial which has been so long in the making. On that day, the lawyers and reporters in attendance rise for the entrance of Judge Campbell as she quickly calls the room to order and begins jury selection.

By the end of it, three of the people sitting in that box would be overweight women. A fourth looks like a conservative married woman. The two men are not young hipsters. One is nicknamed "Old School" by plaintiffs because during voir dire he'd used those words to describe himself. There is no smirking youth culture represented here. This is a jury who would say during the selection process that they got most of their news from Fox News, from the local news, from Yahoo, from MSN, not from blogs, not from Twitter. It is a jury whose fellow residents, eight months later, would go for Donald Trump in the presidential election with a shade over 48 percent of the vote.

This is not a jury of Gawker's peers, though Nick or his lawyers must have had some faith they would be treated favorably, or they would never have let it get this far. It's not a jury of Hogan's peers, either, or hasn't been for a very long time. The median household income of Pinellas County has hovered at or below the national average for as long as Hulk Hogan has been Hulk Hogan. Still, it's a group Hogan is in a better position to work with than anyone at the table across from him. It's one he is *willing* to work with. Because he's willing to do anything at this point. He just wants to win.

More, he *had* to win. He had no other options. Gawker hadn't left him any way out.

There was a cultivated and deliberate sense around Lyndon Johnson, an aide once said of the pragmatic, ruthless man. "There was a feeling—if you did *everything*, you would win." Whatever it took. Whatever was necessary. Even if it wasn't necessary but it *might* help. That's what you did and that's how you would stay on top. This is very different from the sense that Hillary Clinton had that she *should* win. Or the sense around Al Gore that he probably did win. What matters is who does what needs to be done to finish.

As each side paces in their hotel rooms in the final days before the trial, only a single question really matters, and it is a simple one: Who wants it more? *Who wants to win most badly?* Yes, there would be other questions at stake in this trial and the precedents their answers would set. Who has the more persuasive case? Whose rights are more essential to protect—the celebrity's in a private bedroom or the journalist's when they publish? Of the two controversial, battered, flawed participants, Hogan as plaintiff, Gawker as defendant, who is more sympathetic? Or more directly, who is less despicable?

But at the root of all of them, the thing that would determine what the jury and the judge and the public would see at all, and what had brought them to this point after nearly ten years of planning and scheming in one way or another, lay that other, simpler matter of will.

PART III

The Aftermath

CHAPTER 15

The Battle for Hearts and Minds

Professional wrestling is fake. The outcomes are scripted, what the wrestlers refer to as *kayfabe*. Most lawsuits are *kayfabe,* too. Both sides may posture and pretend. There is tough talk and occasionally a good show. But in the end, the outcome is usually predetermined: the case will settle, because the case law is settled, and the lawyers on both sides will win.

There is another wrestling term, a *shoot*, for the rare moments when the script is abandoned and a staged match becomes a real fight. Gawker was in some ways lulled into complacency by a script written by all the lawsuits and opponents it had faced in the past. *This will settle on the courthouse steps.* It won't go to a jury. They never expected there would be real punches, that the posturing was for anything but effect.

Peter Thiel would pass a note along to Terry Bollea by way of Mr. A and Charles Harder in the early spring of 2016: *Gawker thinks this is all kayfabe, but it's about to become a shoot.*

If one were to peer into Courtroom A on the fourth floor of the Pinellas County Courthouse through the rectangular windows of the doors minutes before the trial began on the morning of March 7, they'd see a room packed far beyond its usual capacity. They would hear a slight echo of voices in the cavernous room, and they'd see a jury box looking rather empty, as just six jurors and three alternates sit on Florida civil cases. Strangely, and perhaps fittingly for this case, they'd see in the pattern on the large, green granite stones that line the wall immediately behind the judge what appears to be a crude outline of a woman's naked lower torso. Sitting at their respective tables facing the judge are two sides who have spent close to $10 million each litigating the case, perhaps more. Gawker to the left, and Hogan to the right, closest to the jurors. Hogan sits up close with his attorneys; A.J. and Nick sit in the first row of the worn wooden benches of the gallery, hidden partly behind their team. Only Heather Dietrick, the lawyer and president of Gawker, sits up front as a representative of the company in the courtroom. Mr. A has left town, believing he is unneeded in the actual proceedings. Peter, confident that all is in good hands, is not even on the same continent.

The fate of these characters hangs precariously on the outcome of two weeks of testimony and deliberations in this green-carpeted room. At the beginning of the proceedings, a slow rumbling sound shakes through the two-story courtroom from the aging bowels of the building. "Sorry," the judge instructs a startled jury, "I don't know what those loud noises are." She might not know the source, but the sounds might as well be the thunder gathering on the horizon. On a yellow notepad, provided to him by his team, Terry Bollea writes a note to himself: "I am grateful for today." To the world, he tweets, "All is well. HH."

Harder has spent weeks writing his opening arguments, preparing to bring full circle that day in October 2012 when he had come down to Florida to announce the biggest case of his life to cameras on the courthouse steps. Yet it is not Charles Harder who approaches the dais for the plaintiffs. The call was Hogan's. Is the tall, thin, blue-eyed lawyer who just moved his firm to Rodeo Drive in Beverly Hills really any better equipped to relate to a Florida jury than the Oxford-educated Nick Denton or Gawker Media's D.C.-based representation? No, he isn't, and Hogan has suggested as tactfully as he can that it'd be better if he sits this one out. Their local counsel, he says, should address the court. He's blunter in retrospect: "Charles is not a trial lawyer. He's never been in a trial in his life." It's not strictly true, but Hogan has a performer's eye. He knows the "smoke and mirrors" of the entertainment business, as he likes to say, he knows what it means to love and work a crowd. He had seen Charles defend him ably in his deposition and in front of the judge many times. But a trial is not about a judge—who is an arbiter in matters of law. It's about a jury—who are arbiters in matters of fact, but make decisions, like all human beings, based on emotion. Hogan knew his audience. Charles isn't "Florida people." So on the day of the trial, Harder sits in an overstuffed leather chair behind Hogan and watches another man give the arguments he was supposed to give.

"On October 4, 20 . . ."

The judge cuts off Shane Vogt, the man who is not Charles Harder, the man who is delivering the remarks that should be his. "You're going to need to speak up."

The man begins once more.

"On October 4, 2012, the defendants," he turns and points, "Nick Denton." Pause. "A. J. Daulerio." Pause. "And Gawker.com." Pause. "Gawker Media. Made a conscious decision. They made a conscious decision to expose Terry Bollea naked and engaged in sex and having private conversations in a private bedroom. He was engaged in one of the most intimate of human acts in that bedroom. And they made a conscious decision to expose him in that state to the entire world. This video, which was secretly recorded, which you will hear Nick Denton describe under oath in his deposition as 'pornographic' and 'offensive to view in a workplace,' remained on Gawker.com for six months. For those six months, this man," he points, "stood there naked and exposed to the world. Over the course of those six months, over five million people visited this page. Over the course of those six months, over two and a half million people watched that video. . . . For 203 days, he stood there naked for the world to see. And these people flocked to this website because A. J. Daulerio invited them to."

"If you want to win, 'ego is the enemy,'" Peter would say, "and the anti-ego thing we did was downgrade Harder's role in the trial. Harder was not happy about this. It was the case of your lifetime and you get to have a much smaller part in it than you originally thought? But if we win, you get to take credit."

Shane is much better positioned than a Beverly Hills attorney to present this case as a battle between a media company with offices on Fifth Avenue and a blue-collar athlete, a beloved but beleaguered icon who claimed to have been betrayed and bullied. Vogt was a Stetson Law grad. He went to college right there in St. Pete and was a star basketball player. He wears sport-cut suits and his prematurely balding hair is shaved clean. He has daughters and raises cattle. He's one of them, and as a true local, Vogt can better sell to them that his client, this humble athlete, might be "known professionally as Hulk Hogan, but the plaintiff is Terry Bollea, the man. And he is a man. He is a human being."

Vogt would then tell jurors something that Gawker's lawyers and the media had apparently forgotten in their furor over this perceived attack on the free press. He tells them that in this case, in any civil trial in the state of Florida, the standard of evidence is not high. It's not a matter of *beyond a reasonable doubt*. It's simply a matter of more likely than not. Did Gawker know the tape was recorded without consent? Did they act recklessly, callously? That's all. That's all you've got to be convinced of. And then his remarks are finished.

Gawker's legal team, though they would later concede the savvy in Hogan and Thiel's decision to cede the stage to the local counsel, made no such move. It would not be Gregg Thomas of Tampa making the opening arguments twenty minutes after Shane Vogt, it would be Michael Berry, a young-looking attorney with light brown hair from Philadelphia, on whom the critical first impression—the embodiment of the *thesis of their case*—would depend. Despite Thiel's immense resources, despite the narrow legal argument that the conspirators had staked their strategy on, Gawker still has a chance. There is still time, as there has been at so many junctures of this conspiracy, for Gawker to save itself. If Michael Berry could convince the people in that box that his clients were humans who had made a mistake, and that they did not deserve the financial death penalty that Harder had called for on those Florida steps so many long years ago, if Gawker could appeal to the hearts and minds of those people, perhaps they could snatch victory from the jaws of defeat.

George Washington had done such a thing quite simply and masterfully in New Windsor, New York, at the end of the American Revolution. The war had been won but the peace had been bungled, and angry veterans were without their pensions. They had plotted and schemed and were on the verge of overthrowing Congress. Washington had been preoccupied and let the situation sneak up behind him. Congress had been entitled and unaccountable and also had not taken this threat seriously. A meeting is called of all the officers in the army. The mood is tense. The very existence of civil authority in America hangs in the balance. Washington knows he does not have much time and surprises the men by walking into the meeting. He asks quietly for the floor, and he begins to speak to his men impassionedly, begging them not to be swayed by these wicked plans. Then, simply, he reaches into his pocket to read a letter from Congress. He moves slowly, fumbles on purpose with the letter, and says, "Gentlemen, you will permit me to put on my spectacles, for I have not only grown gray but almost blind in the service of my country." His display saps the men of their anger—this man, their leader, he has suffered, too. He has been worn down by the same service that they are demanding compensation for and he has not offered a single complaint. As Washington expresses his confidence in Congress and makes his case, the conspiracy collapses with each word. It had been perfectly timed, the sympathies perfectly played, and a solution is quickly worked out. The Newburgh Conspiracy, as it would later come to be known, the one that could have killed the country before it really began, is dispatched to nothing more than a footnote in history.

But as Berry, friendly and baby faced, addresses the jury, it's quickly clear he lacks the gravitas to tug at the heartstrings of the people that the fate of his client has been tied to. He opens with an awkward, pandering "y'all" to the jury. He is quiet, low energy. He talks about leaving his family to come down to Florida to try this case—"Why do you need to be away for so long, Dad?"—as if he were doing everyone else a favor, as if this trial were an inconvenience for him that should be factored subconsciously into their final verdict. Like an internet commenter struggling for solid ground in an argument, Berry soon finds himself overreaching and mentioning the Holocaust, informing the jury that "Mr. Denton grew up with parents who've seen firsthand what happens when speech is suppressed." "Gawker did not post the Hulk Hogan sex tape," he tells the jury, and there is a flicker of interest. They only posted a "*highlight reel*," he says. "A highlight reel of those unglamorous moments." When he does, at long last, begin to hit his stride, Berry is interrupted by a procedural objection from Hogan's attorneys. He looks at the judge. He looks back at the plaintiff's table. Back at the judge. The look on his face: What is happening? I am not in control here. Berry is the opposite of Shane Vogt, not relatable or confident. He is everything Harder would have been stereotyped as if he had opened the case: a foreigner, a carpetbagger, someone we're not sure we like. More, he is not in command. And his opening statements still have ten minutes left to go.

If the two parties had gone into 2016 as two boxers seemingly evenly matched and the first rounds had presaged a fair fight, that impression started to collapse as soon as arguments began. Underneath there had been an undeniable truth, that one boxer was punching himself out, the other deliberately encouraging him to do so, waiting for his chance to begin to pick him apart. And now that chance was here.

"They were in my ring," Hogan would say. "They screwed up. Getting in front of real people. That's where they screwed up." The confidence rises with this realization. This is the moment he had demanded, that Gawker had alternatively avoided and dismissed, and it is unfolding better than the conspirators could have hoped. I have heard Peter Thiel say over and over again that in the trial, Gawker argued the law while Hogan's case argued the facts. "You argue the law to show how much you know about the law," he would say, "but it's not how you win a case in front of a jury." Thiel the nonpracticing attorney grasped this instinctively in a way that the professional lawyers for the defense clearly missed. Facts are stubborn things, and no amount of legal maneuvering could blunt them fully, not in court anyway. The person who wins the jury is the one who tells the most compelling story. Whoever is most human and personable wins. The fact of what Gawker did—running that tape that Hogan was believably claiming he never wanted to be public—was ever present in the courtroom. Who they did it to was real and indisputable, too. Gawker's strategy was to insist that it was *allowed* to do what it did, and leave the implication to hang there. There had been no denying it, no effort to—they'd run the tape, they'd made no effort to verify the tape, no effort to blur the tape, had no consideration of the person on the other side of the computer, who was now in the courtroom with them. No explanation for why they hadn't done these things. They believed the law did not require it. This would be a fatal miscalculation to make when your fate rests on the decision of six ordinary people who aren't inclined to make a distinction between immoral and illegal, who aren't being asked about the First Amendment but about whether someone's privacy had been gratuitously violated.

All of Gawker's delays would work against it at trial, too, not because the jury knew how long and hard Denton's lawyers had fought to prevent this day from happening, but because of what had transpired in the intervening years. The internet was no longer new and exciting, but a part of normal life. New norms, new concerns about technology and privacy had developed in that time and they were conservative norms. Many were established in response to some of the horrible events that had happened publicly via blogs and social media. A young man named Tyler Clementi had committed suicide in 2010 when his college roommate filmed him kissing another boy with a webcam and mocked him on Twitter for it. For years the prosecution of his bully roommate led the news, changing attitudes slowly along with it. States had begun to pass anti–revenge porn laws. Even as the Hogan and Gawker trial began, another jury was out deciding the fate of the man who had recorded peephole footage of the sportscaster Erin Andrews through the wall of her hotel room. They would award her $55 million. What Gawker could have justified in 2007 when it was still a small company and outed Peter Thiel, in 2012 when it posted Hogan's sex tape, even in 2015 had the trial proceeded as scheduled, was no longer the same. The world had changed, and Gawker's place in that world—a company with millions in revenue, with a valuation in the hundreds of millions—had changed, too. What would ultimately be the undoing of Gawker was the simple fact that they came across as genuinely unsympathetic. To the jury, to their peers, to the public following the events through the headlines and via live stream, what they stood for was incomprehensible.

After opening statements, both sides switch their attorneys, but the disparity is still obvious. Michael Sullivan, who represents Gawker, is grandfatherly and calm. An effective and capable lawyer, he is not the bulldog you would expect to speak on Gawker's behalf. He is Midwestern, soft and conciliatory. Ken Turkel, another local attorney who represents Hogan, is beefy and loud. He is confident and reasonable and still youthful. Both look like school principals—one of which you might confide your problems to and respect, the other you would lie to with ease and snicker about when he wasn't looking.

The witnesses are paraded in front of the jury. First it's Heather Clem, shown via video from her deposition. Then it's Hogan, in person, dressed in all black. It's unclear whether this is normal wrestler's business attire or if he's in mourning for the loss of common decency. The man knows how to work a crowd. He walks slowly, achingly to the front of the courtroom, the toll of his back and knee surgeries plainly visible. He squeezes into the tiny witness stand, the closest to a celebrity that many on the jury will have ever been. Harder had been set to question Hogan, too, had come to his hotel room a few days before with a binder full of material to prep, and gotten the bad news again. "I'm not feeling it," Hogan had said. "I don't love you." Not the way he loved Ken Turkel, or the way he knew the six jurors would love them together. On the stand Hogan is playing a role he does not often play in front of a crowd: soft-spoken, vulnerable. He is a man here, not a celebrity. He grabs his fingers nervously. He introduces himself: "My name is Terry Gene Bollea, born in Augusta, Georgia, August 11, 1953." He has one job on the stand. To be human. To sell his lowest, lowest point, and to survive cross-examination. He does both. Gawker's attorneys wince as they feel its effectiveness.

In a trial, almost nothing new happens. All of the information presented has been proposed and reproposed and discussed and fought over a hundred times. All of it has been practiced in the mirror—the trial is just the performance of all that practice. Yes, Caesar was killed by the senators' dagger thrusts, but his fate had been decided long before that. It was not an *if*, it was a *when*. The only questions that remained were *how* and with *what*?

For Gawker, the trial is the how—the event preordained that now must be made real. It is real when A. J. Daulerio takes the stand. This is the *what*—the knife that slips under the ribcage and pierces the beating heart. A.J. is questioned first by his own lawyer. Ostensibly it is a chance to anticipate the hard cross-examination coming forthwith, to humanize his client before he is attacked, but it isn't taken. Sullivan's difficulty connecting with the jury becomes clear. Even in his questioning, he comes off as lecturing when he doesn't mean to, punctuating every sentence with an obnoxious "Okay?" and "Do you remember that?" The jury has drifted, they are not buying what has been sold. That boredom is about to be banished.

After an hour and a half of slow questioning by the defense, Shane Vogt is let off his leash and set upon his target. The full brunt of years of denied accountability, of bad legal strategy, of growing, building resentment against the media is going to pour down upon Daulerio. This will not be easy.

"If I understood your testimony a moment ago," Vogt says, hardly taking even a moment to flip through his papers, he is ready to set a new pace, an aggressor's pace, "when you referenced your standard of newsworthiness of any child celebrity over the age of four, you were joking? Is that what you just said?"

"I did say that, yes."

"You think that's a funny topic to joke about, child pornography?"

"No, not at all."

"At the time you made that joke, you were in a deposition, right?"

"Yeah."

"You were in a deposition and you were asked a question about one of the central issues in this case, were you not? Newsworthiness, that's your defense, is it not? And when you were asked a question about newsworthiness you made a joke, is that what you're telling this jury here today?"

"No."

"You just said you were making a joke. You were joking about child pornography, were you not?"

Imagine what this must be like, there, in that witness box. You're defending a post you wrote more than three years ago, you're defending remarks you made in a deposition that you've nearly forgotten, you're defending a company you don't even work for anymore. Yes, you posted clips of a sex tape, but you're not the one who recorded it and you were at least half sincerely making an editorial point about the mundanity of celebrity and sex with the writing that went alongside. Now you are being depicted as some sort of rogue operator, a lawless maverick in an otherwise well-run and decent company, when in reality you were doing your job, a job at a company whose lawlessness and flippancy dates back far further than your own employment, a job like most jobs where the majority of the upside went to your bosses and not you. Had some other Gawker writer gotten the same tip, they'd have run the story just like you did, but it fell in your lap—or your inbox, as it were. Everyone you knew at your company celebrated you for it at first, and now—now you're here. You're just months out of a stint in rehab, you're struggling to remain sober, and yet there is the specter of a $100 million judgment—which you of all people cannot remotely afford—dangling over you, threatening to destroy the little bit of a life you've recently reassembled.

While some critics might be inclined to categorize all this as just desserts, it is also true that only the decision to *publish* the piece had been Daulerio's. It was Denton who had decided to ignore the cease and desist, it was Cook who had escalated Gawker's war of words against the judge, it was Dietrick who had attempted to intimidate Hogan into dropping the case. Yet the heat would fall disproportionally on Daulerio, as if he were the sole decision maker.

"It is as if the universe is playing a huge cosmic prank on me," A.J. would say. "How is this all happening to me while I am trying to get sober?" How nice a drink—or any substance—would have been when the animus of an entire courtroom is directed at you. It would have taken the edge off the dread that a journalist would feel in that moment, knowing he was about to be on the other side of a process he had seen so many times himself: The articles. The tweets. The outrage on TV. And it's all coming at you, the one who warned your lawyers that this would happen, who begged your bosses to settle. "I felt like I was in a *Black Mirror* episode, trapped in my own Gawker story and I can't say anything," Daulerio told me. "The part I couldn't understand was that the lawyers were letting it happen."

This interpretation may be somewhat self-serving, but he's not wrong. Only when Vogt gets A.J. to admit he was smirking and laughing during the deposition, "because you don't think the First Amendment is that serious," do his lawyers finally intervene and object. Defending the First Amendment was easier than defending their clients. Even his opponents are pitying him, even as they gratefully rack up points at his expense. One of Gawker's lawyers would tell me that of everyone involved, A.J. got the rawest deal. But the deal was one still largely of his own making.

"You knew though from the March 2012 reports that Mr. Bollea was claiming he was secretly recorded, right?" Vogt asks, already knowing the answer, already having seen tape from the deposition and read the interrogatories, but looking to stun the jurors with the reality of it.

"Uh, yeah."

"And you did no investigation whatsoever into the motives of the person who was providing you this DVD of him, right?

"Nope."

"And you didn't care, did you?"

"I didn't care in regards to the story that I was going to write."

Shane Vogt had read emails from the girl pleading for the removal of a video posted by Daulerio showing her visibly drunk and having sex—likely involuntarily—on a bathroom floor in a sports bar in Indiana. Though he would eventually take the video down and come to regret posting it, this exchange had rested there, like a time bomb with a long, patient clock, since Harder and Mr. A had discovered it, held it, waited for their opportunity to use it in court.

"You gotta understand," the girl's father had pleaded with A.J., "I've just been dealing with watching my daughter get fucked in a pile of piss for the past two days." A.J. had told them "not to make a big deal out of it" and that things like this pass. All of this had been private, one of those things that had made sense to him at the time, and now it was public and he could not seem to say anything that would make it make sense again. A reporter would write of a "palpable sense of shock rippling through the courtroom" during A.J.'s testimony and the reveal of the emails. If they'd looked closer in that moment, they'd have noticed a juror's knuckles grip intensely on the bar in front of the jury box, restraining anger as the callous words of the defendant were read onto the record just a few feet away.

A.J.'s lawyers can't be blamed for his answers. They can't be blamed for what he did, even if he had come to regret it. Their job is to defend speech and their clients have not made that easy. Gawker's lawyers can't control what he said in those private conversations, and they don't get to choose what evidence makes up a case. Bad client, bad attitude, bad timing. Still, they do choose how their evidence is delivered at trial and how their clients are prepared. This is what they have been paid millions of dollars for. It is their responsibility. A.J.'s tone is flippant; even his body language suggests a kind of reluctance and contempt for the proceedings. As he leans his neck forward to answer each time, he seems like the teenager who just cannot seem to see that he did something wrong. The kind of teenager you want to send a message to, the one you think you need to smack for his own good. How did they let that happen? Shouldn't their strategy have taken these liabilities into account? Isn't this what witness preparation is for?

A.J. describes the instructions he got going in, which did not begin until he arrived in Florida for the trial. He had shown up where and when asked, then he was given a stack of his own articles and told to prepare to be raked for them. "Get off the stand as quickly as possible" is what he claims he was told. One can imagine a buck private in the trenches of World War I looking back to his commanding officer for words of wisdom just before making his charge across the no-man's-land and being told, "Don't get killed." A.J.'s lawyers might as well have said, "You're on your own, buddy. May God be with you." Nick Denton tells me that the jurors aren't the only ones whose jaws drop at the courtroom reveal of A.J.'s remark about four-year-olds and celebrity sex tapes, *it was news to him, too*. His lawyers had kept it from Denton, had failed to inform him that it was coming just as they had left A.J. alone to defend himself. They said it was to keep everyone's testimony uninfluenced, but it seems more likely that they had simply held on tight to the ticking time bomb, praying, perhaps, that it might turn out to be a dud.

The great sin for a leader, Frederick the Great once observed, was not in being defeated but in being surprised. How did Denton not see this? How did Gawker's chief strategy officer not see that this was a fight they could not win? Where was their publicist? Heather Dietrick, the one they had chosen to sit in the courtroom for them, who had been privy to every part of this case from the beginning—where had she been? Denton would say in retrospect that Gawker's "audience share in Williamsburg was not decisive." It didn't matter what his friends in Manhattan or his readers in Brooklyn thought of the trial, what mattered was what the jurors thought. What mattered was whether they believed Hogan on the stand. "Hogan used language—and the trust his brand engendered—to make his own reality," Denton said, intellectualizing his own decimation. "We were reminded that he had many more followers than Gawker did—both in the jury and in the general population."

"PR can be powerful, it can be effective, but it can always backfire when you start to believe it too much. They needed to say they were sorry. If they had done that, they would've survived. Instead, they insisted on the right to be evil," Thiel explained. The word "sociopathic" has been used on occasion to describe Gawker, but even sociopaths are generally better at judging situations, at reading people, at extrapolating how things are likely to go, than anyone associated with the Gawker team seemed to be in this moment.

This trial was an exercise in stupidity. A smart person would have seen that even an insincere apology would have made all the difference. A smart person would never have let it get this far. Whether the conspirators were brilliant or just rich can reasonably be argued, but what is indisputable is the fact that their victims marched toward their fate quite sure they were heading in the other direction. To try to argue newsworthiness when the tape at issue was illegally made, illegally procured, without the consent of the aggrieved? To say that this guy didn't deserve privacy even in his most intimate moments because he was famous? Seeing Hulk Hogan outside the courtroom early on in the trial, Gawker's lawyers see him interact with a few of the groundskeepers and employees. They see how much these people like him, how Hogan has cultivated that connection through his image. There is always a danger in letting a case go to a jury, but to put this case, with this defendant, in front of these jurors was suicide.

Too late to change course now.

With a few more days of testimony, the visceral anger created by A.J.'s excerpted deposition testimony seemed to gradually accumulate into a tangible sense of repugnance toward Gawker in the courtroom. There is Denton on the stand, forced to read back passages of the story, forced to explain the insouciant remark in his deposition that A.J.'s article was perfectly judged, sweet and sympathetic and humanizing. And what did he mean when he said that he was a believer in total freedom and transparency? That he was an extremist about that? Nick can feel repugnance to that now. He could feel the jury questioning: Who are these people? What planet do they come from? He could see that his message wasn't landing, that they didn't care about free speech or transparency, not like he did. They didn't understand him or the importance of what he did—nobody cared that the rumors Gawker posted often *did* become tomorrow's news. He could look at them and feel angry at their hypocrisy, knowing that each one of the jurors in that box had probably clicked on or shared one of the types of stories they were demanding he explain.

Denton would later describe how overwhelming this feeling was, how lopsided it felt. The pressure first begun in the public relations battle in 2014, the efforts to separate Gawker from the herd, to turn its peers in the media against it, were hitting a crescendo in that courtroom. All the good work that Gawker had ever done, all the real news Denton's writers had broken, the stuff Nick was rightfully proud of, was being erased. It was being replaced by Denton's own heady, tone-deaf musings from years before and the flippant words of A. J. Daulerio, who "was being tarred as an 'aspiring child pornographer'" for his comments, according to Nick, even though he had an explanation for them. Of course, it was an explanation that even he would admit was "too complex to overcome that shorthand." They had sowed the wind and were not reaping the whirlwind. Still, it felt so unfair, so unfamiliar. It was impossible to combat. Does Nick feel in that moment, the way A.J. had, what so many Gawker subjects had felt over the years? Does he understand now what his own medicine tastes like? Does it matter?

In the courtroom the body language of the lawyers has begun to function like one of the prediction markets that a person like Peter Thiel would look to for insight, one side seemingly resenting the entire proceedings, the other starting to enjoy holding the stage. One side growing more confident, the other more clearly aware of their fate. One side feeling the burden slowly lift, the pressure dissipating, the other feeling the full weight of all these years of maneuvering, the deferred reality finally becoming inescapable. David Houston would look over at his opponents as the trial plodded on and see disarray. There was only, he said, "the debris of defeat."

The hearts and minds have been won—the ones that matter, anyway. It was no longer a matter of who would win, only by how much. Machiavelli would say that a coup or a conspiracy can succeed only if the will of the people is on its side. "If you can convince a jury in Tampa that this is not the way the technological future should look," Peter says to me, "they can tell history to stop."

Now all that was left was to seal the legacy, to tell the jury a story about how bad this all really was and why these people from New York City deserved to be punished. It is Turkel, not Harder, who is chosen to give the closing arguments for Terry Bollea. Turkel would claim in his arguments that he didn't want sympathy, that he simply wanted the law to be followed, because the law was why they were there. But of course, sympathy is exactly what he wanted. His entire strategy depended on getting it, and on stoking a desire to send a message in the process.

"Daulerio says," he would say, motioning to the other side of the courtroom, "'the internet has made it easier for all of us to be shameless voyeurs and deviants.' I'm not so sure all of us *are* shameless voyeurs and deviants. They may be up on Fifth Avenue at Gawker, but that's a little bit of an assumption for the rest of the world. And they say we watch this footage because it's something we're not supposed to do. What could be a better admission that it was gratuitous than that?"

Sullivan follows, in what is the last chance for Gawker to make its case: "What we ask you to do is hard. It's very hard, but ultimately it is right. We ask you to protect something that some among you may find unpopular. We ask you to put aside passion and prejudice and sympathy and follow the law, the law that has served our country well since our founding, law that allows our citizens to write, to speak, to think about all topics, to hold public figures accountable as people who warrant the privileges we've bestowed upon them. I realize this may be hard, but it is right in the long run for our freedoms."

It is a lecture and not a call to action, but he can sense this in their reactions; perhaps he sensed it even when he was writing the words. Because his next line all but apologizes for the way Gawker has made its uninspired case. "Shortly," he concludes, "we will come to the point where the voices of the attorneys will finally be still."

Finally, they are still. The judge reads the jury their instructions. Before they depart there is a question. It brings both lawyers to the bench. One juror wants to know if community service is an option. Wouldn't that have been nice? If there was some way out for everyone involved that didn't mean the financial death penalty for a group of journalists? It was, as Hemingway once put it, pretty to think so, but sadly no more than that.

"I think," the judge says with a sigh, "it's not that type of case."

It will not be that kind of verdict, either.

CHAPTER 16

Managing the Aftermath

After the trigger is pulled and the gun explodes in recoil against the shoulder, after the drive to the basket and the shot is flipped up, after one's arguments are made, following the cessation of activity, there is a brief period of unknowing. Whether the bullet will hit its mark. Whether the ball will go in. Whether the jury will come back with the verdict you expect.

This period can be a half instant, in the case of a gunshot, while the ringing subsides and the eye refocuses. It can be the second it takes to come under and around to the other side of the rim. Or it can be however long the jury takes to deliberate, the judge to rule.

The thrust of the conspiracy is made and then the results will be what they are. The bomb goes off in Hitler's conference room in July 1944, the windows are blown out and most of the roof comes down. Everyone is thrown to the ground, and as the survivors stagger back to their feet and peer through the smoke, the verdict of the deed awaits the man who had snuck out, convinced in every way of his success. If only . . . The conference table had absorbed the force of the blast. Hitler lives. He is bruised and singed, but the man lives. In fact, the blast cures the palsy in his arm and hand—and now he believes God has spared him. Seven thousand alleged conspirators are rounded up by the Gestapo. Nearly five thousand are executed. Fighting continues for another nine months.

In Pinellas County, on March 18, Hogan had made his case to the jury and now would be making one to his own God while he waited along with his lawyers in that pregnant pause between action and result. He would tweet one word to his 1.42 million followers: "Praying."

The conspirators would not wait long for an answer. Six hours. Less than an hour for each year Thiel has been plotting and scheming. Barely enough time to drive back to their hotels, to collapse onto the sofa and consider what has happened over the last two weeks and what rests on the decision of these ordinary people. Both sides make their way through security, take turns loading into the elevator and return to Courtroom A. The jury leaves their small quarters off the hallway and follows the lead of the bailiff back into the courtroom. As they file back into the jury box, the unknowing is over, and so, too, is Gawker.

"We thought we might get a spanking, not a mortal blow," Denton says of his mindset prior to the verdict being read. "Something proportionate to any harm done." A nervous energy ripples through the courtroom. One juror winks to Hogan. The verdict on all five counts is in his favor. The award is $115 million. So much for proportions. Within a week, another $25 million would be added in punitive damages—$10 million of it to Denton personally, and another $100,000 to Daulerio. It would have been higher, a juror says after the trial, had A.J. not already been broke. "We would have hit A.J. harder, but we just didn't think you could get blood out of a rock."

The conspirators have not just won the hearts and minds of the people, they have turned them into the executioners. Their message to Gawker, and to the media which has grown to sympathize with them as Hogan's flaws were exposed and the verdict drew closer, is resounding: We want these people gone.

Gawker is stunned but tries not to show it. One post out of so many has brought them here. They were convinced they had a case. Or rather, that the other side absolutely did not, and they acted accordingly. "I did not know how devastating A.J.'s joke would be, nor how strongly Thiel's local lawyers would play on the culture war," Denton says by way of explanation and possibly a little blame shifting. "Our lawyers—traditional First Amendment lawyers—were not prepared for that."

Pede poena claudo—punishment comes limping. The original sin of Gawker, for which accounting was so long delayed, deferred, forgotten. Grains of gunpowder spilled long ago, exploding only now, devastatingly. $141 million. No, they don't have that kind of money lying around. Who does?

Nick pats A.J. on the leg. "We'll appeal." But he won't—they can't. Denton has forgotten or miscalculated because the buy-in to appeal in Florida is a bond equal to the verdict, capped at $50 million. Perhaps if they'd better prepared for the contingency of losing this badly, there would have been some way to wriggle out, to post Gawker's Cayman Islands stock as collateral instead of cash, to survive long enough to get reinforcements, to persuade the judge who they had shown so much contempt for to stay the bond to allow an appeal, possibly even to swallow their pride and apologize, but they hadn't. Gawker bet it all on this one chance; it won't be getting another.

The jurors are given a certificate of appreciation from the judge for their service and sent home.

Hogan sits silently sobbing at the table he had occupied for the last two weeks. *They believed me*, he says to himself. *Finally, people believed me. That I didn't leak this tape myself. That I didn't want this*. The failed sting is now a distant memory, his decision to pass on a $10 million settlement recedes behind him, the risk of it all disappearing into history. David Houston, the lawyer he began this journey with before anyone could have hoped for any kind of intervention, pats him gently on the back. Finally, Hogan stands, he and Houston embrace. Harder stands behind them, waiting as a parade of congratulations comes to his client. Finally, he approaches. They shake hands, and Hogan clutches his own heart as he says to Harder, "Thank you. Thank you." Mr. A watches it unfold live via online broadcast of the courtroom. The quiet operator is mad with glee and pleasure. He picks up his phone to call Peter Thiel. It's the game of telephone, from the courtroom to the safe house, until it reaches the mastermind, away in China, teaching a class of university students who have no clue what their professor has been working on.

There was much left to be done—many reams of paperwork left to be prepared and paid for, more lawyers to hire and hearings to attend, but he has done it. At last he has done it. The bet paid off. In *Gatsby*, Carraway had been in awe of Wolfsheim. "How did he happen to do that?" he asks of the 1919 World Series plot. Gatsby answers: "He just saw the opportunity." Thiel had seen the opportunity where no one else had. He had taken it. Legally. And he had won. He had proven that "nothing you can do about it" is just what people who don't want to do anything about it like to say to make themselves feel better about their inaction. Peter Thiel has done what presidents, robber barons, and folk heroes have been unable to do. He has fought a battle with the people who buy ink by the barrel and come out the better for it. On the day of the verdict, the *New York Times* editorial section would publish a debate of experts, asking about the implications of the case. Two of the three experts would come down against Gawker and for Hulk Hogan, underscoring Thiel's early goal to predicate the dispute on privacy, not press freedom. One, a law professor and former journalist, wrote, "When human dignity is degraded by depictions of sex, nudity or medical conditions the 'journalism' should not be called newsworthy." The next day the former assistant general counsel of the *New York Times* would be quoted in another piece published in the paper: "I think the damages are crazy, but I just don't see this as a terrible blow to the First Amendment." The dean of the law school at UC Irvine would follow in the same story: "I think this case establishes a very limited proposition: It is an invasion of privacy to make publicly available a tape of a person having sex without that person's consent. I don't think it goes any further than that and I do not see a First Amendment basis for claiming that there is a right to do this."

What had begun as a petty squabble between two similar, strange men had become something bigger, a chance to draw the line about what was allowed in the public sphere. Thiel had set out to destroy this thing that he thought was destroying an important part of society, of culture. There was revenge in this, too, absolutely. Nick Denton had said, "Peter Thiel makes me sick," and the feeling was mutual. Now Thiel made the world feel the same way about Nick Denton and Gawker. He had humiliated Denton as he had been humiliated years before. Better, *no one even knows he was the one responsible. All they knew was that it felt like justice had been done.*

Who is the high-agency individual now?

If we could stop the story here it might be one of the most incredible conspiracies in history. But if it had stopped here, we might never have known how any of it had transpired, so we cannot stop here.

A conspiracy is possible only with secrecy, but secrecy is subject, like all things, to the law of entropy. For some time Thiel's secret had been decaying, his grip on the absoluteness of it had slipped. Though he'd told very few people what he was doing, in the course of a decade, the list of names added up. As victory approached, caution had relaxed into confidence, which was eventually replaced by carelessness. Thiel has said there is always the temptation to "brag about these things you're not supposed to do." It was after the trial, "after we won in

March," he said, "that I thought it was maybe a bit safer because you wouldn't have as much focused attention." Maybe he wanted people to know, maybe he wanted them to be awed by what he was doing, maybe he wanted them to fear him. Mr. A would say, "I had a sense—whether Peter knew it himself—that he wanted to be known. He wanted to do it quietly, but after this great victory he wanted to be known."

Why else had Peter begun to make that silly prediction from time to time at dinner, the thing he believed that few others believed—that Gawker would be out of business within a year? Why had he smirkingly asked friends who knew just loud enough to be overheard by other friends, *How do you think our project is going?*, and let the mystery of what he was up to this time just hang there? In 2015 this was innocuous fun, a risk to be sure, but forgotten just as quickly. In early 2016, his comments would have seemed unlikely but contrarian. Looking back at it in March 2016, it suddenly takes on a different context to the people who had heard it. *Did Peter know something? Could he have something to do with this?*

Perhaps Peter Thiel would have gotten away with even this sloppiness, with what he would call a "catastrophic mistake in retrospect," but the conspirators make another miscalculation on top of it. In the weeks after the trial, another case is filed against Gawker. Harder is representing a man named Shiva Ayyadurai who claims to have been the true inventor of email. Ayyadurai claims he is paying his own legal bills and that Gawker slandered him in 2012 and 2014. In January 2016, Harder had filed what appeared to most people as another flimsy suit against Gawker, this time on behalf of a journalist (both cases are for libel/defamation, a violation of Thiel's earlier strategy). Whoever is picking up the tab, there is no question that the cases were approved by the conspirators. This is a conscious effort to move in for the kill, rushing to file more cases before Gawker declares bankruptcy, hoping to ensure that there is no way the site can get back up on its feet in a fighting posture after the decisive verdict. "We thought it was reasonable to bring those cases because Harder had just won and presumably there would be a lot more people talking to him and more plaintiffs looking to file with him after he had this spectacular success," Peter says.

But the unintended result is a showing of their hand, an overplaying of their hand. Two more cases, so close together, so much less sympathetic than a stolen sex tape, harder to write off as simple justice. The decision not to simply slip away during the chaos, but instead to give away too many clues by talking about the conspiracy, would come to haunt Peter. It would be his biggest mistake. Especially against this opponent, the one who knows what to do with suspicions and speculation.

Machiavelli would say that when overconfidence enters men's hearts, "it causes them to go beyond their mark . . . to lose the opportunity of possessing a certain good by hoping to obtain a better one that is uncertain." In plain language: perfect is the enemy of good (or good enough). Clausewitz warned generals about the "culminating point of victory." A point where, if blindly ridden past, flush with the momentum of winning and strength, you imperil everything you have achieved. The decision to attack one additional city, to charge after the enemy who has retreated, or to extend the battle for one more day might not just be subject to diminishing returns, it might snatch defeat from the jaws of victory. Every conspiracy runs this risk, and often, the conspirators know they have passed it only after it is too late.

There had been an effort after D-Day to make the Nazis believe that Normandy wasn't the real landing, that it was the feint. The Allies hinted at other landings, made it look like they would be landing elsewhere, to keep the German generals from fully reinforcing their efforts at the place where it mattered. But there was little value in these extra cases to Thiel—they had already won.

What ultimately tipped Denton remains a mystery. Perhaps it had been those loose lips at dinner parties. Or perhaps someone was seen coming out of Harder's office. Perhaps one of the lawyers said something by accident. Perhaps there were simply too many people involved now for a secret to be kept. Or perhaps it was a combination of all these things—the way that paradigm shifts are said to happen in science. Enough disconnections add up that a stunning new theory must be proposed: *Eureka, I have it! Someone is behind all this!* One lawyer representing all these clients? What are the chances? I know of at least one person, a friend of Peter's, who managed to guess the existence of a conspiracy sometime in 2015. He is hardly a detective, but he put the pieces together after meeting Mr. A at Thiel's house in Los Angeles. A few months later, he noticed a picture on Mr. A's Facebook page. The place? Pinellas County, Florida. Suddenly the offhand remarks, those predictions about Gawker being out of business, all make sense. And the secret becomes a little less secret until eventually it explodes into view.

The question for Gawker and for the media then is who? Who could have done it? "We all had to kind of sit back and jog our memories," A.J. would say. "Who are rich and powerful people, who each of us may have pissed off, in a possibly apocalyptic way?" Even then, as one source would describe it to me, there was no shortage of people whose fingerprints could be on the knife. These were questions that should have been asked in 2012, in 2013, in 2014, in 2015, and in early 2016, but the time for should-haves and could-haves is officially over. There's nothing they can do about that now.

Within a month of the court's decision, Nick Denton begins to float a theory to reporters: What about Scientology? Denton had personally broken a number of embarrassing stories about the famously vengeful and protective religion. The church is headquartered in Clearwater, Florida, not far from the courthouse. Could they, with their deep pockets, be behind it? Maybe. But off the record, to friends, Denton floats a name: Peter Thiel.

"Mr. Denton has begun to question whether Mr. Harder has a benefactor, perhaps one of the many subjects of Gawker's skewering coverage," reads the *New York Times* piece from late May. But it's Denton's quote that matters: "My own personal hunch is that it's linked to Silicon Valley, but that's nothing really more than a hunch. If you're a billionaire and you don't like the coverage of you, and you don't particularly want to embroil yourself any further in a public scandal, it's a pretty smart, rational thing to fund other legal cases."

Once the what and the where had been established, confirmation of the *who* was only a matter of time.

On May 24, 2016, *Forbes* wins the race: "This Silicon Valley Billionaire Has Been Secretly Funding Hulk Hogan's Lawsuits Against Gawker."

One of Denton's classic slogans—today's gossip is tomorrow's news. Two days after the *Forbes* piece runs, Thiel himself confesses to the *Times*. The controversy is immediate and immense. For the first time, coverage of the most media-centric story of the year is no longer tinged with amusement about the lurid details of a celebrity's private life or whether sex tapes were newsworthy, but rather with anger and rage and anxiety. Now it was: *Should people be able to do what Thiel had done? Is the entire right to a free press imperiled?* The *Los Angeles Times* would say that of all the possible twists in the story, "few developments could be more frightening," and *The Guardian*, publishing across the Atlantic in a country with historically more accessible libel laws, nonetheless predicted that Thiel had given his fellow billionaires a playbook and that the case was "a chilling taste of things to come." And the *New York Times*, whose experts had just weeks before been talking of the positive or minimal effects of the verdict, would publish six mostly negative pieces (some hysterically so) in the next seven days. The coverage had turned and only one fact had changed, the fact about who had paid Charles Harder's legal bills.

Even the conspirators, long in the dark, are surprised by the news. *The guy from PayPal? The libertarian billionaire who tried to make seasteading happen?* Perhaps some unconscious version of Occam's razor had set in (the simpler explanation is more likely) among the conspirators and they had begun to assume there was no mystery man at all, that Mr. A *was the benefactor.*

A decade of secrecy has been undone in less than ninety-six hours. Along with it, much of the carefully constructed narrative that Gawker was unique and evil, that it deserved this, that this was a grassroots and organic rejection of a culture gone bad, teeters on collapse. A painstakingly plotted story takes a turn that a screenwriter would have been reluctant to invent for fear of the note, "C'mon, that's a little far-fetched."

"It was scarcely believable that something so cinematically vindictive and conspiratorial and underhanded could have actually happened," John Cook would tell a sympathetic documentary crew about the case. Which, undoubtedly, is why it happened. All those adjectives fog what happened as it was happening, right in front of Cook, in front of Nick and so much of the rest of the world. But now that it was clear that it had, the optics changed, too.

Thiel is just as unprepared for it. "We didn't think it was going to happen, so yes, we were caught by surprise." He is caught by surprise not only by the news, but by the direction that news begins to go. Though on May 25, the hashtag #ThankYouPeter would briefly spike on Twitter—driven mostly by alt-right and Gamergate accounts—and many of his Silicon Valley colleagues would cheer the audacity of what he had pulled off, the reaction from the rest of the media was almost overwhelmingly negative. The revelation of Peter's name immediately flips the narrative that many reporters and commenters had been running with. Now all of a sudden, it wasn't Gawker, the bully, beating up on Hulk Hogan, it was a megalomaniacal billionaire threatening free speech. The idea that Gawker could have perhaps quite handily prevailed at trial with a better legal strategy was immediately replaced by the perception that Gawker never had a chance.

The once invincible Soviet Union falls and suddenly everything that happened in the Cold War seems silly and overwrought. All the fears seem misplaced, as if the threat were never real. The bomb is dropped on Hiroshima and the war ends. Now the country that dreaded up to a million casualties from a direct invasion of Japan, that had already begun to manufacture the Purple Hearts to give to the families of those men, is forced to explain how it could do something so cruel.

Denton, furthering a sort of Lost Cause mythology of his former empire, would say, "The idea that Thiel was terrified of the next Gawker piece is still absurd to me—and given how things turned out, we had much more to fear from him than the other way around." Hogan is no longer the little guy who fought and won. Hogan was the big guy. He had a billionaire on his side. The fact that Gawker had willfully published a sex tape that was known to have been recorded without consent, that it then had declined every opportunity to take it down and spent millions trying to deter Hogan from seeking his day in court was all forgotten. Gawker had, at one point not long before, been almost appalled that anyone would be so stupid as to sue it and think they could win in court. The fact that a judge had ruled the case legitimate and a jury had found for Gawker's opponent—all these realities of recent history disappeared. And the hope of a clean victory went with them. Going into the jury room, Gawker was the bully. By the time they left the courtroom, they were no longer, they were the victim. That's the new narrative.

Machiavelli warns conspirators that the most dangerous time is after the deed is done. It is as if Peter and Harder did not fully consider this. "We thought the point of maximum tension would be the trial and once we were done with that, you know, if they couldn't figure it out at the trial they never would," Peter says. He would also say that he thought *the end* of the trial would put them past the "point of maximum danger." In fact, this was exactly the point of the highest vulnerability. Loss inherently makes the loser sympathetic. We can easily be made to feel bad for the person on the other side of a true catastrophe, even if just minutes before we thought they had it coming to them.

Thiel and Mr. A, both foreign born, had forgotten that essential quirk of the American character—the inclination toward rooting for the little guy. Had Thiel been able to talk to Hogan more, perhaps this could have been avoided. Hogan, the showman, the American, knows how fickle crowds in this country are, how quickly they turn. In a wrestling match, he would say, when one wrestler begins to beat too unfairly on his opponent, they switch sides. They stop shouting, "HULK, HULK, HULK," and a rumble begins to grow in favor of the one who is being beaten. In overreaching, this is what the conspirators had done. They'd delivered too many kicks to the body while their opponent was on the ground. They had no public story to explain why they had done what they did. Hogan had his story—Gawker had pulled down his trunks in the middle of the ring, so to speak; they'd humiliated him and he wanted his day in court. Thiel did not.

It wasn't until August, nearly three months after his identity was made public, that Thiel began working on a *New York Times* op-ed—after he had spoken at the Republican National Convention and opened himself up to significantly more attention—to explain his motives behind the Gawker lawsuit. It was here for the first time that he would try to explain that he saw this as an act of philanthropy and not malice, that he intended to liberate, not destroy, that the destruction was constructive. It was the first time his case was made directly and the first time it was made to someone other than that jury in Florida. In October, he would give a press conference at the National Press Club in Washington, D.C., to answer questions about it, to justify his thinking, to describe Gawker as a "singularly sociopathic bully." In both cases, he was on the defensive, no longer dictating the narrative but reacting to it. Denying that he was evil or vindictive. It is not a good look.

In a conspiracy that was so brilliantly planned and orchestrated, calculated in every way down to its probabilistic decimal point, where no expense was spared, this can't be seen as anything but little and late. If we are to flash back to 2012, as Mr. A and Harder are meeting for the first time, as Thiel strategizes with them from afar, we find the roots of this mistake. They had considered so many different variables. They thought about Gawker's weaknesses and how to exploit them. They explored a dozen different routes to the endgame—a decisive legal judgment against Gawker. But like so many conspirators, they seem not to have stopped to ask, *Okay, then what?*

A close friend of Peter's told me that some friends had warned him against pursuing Gawker, explaining that were he to succeed, the rest of the media would hate him for it. This didn't compute for Peter, the friend would say, he didn't understand that the media was just as tribal as any other group. Peter had read the average citizen correctly. (*Vice*: "Most Americans don't care that Peter Thiel crushed Gawker.") What he missed was that to take down one media outlet would make him an enemy to all the others, even if they never liked Gawker to begin with. That it would be seen as an act of retribution and would invite retribution in return. "Peter genuinely believed the media would cheer him on," he said. He didn't think the media would consider Gawker one of their own. He thought they'd appreciate what he'd done. He had no contingency plan, it appears, because he thought it illogical that he'd need one.

Peter, too, seems to have thought that victory would be the end in another way, that the public wouldn't have wanted to know *how* this happened. While we may not live in a world of conspiracies anymore, our desire for *conspiracy theories* is endless. If someone like Hogan beats someone like Gawker, people are going to try to figure out how he did it and they're not going to stop until they're satisfied. A student of history should have known that.

Did Peter really think that things would simply go back to how they were before? That with his money and power, he could make the world return to the halcyon days before *Valleywag* had written about him at the end of 2007? Before 2002 when Nick had launched Gawker? Way back at the beginning, Thiel and Mr. A decided on limiting themselves to ethical and legal means of remedy against Gawker, because as Thiel had said, secrets often have expiration dates. Mr. A had begun exploring bankruptcy lawyers in anticipation of a favorable verdict as early as 2015, but he had made fewer preparations for a favorable verdict where the curtain was pulled back and the puppet masters revealed. Where was the contingency plan? Why hadn't a draft of the op-ed been written long in advance? Why hadn't an entire public relations plan been developed for the endgame? The argument would have been convincing: if Gawker can do what it did to Hogan, if it could take this case down to the wire, require millions of dollars to defeat, what do you think it could have done to you? Had Harder realized that their legal strategy would become more sympathetic had they presented Heather Clem, the woman in the tape, as a kind of victim, too, Hulk Hogan would not have loomed so large in post-trial press. Had Thiel written anywhere about the effect that being outed had on his personal life, had he set up interviews with sympathetic publications in the days immediately after the story broke, he might have been able to place that narrative. But that hadn't happened. If Gawker never thought this case would get to trial, then it might be said that Thiel had not thought much *past* the trial. And now, as a result, he is the petty one, the one motivated by a personal grudge, the one who hurt people and took their stuff and saw his image go from genius billionaire tech investor to ruthless plutocrat and enemy of free speech. Cunning and resources might win the war, but it's the stories and the myths afterward that will determine who *deserved* to win it.

How one rides out the chaos in the aftermath of a deed is everything. Winning, succeeding, pulling off the complex operation is the last step of one journey but simultaneously the first step in the next one, one arguably more important and more difficult than what came before. The next step is *holding on* to the victory. No matter how brilliant you are, how impressive the conspiracy was—it will be defined by what comes after. Charlie Wilson worked with the CIA to fund a guerrilla resistance to the Soviets in Afghanistan and won. There wasn't much of a plan for what to do with these trained and armed fighters afterward. He would say, "These things happened. They were glorious and they changed the world. And the people who deserved the credit are the ones who made the sacrifice. And then we fucked up the endgame." Those same fighters became the Taliban and sheltered Osama bin Laden. Soon enough, they became the bane of U.S. soldiers, just as they had been to the Soviets, and as their great-grandfathers had been to the British.

Thiel knew the importance of finishing. He had written it in *Zero to One*. "It is much better to be the *last* mover," not the first mover. "Grandmaster José Raúl Capablanca"—Thiel's favorite chess player—"put it well: to succeed 'you must study the endgame before everything else.'" The conspirators had studied it, but only so far as their maneuvering took to get the other man's king on its side. What they failed to consider was that in any chess match between masters, there is always more than one game. Each requires its own unique plan.

CHAPTER 17

The Art of Settling

In the Girardian view, violence is reciprocal and imitative. It escalates in a never-ending cycle, often taking society along with it. Hamlet avenging the murder of his father, until he is killed in turn. Saddam Hussein and Bush Sr. Bush Jr. and Saddam Hussein. The noose is put over Saddam's head, but it gives way to the next feud. Shiites and Sunnis. Americans and ISIS. Sworn blood feuds lasting for generations.

And how will this conflict end, this fight between Denton and Thiel, which had now broken into a public war? Will it escalate? Can it be maneuvered to a conclusion or will the gains be clawed back?

Of the dangers after a successful conspiracy, Machiavelli would say, "there is only one, and that is when someone is left who may avenge the dead prince." For this reason, Robert Greene warns, one must "crush your enemies totally." Remember, after David fells Goliath with his well-placed stone, that's not the end of it. Then began the gruesome work of hacking off the giant's head with the man's own sword. The point is: you can't leave them even an inch to come back at you.

Peter sought from the beginning to land a decisive blow, but in the modern world, short of murder or imprisonment, there is no such thing as decisively silencing an enemy. Nick retained his ability to speak publicly, his reporters would be as reckless and vindictive as they always were, and for some time while the details of the case and verdict were being finalized, Gawker would remain a powerful publishing platform. Peter may have won in court, but what would he look like in victory? And how would Denton act in defeat?

In May 2016, after Thiel reveals his role to the *New York Times*, Nick writes an open letter to Peter on Gawker that presages precisely the cycle that Girard had warned against. "We, and those you have sent into battle against us, have been stripped naked, our texts, online chats and finances revealed through the press and the courts," Denton would say, but "in the next phase, you too will be subject to a dose of transparency. However philanthropic your intention, and careful the planning, the details of your involvement will be gruesome. . . . We have our devices," Denton would hint, "you have yours."

"I'm not a fighter, I'm a waiter" is how Walter Winchell opens his memoir, addressing the enemies who had prematurely ended his career and toppled him from power. "I wait until I catch an ingrate with his fly open, then I take a picture of it." The gossip columnist Louella Parsons, driven from relevance by studio heads tired of her tyranny, dragged down by lawsuits at the end of her life, would retreat into literal silence in protest. The last ten years of her life, it was claimed she never said another word. Which would it be? What would be Denton's path?

The coverage that followed the verdict showed Denton's devices—that he could influence the press, that his friends could make the man's life miserable. *Wired*: "How Can We Make You Happy Today, Peter Thiel?" *Vanity Fair:* "Peter Thiel Wants to Inject Himself with Young People's Blood." *Paste*: "Peter Thiel Is a Petty, Vindictive, Dangerous Human." *The Advocate*: "Peter Thiel Shows Us There's a Difference Between Gay Sex and Gay." Thiel had set out to reduce the power of Gawker and to regain his private life and it began to appear that the former had come at the cost of the latter.

To the media, Denton in defeat was made once again into one of their own. Even if he hadn't been before, he was by nature of his circumstances more sympathetic than ever, falling from publishing kingpin to reluctant landlord, renting out his Manhattan loft on Airbnb to cover his bills while the details of the verdict were being sorted out. Harder told me that he found the media to be like a pack of crows, "If you kill a crow outside your house, the whole pack will descend upon you and never leave you alone. If you go for a walk, they will attack you. That's the media that would help out Gawker."

Though Thiel would receive many private congratulatory messages from CEOs, celebrities, actresses, investors, and even other journalists when the story originally broke, as the coverage wore on, members of his billionaire class turned on him. Jeff Bezos, the founder of Amazon, would be asked about Thiel's campaign. What could he say? Certainly not that he thought billionaires should do things like that, not unless he wanted to invite the crows over to his house, too. "Is that really how you want to spend your time?" he asked half rhetorically. "As a public figure the best defense to speech that you don't like is to develop a thick skin." True, but even Bezos would have to agree that there is also a time to, as Amazon's policy toward publishers was once articulated, chase one's opponents down "the way a cheetah would pursue a sickly gazelle."

With the balance of power now in flux, and Denton with some much-needed public leverage, it began to occur to Nick that his best move might be to confront the architect of his defeat in person. In late June, Thiel and Denton would be in the same room together, in the home of the friend who had last tried to connect them back in 2014, when Denton's lawyers suspected some sort of conspiracy and Denton had taken a flier and sent Peter that email about getting coffee. But why now? Why would either want to do this? Curiosity, perhaps. Self-interest, almost certainly.

"You can understand that we were on a mutually destructive path. Damaging for Thiel, possibly fatal for me," Denton says. "Others were keener to pursue the fight at that point than we. There was a mutual interest." Denton would like to save himself financially, Thiel disdains the public eye. It matters little that Thiel has won and that Gawker has been humiliated in court if Denton's will to fight is not broken. He could continue to harass Peter publicly, he has the power to hurt him with the drip, drip, drip of exactly the kind of gossip that first stung Thiel as unfair in 2007. Thiel has plenty of leverage, too; Denton can see that Thiel can keep coming and coming at him. Now that Thiel and Hogan would be Gawker's lead creditors in bankruptcy, Thiel could fight every expense, simply to punish Gawker—and so far he had, prompting a bankruptcy judge to admonish Thiel's lawyers for spending thousands of dollars in fees to fight the budget of Gawker's farewell party. In the end, Denton found himself with only one thousand dollars to toast the end of an empire once worth nearly $300 million, and promptly running out of alcohol with which to do it. Denton and his lawyers could repay this humiliation by eating up millions of fees on their end, essentially burning the city as they retreated, until there was nothing left to pay even part of Hogan's judgment. Thiel had the resources to chase Denton for a lifetime. Both sides could keep pulling the rope of war from their respective ends, wrenching the knot tighter and tighter. Or they could meet. And so they did, first in a private home in San Francisco, then again later in the offices of a New York law firm.

History affords us few similar moments with which to make comparison or to draw parallels. Orson Welles and William Randolph Hearst had been locked in a public battle over the fate of what would go down as one of the greatest movies of all time. One had made it and wanted the world to see it. The other believed it had stolen and perverted his likeness and used every ounce of his power to prevent anyone from seeing it. Hearst had tried to buy it, tried to destroy it, tried to beat Welles bloody in his newspapers until he gave in and stopped. Now, by sheer chance, the two found each other in the same elevator of the Fairmont Hotel in San Francisco. Will one wrap his hands around the throat of the other? Will they make peace? Welles breaks the silence. He invites his tormentor to the premiere of *Citizen Kane*, the very movie Hearst had attempted to destroy. Hearst declines. Is it a trap? Is it a real gesture? Welles, as he leaves the elevator, jokes that Charles Foster Kane, the character based on Hearst, the one Hearst so loathes, would have agreed to come. The two never see each other again.

It is Grant and Lee at Appomattox Court House, Grant caught by surprise at the request, showing up in a dirty field uniform and mud-flecked boots, Lee showing up in full regalia and a sword on his belt. Two men who had battled each other on fields and in forests across the country they both loved, men who had seen carnage and death in the course of a war neither had wanted. Now they were together. Grant tells Lee that they have met before, once, when they served in Mexico, and how his striking appearance had stayed with him. Lee, slightly embarrassed, says he has often searched his memory about this encounter, knowing that they crossed paths, but has always struggled to remember. They hash out surrender terms; the occasion is so momentous that a trembling aide cannot steady his hand enough to write them. And as Lee leaves, bearing a heavy sadness, returning to his troops to tell them that this long Civil War is over and that they have lost, Grant salutes him. Lee saves face; Grant saves the county.

One of those moments is a fun story in the history of showbiz, the other one of the most important scenes in American history. One successful, the other not. Both share the same fundamental awkwardness, the same unusualness when combatants find the distance between them suddenly evaporated. So we might, without overstating it, add to the unique pantheon these moments between Denton and Thiel. Denton had initiated, half motivated to try to end this ordeal that had taken up so much of his life and destroyed his finances, half by sheer curiosity, a desire to meet the man responsible for it all. Thiel would say it was something he felt he had to do, that he owed it to Denton as a man. Denton felt like he might be able to make a case in person that could not be made through lawyers. Perhaps he wanted simply to put a human face to it all, to *see* the person who had done this to him. Part of him must have wanted to deprive Peter of the shield that had let him get this far, the protectiveness of seeing Gawker as the MBTO and not acknowledging his and Denton's shared beliefs, personalities, and background.

Picture them sitting across from each other. Two men who had hated each other, made each other sick, spent north of $20 million battling each other, who had written and said such terrible things about each other. One had embarrassed the other, haunted him. So the other drives him from his home and leaves his life's work teetering on the edge of destruction. Each is still trying to judge the other's intentions, each wondering where this will end, whether the other is exhausted or if this will keep going. Thiel has the upper hand, yet Denton is not without resources, his *devices*. He must still have struck some fear into Thiel or he wouldn't be here. Thiel expects to meet a sociopath, intent on manipulating him. "How do you negotiate with a sociopath? That was the question at the back of my mind," he recalls. It is a question to which he actually had an answer. "You have to box them in, and make sure they have no leverage, because they will look for a way to wriggle out and double-cross you in one way or another." Thiel clearly does not expect to see a human being walk in and sit down across from him. Denton, for his part, expects to find a domineering, angry man, not the almost bashful Thiel who only reluctantly makes eye contact.

Neither will say much about this meeting, both intent to protect the sanctity of what happened. At the front of Peter's mind would be not only the theories of Girard, but the warning he had received many years before: "Be careful who your enemies are, because you will become just like them." *Lie down with dogs* . . . How similar were these two, both mercurial, both driven by deeply personal motives that had become intertwined with larger, more philosophical justifications over time. "It's weird that I dislike him so little," Denton would tell me. "There are many people on many sides that aggravate me far more. There is some kind of meaning. We are similar in some ways and diametrically opposed in others. It's too uncanny not to have some narrative purpose."

The status quo was once a world in which Nick Denton had the throne, the media throne that gave him immense power, and now the positions had been undeniably reversed. Peter was one of the most powerful people in the world. He was a billionaire many times over. Palantir was a national security juggernaut. Facebook was the most popular network of humans ever assembled. He had thirsted for revenge and justice against this man for so long, he had schemed for it from afar, but now it was right there in front of him. To try to break a man is one thing, to see him broken before you is another.

Denton emails Thiel afterward, expressing optimism about this new line of communication between them. "Feel free to signal your gameplan to the extent you're comfortable and it is useful," Denton tells him as if this were a chess match and not an attempt to save himself financially. "If we're to preserve value for the protagonists rather than the lawyers, it would help for each of us to understand the other's calculus. (Though no doubt there will be some gamesmanship too!)" Peter replies that he, too, found it "helpful to exchange views" and promises to think "a bit more about what sort of resolution makes sense for us." But it is the note from the mutual friend, the mediator in a sense, that best captures the tone of that meeting: "Life is short and I want each of you to have happy, wonderful and long lives. For that reason I sincerely hope you two are able to resolve this conflict soon."

But here is the paradox: if Thiel is too lenient, then all of this has been for naught. Denton can move on and start another gossip site. Thiel said in his *Times* interview that he had been after *"specific deterrence,"* a legal term. It means: Gawker won't be able to do this kind of crap anymore. Ever again. To let Denton off the hook out of empathy, because the man's suffering was now real to him, would be to undermine the goal. From the outset, he had steeled his heart for this very moment, as all conspirators must. And yet to push too far, to give in to emotion and bloodlust, would undermine it all the more. "There were a lot of other people who had been destroyed and on some level it would be unjust for me to be too merciful," Peter would say.

But to be too firm, too unyielding, is to prolong the conflict or worsen it. Franklin Roosevelt had universally angered almost every one of the Allied generals at Casablanca when he told the media that he would accept only one outcome from the Germans: *Unconditional Surrender.* He hadn't been thinking of policy, the words had just popped out in a press conference, but he could not take them back. The people who actually had to do the cleaning up, who needed to fight the war to a close, knew that this kind of language would only make the job harder. It had deprived Germany of a way to end the war earlier, it had united a collapsing enemy in desperation. Without a way out, tensions only increase and combatants have no choice but to fight on. Scipio Africanus, the general who defeated Hannibal, would say that an army should not only leave a road for their enemy to retreat by, they should *pave it*. The Romans had a name for this road, the Gallic Way.

Having activated powerful forces, sold his team on the crusade, the final needle to thread for Thiel was how to end it without disappointing them or earning himself an enemy willing to fight until there was nothing left for anyone. "The goal was not to send Nick Denton to the poorhouse," Thiel would say, and so he would complete his *spolia opima* by negotiating an end to the fighting while there were still spoils to distribute.

They had met in person in June, and in October there would be a three-day meeting of all the lawyers in New York City to finalize terms. By November, everyone had been wrangled into the right place. Gawker Media would settle with Terry Bollea for roughly $31 million. Ashley Terrill and Shiva Ayyadurai, the defendants in those two cases Thiel and Harder had rammed through at the end that had contributed to Thiel's exposure, would receive $500,000 and $750,000 respectively. A.J. walked away without any real financial burden. In March 2017, Denton settled with Bollea, who, dropping the $10 million jury award against Denton, would let him emerge with roughly $15 million based on his shares in Gawker Media. The media firm Univision acquired Gawker Media for $135 million in a bankruptcy auction. "My own sense is that if Hogan ended up with more money from it than Denton," Peter said of his plan, "that would be enough to count as a very solid win."

Gawker.com itself ceased publishing on Monday, August 22, 2016, two days before Denton's fiftieth birthday. All but a few of the most offending posts still stand, never to be touched again, lingering, Nick said, "on the web like a ghost ship, the crew evacuated."

He was smart enough, resilient enough, to accept this as a tolerable outcome. "I have been reminding myself how bad it *could have* been," Denton would tell me. "Backer still in the shadows, never revealed. Not enough in proceeds to fund a family and my ideas . . . The prospect of another four years of litigation . . ." He'd come to have a certain fatalism about it, that if the end had not come here, it would have come soon enough elsewhere.

Peter had left him a way out, a line of retreat, a way to exit with dignity, and he'd taken it. Not that Denton wouldn't once or twice fantasize about something horrible happening to Thiel. But that would be a thought he would find better to keep to himself, not a comment he needed to pin to another look into Thiel's private life on Gawker.

There is a moment at the end of the Roman Civil War when Pompey is defeated by Caesar's armies. Pompey, formerly Pompey the Great, finds himself simply walking away from the battlefield at the end of it. Nowhere to go, no country left, unnoticed even by the soldiers around him, having lost a lifetime of power in a single afternoon. So, too, on November 2, 2016, Nick Denton would post on his blog that the saga was over, that he had settled, and that he was simply fading back into civilian life. *A hard peace*, he would call it. A surrender.

Left alone during these months of limbo is A. J. Daulerio. He is not invited to any sort of détente, probably on the calculation that he would either destabilize it or add little value. The headlines about him as the verdict recedes into the rearview paint a picture of a man in increasingly desperate straits. *Forbes*: "Former Gawker Editor Lashes Out at Peter Thiel, Calls Freeze on His Checking Account 'Ludicrous.'" and "A. J. Daulerio to Peter Thiel: Do You Want My Rice Cooker and Dishes?" *Above the Law*: "Too Poor to Pay Million-Dollar Judgment, Former Gawker Editor Offers Up Rice Cooker, Dishes." A.J. had woken up one morning to find a $230,200,000 legally ordered hold on his bank account.* This isn't just a person with nothing to lose—it's a person increasingly with no way out.

An interview A.J. gives in September on the *Longform* podcast

* While the actual amount owed was disastrously large to A.J., it had likely been compounded by an extreme banking error, as the hold was for exactly double the size of the entire verdict.

rattles Thiel and Mr. A, and Hogan most of all. A.J. seems backed into a corner. Desperate. Crazed. Had they gone too far? Is this a new enemy, one to fear even more than Denton? Nearly a year after the verdict, A.J. still wouldn't have access to his own checking account. How bitter would this make him? To what lengths would he go to get even? Or would sobriety and the humility visited upon him by the verdict his deposition testimony helped secure also help him turn his life around? It would remain to be seen. "I work hard every single day to rid myself of revenge fantasies. It's pointless. Peter and Nick settled so that's supposed to be it," he would tell me. Would he continue to do that work on himself? It is up to him. It's a going concern against which Thiel must always be on guard.

But Nick, at least Nick, was handled.

Three days before the end of 2016, Charles Harder is on the West Coast with his family. An email alert comes in from the bank. A wire transfer for roughly $32 million has just been sent to the firm's client account.

The bounty has been paid. Yet no conspiracy ends that cleanly, not with any of the parties or their allies still living. The debtors who had taken over Gawker's finances would not simply go quietly into the night. Just months into the new year of 2017, they—without involvement from Nick Denton, it should be said—would begin to discuss suing Peter Thiel for having funded the lawsuit against Gawker. They would ignore the settlement and try to have it overturned. "Like soldiers stranded on islands after hostilities have ended, debtors persist in fighting after the war is over," Harder would have to write in a filing. In the last months of 2017, the advisers overseeing the bankruptcy of Gawker announced that they were considering putting up for sale the company's potential multimillion-dollar claim against Peter Thiel for his efforts to destroy the company. Meaning that another backer, some other interest could now be reversing the roles, financing a lawsuit against Peter Thiel on behalf of Gawker, not so much out of any sense of justice but because there was money in it. In other words, perhaps the battle was not quite fought all the way out.

The conspirators would find that victory required a kind of defensiveness still. Mr. A would ask that we keep no documentation of our discussions, lest it be used against him personally in court. Hulk Hogan, once celebratory, would avoid interviews for fear that it complicated the still-ongoing proceedings. Even Peter would begin to watch his words: "What can I say here?" "How should I put this?"

Peter had hoped to avoid something interminable. He had said to me, "Whatever misgivings I have about Denton, at the end of the day, my judgment is that he also wants to end it," and yet maybe it wouldn't matter. It could still become exactly the endless, irresolvable feud he had feared.

CHAPTER 18

There Are Always Unintended Consequences

The historian E. P. Thompson said that history never happens as the actors suspect, that history is instead the "record of unintended consequences." The assassination of Julius Caesar does not restore the Roman Republic, it leads to a brutal civil war and, at the end, another emperor. The Allied powers destroy Hitler and Germany but empower Russia and Stalin and create a new Cold War to follow the conclusion of the hot one. There is always something you didn't expect, always some second- or third-order consequence.

Peter Thiel's conspiracy had achieved its intended outcome. A negotiated peace had been found. Gawker.com would cease to publish. A new leader was in charge of the rest of the sites, some of the offending articles would be removed. But what would the consequences, intended and otherwise, of it all be? What had this brilliant, independent mind neglected to see? What, if anything, would come as a surprise? His own power and strength for one.

The nineteenth-century French economist and libertarian thinker Frédéric Bastiat would say there is just one difference between a good economist and a bad one. "The bad economist confines himself to the visible effect; the good economist takes into account both the effect that can be seen and those effects that must be foreseen."

Many were outraged by what was visible in Thiel's conspiracy against Gawker. They worried about a "chilling effect" on the media. They worried that people would be less free to say what they think and feel for fear of being held accountable for it. They worried that reporters would be less likely to take risks on important stories. They worried that Gawker had been deprived of its constitutional right to appeal because it couldn't afford the $50 million entrance fee, and this is not an unreasonable concern. "You live in a country where a billionaire can put a publication out of business" is how one Gawker writer put it in Gawker's obituary of the site. "A billionaire can pick off an individual writer and leave that person penniless and without legal protection."

In the years he conspired against Gawker, Thiel would come to see the U.S. legal system differently. He later said that, before the case against Gawker, he had believed that the problem in America was too many lawsuits and too many lawyers. Like many media outlets, Gawker's legal strategy had been to lean into that understanding—to be the black hole of time and money whose event horizon no one could afford to confront. With his immense resources, Thiel believed he had simply changed the equation. The fact that Hulk Hogan, a "single-digit millionaire" as Thiel put it, would not otherwise have had the funds to pursue a case like this means that there might be many other legitimate legal precedents or cases that have otherwise gone unpursued out of intimidation or lack of funds (it cannot be said with a straight face that A.J. and Nick did not have "legal protection"). Having actually gone through the system, Thiel would come to believe that maybe there weren't enough lawsuits. *That people should try more.* And so he puts more money behind the idea, funding in 2016 a start-up called Legalist, conceived by a Thiel fellow, dedicated to bankrolling lawsuits with a high probability of winning and possibly setting new precedents.

He learned another important lesson in that Florida courtroom, this one also about America—that average and ordinary people cared little for the assumptions of the so-called elites. I think he also learned something about his own willingness to put up a middle finger at those elites, and how vulnerable they might be. There was a pleasure in making these people howl, in taking real action and, as he had said, finding oneself capable of the power to "tell history to stop."

For once you do something like that, you're no longer like other people, content with the status quo, respectful of how things are or have been. Reality seems, somehow, more malleable than it did before.

Perhaps it was this surreality that lent itself well to the world of Donald Trump, which is the only word that captures the campaign from the moment it began in the lobby of Trump Tower—with Trump's descent down the escalator, followed by his denunciation of Mexicans as rapists, and then careening from divisive issue to divisive issue from there. But Thiel and Trump agreed in theory on at least one thing: that America had lost some form of its greatness and could be made great again. Conspicuous among Trump supporters for being at least halfway sane and respected, Thiel would be asked to speak at the convention, giving a frenzied six-minute address to a television audience of some thirty million. Many who knew him would observe that it was the most excited they had ever seen him—that he was almost breathless, vibrating with energy onstage. If Peter were capable of mania, this would be the closest he ever got to it.

That his advocacy for Trump as a business leader and his campaign against Gawker as a cultural menace would combine to create a wicked, almost unanimous backlash seems to catch Thiel on his back foot. The venomous way his support is received comes in wave of surprise after surprise. There may indeed be too few lawsuits in America, but there is plenty of outrage to spread around.

Thiel must have known that supporting Trump would be controversial and that his advocacy would come at a price. The coverage that followed was overwhelmingly negative, as were the opinions of many of his friends and colleagues in Silicon Valley. Members of Facebook's board jockeyed to remove him. Prominent start-ups vowed not to take his money, or money from funds even remotely associated with him. Peter had gone after Gawker because he believed that he was a private person and deserved a private life, but the great irony of his victory over Denton was that it had made him a celebrity—one whose every action was now, by definition, news. Whom he donated money to, what causes he supported, that his doctor was an advocate for a process known as parabiosis which transfers youthful blood into patients as an antiaging treatment. Thiel's victory over Gawker had proven Gawker prescient: that he was deserving of coverage and that people would love to hate him.

"There are worse things than being disliked," the novelist Walker Percy once wrote, "it keeps one alive and alert." I saw Thiel in his office in San Francisco a few weeks before the election, when his bet on Trump seemed at its most ill advised. He was slightly frazzled and overwhelmed by recent events, but also invigorated and excited by the energy of it all. He was willing to entertain that he was wrong, that he might have stepped on a land mine, but he also suspected that he might not be—that he might be onto something. Soon he would double down on Trump and make a $1.25 million contribution to the campaign. Jeff Bezos had also felt the need to opine about Peter's politics: "Peter Thiel is a contrarian, first and foremost. You just have to remember that contrarians are usually wrong." It certainly looked that way, until November 10, and then I would get an email from Peter: "Contrarians may be mostly wrong, but when they get it right, they really get it right."

Thiel is once again in the catbird seat, having taken the world by surprise one more time. He had proved not only that we live in a country where a person can conspire to put a publication out of business, but that we live in a country where the media would give literally billions of dollars of free publicity to a candidate they despised and were then shocked when the man ended up being elected.

If one looks back at that fateful choice, the choice to follow his secret campaign against a media bully with few friends, then to *publicly* support the campaign of the most contentious presidential candidate in history—a candidate with even fewer friends—it appears at first to be a disastrous public relations blunder. But this implies that these are distinct actions, that there was a separation and a choice. Mr. A would say, looking back, that perhaps their actions would have been better received had they not been stained with Trump, "but Peter endorsed Trump *because* of the trial. It gave him an appreciation for the dynamic of the country and for Middle America. I don't think there is an alternate reality where he wins and doesn't support Trump. I don't think Peter Thiel would have been involved with Trump at all without this case." Nothing would quite make this connection so clearly as a photo Thiel would send me of him at a post-election costume party put on by the billionaire donor Robert Mercer. Donald Trump was dressed as himself, and Peter Thiel was dressed in a red bandana and blond wig, as the one and only Hulk Hogan.

Yet the differences between the two efforts and personalities are too significant not to point out. In pursuing Gawker, Thiel had been patient and methodical, he had drawn ethical lines and chosen his associates wisely. In supporting Trump, he was rushed, he is operating out in the open, not in secret, and willing, in a sense, to associate with anyone he thought had a chance to win, anyone Thiel thought could help advance his unusual goals as a businessperson, a private citizen, and a contrarian thinker. Nothing shows that better than his uncharacteristic speech at the convention, or the list of fools he shared the stage with. There was little in the way of higher purpose in supporting Trump, no matter how Mr. A would spin it. There was something different about it, something written in scarlet letters, not just for Thiel but for all of them. One is a conspiracy, the other a crime of opportunity.

Harder himself would be sucked into Trump's orbit, through Thiel, and come to represent the First Family in a number of cases, apparently finding no irony in helping champion Melania Trump's campaign against cyberbullying while her husband bullied people on Twitter from the White House. Harder would, during the election, find himself sending Gawker a threatening legal letter over a story it wrote about Donald Trump's alleged hairpiece. He would find himself threatening to sue the *New York Times* on behalf of a movie producer accused of heinous acts of sexual harassment, and for Jared Kushner, accused of conspiring against America with Russia. Working for Peter Thiel has been good for business, if in part because his reputation as a slayer of media outlets makes him very attractive to powerful people who have done bad things.

I would ask Mr. A what he thought of Trump, what he made of it all. He would smile and tell me, "I don't care about politics, I only care that my friends are in power." Thiel himself would take to quietly predicting to friends that there was a 50 percent chance the Trump presidency would end in catastrophic disaster. Just as two wrongs don't make a right, does being right twice excuse the risk of how badly it could all go wrong?

And so we have the inexorable march of unintended consequences bending the moral arc of the universe in god knows what direction. A young man and an ambitious lawyer pair up with a billionaire to deal with a gossip blog and find themselves backing a presidential candidate they couldn't imagine backing under any other circumstances. They find themselves involved in forces they can themselves barely contain or comprehend. In the war against Gawker, Thiel had flirted with, flirted with but perhaps didn't touch, members of the

#Gamergate mob that would become the alt-right. Their style of attack: loud, insistent, delusional. Their demographics: predominately white, male, disaffected, bitter. Their tools: social media, trolling, secret coordination, and money. All of these tactics would also be used in Trump's campaign. Many of the same personalities would crop up: Mike Cernovich. Milo Yiannopoulos. Vox Day.* These guerrilla fighters had simply moved from one battle to the other. In the 2016 election, Hillary Clinton, too, had crumbled against the onslaught of attacks from every angle, and an opponent who wanted it more than she did. Eighteen years earlier she had claimed to be the victim of a "vast right-wing conspiracy" and apparently did little to defend herself against the return of such energies.

But just as Nick Denton had learned watching Gawker evolve through the years, Peter would find in the months after his conspiracy that unleashing such wild, chaotic forces is a dangerous bargain. Thiel might be gay, an immigrant, libertarian, and generally civilized and thoughtful, but the people on the alt-right he found himself partly aligned with were not. His arguments for Trump at the convention were reasonable and counterintuitive. Theirs were not. Trump's supporters used the same nastiness and traded in the same half-truths and identity-style politics that Gawker once had.

"These people," Thiel would lament, six months into Trump's presidency, about the alt-right leaders he was now tainted with by association, "they are the most like Gawker. It's not that they are willing to do anything in the name of the ideology, that's the ends justifying the means. . . . The similarity is the nihilism: a mask for no ideology at all."

Peter had pursued legal and ethical means in his conspiracy

*It was these figures who would also create the #ThankYouPeter hashtag which briefly trended on Twitter in May 2016.

against Gawker. Not everyone else he had empowered would have such a commitment. Chuck Johnson, who had also sued Gawker and claimed to have Trump's ear, would tell me that he was not content to let Nick Denton alone as Thiel had been willing to do. "My goal was to bankrupt Gawker and Nick Denton and Peter Thiel did both. So now it's left for me to mop it up," he would say. "In a just world, I'd have them killed. But we are not there yet." Nor was Johnson the only person caught up in reactionary craziness. I would write in a column for the *New York Observer* that would eventually come to Thiel's attention and lead to this book that the Hogan case was an example of the timeless reminder that actions have consequences. A writer for the site Vox.com saw things differently, and writing on Twitter, repeatedly called for someone to engage in a covert lawsuit to destroy me for saying so (Peter replied to me, "It's not as easy as it looks. Not nearly as easy . . ."). The writer would later be suspended for calling for acts of violence at Trump rallies during the campaign. Another Gawker writer would say that the judge in the case deserved to be disbarred, and that Thiel should go to jail for what he'd done (using the civil court system).

Many people were radicalized by the conspiracy and the campaign. Where that energy will go is an alarming unknown. Peter thought he'd be greeted as a liberator, that Gawker was a scourge that once eliminated would allow for open, collaborative discussion. If anything, the opposite has happened. The candidate he helped put in office embodies many of the bullying traits that Thiel claimed to abhor. Trump would also come to actively stymie expression, threatening to "open up" the libel laws in this country and pressuring NFL owners to fire the players who kneeled during the national anthem. This must hit Thiel sometimes, perhaps in the quiet cabin of his Gulfstream, that the man in the White House is essentially the opposite of everything he had spent his life believing in, that Trump threatened the very libertarian freedoms and open civil discourse that Thiel had spent his money protecting. To know he is associated with that, in certain ways responsible for it, might be the most unintended consequence of all.

In Maui, where Thiel has a home and spends a good deal of his time, officials once introduced a species of mongoose to kill rats. Only after introducing them did it occur to anyone that rats are nocturnal and mongooses are diurnal. A bad problem became worse, a rat problem became a mongoose problem. You launch a conspiracy to protect your privacy and make yourself famous. You seek to rid the world of a bully and you find yourself with Trump. The nihilists on the left are sent in a diaspora from Gawker to other media outlets, matched tit for tat by the nihilists on the right. And most of them hate you.

The CIA coined a term to describe this: *blowback*. The word was first used in print in 1954 . . . and the next fifty years would vividly paint its tableau. Teaching a generation about why you don't intervene, why you don't get involved. Because the end of a conspiracy can be not unlike the beginning of it: an intolerable status quo. Perhaps even for the same people. But Thiel knew this going in. He had read that Shakespeare line about fires trodden out and figured that it was still worth the risk.

Did the public learn anything from what happened here? Or did we just go from gawking at Gawker's posts to gawking at Gawker's comeuppance? Did we enjoy A.J.'s ordeal in a real-life Gawker-story nightmare because it was justice or because it was entertaining? "I don't blame people for getting some satisfaction when the tables are turned," Denton would reflect afterward, "and when the media figures get a taste of their own medicine. It would be a little more elegant if the reading public recognized their own contribution, that they get precisely the media that they click on and talk about." I'm not sure that happened. I wish it would.

Maybe all of it is a wash, then. Maybe all that the end of Gawker meant was that Gawker wouldn't out people anymore, that the heel was banished from the media. There is still significance in what happened.

It is said that the weapons invented at the end of one war become the dominant killers in the next one. In pursuing Gawker, Thiel hadn't exactly invented any weapons. Champerty—the funding of lawsuits you have no direct interest in—dates back to at least medieval times. Persistence hunting, attrition, these are concepts that go back to man's earliest days. Scapegoating is one of Girard's most basic theories. Yet it was the combination of all these things, directing them at a media outlet, battling them in court and in secret, that made for something new. A new way of moving the chess pieces. A new model for enacting change, using very old means. The unexpectedness of it is what made it all so effective. *There really was someone working behind the scenes. People really are trying to change things.*

What remains, then, is what will become of this playbook for conspiracy and how it will be used in the future. At what cost will it come to society, to the people it would be used against, to the inventors themselves? Forces, once unleashed, cannot be contained. Genies do not go back into bottles. A smart man observed that inertia is difficult to overcome in politics, but once it has been, momentum is even harder to stop. Where would it go next? Would freedom fighters become a new kind of Taliban? Would the guerrillas return to their farms after the war or would they find they liked the fight too much? Would the mob turn on its creator?

The most insidious and timeless question is what happens to the conspirators when they come to power. The prince is dead, long live the prince. What will the association with Trump do to Thiel? Thiel had big ideas for changing the world and believed that an outsider like Trump had a better shot at implementing them than anyone else. Did

Thiel think that Trump would be another Hogan, a vehicle through which he could enact his goals? Did he think that Trump would go along with his plans and defer to the more experienced people in the room? Thiel wouldn't have been the only smart person to believe that, or to find himself regretting the ego of that belief. Trump would be, in the end, as completely incompetent as the incumbents Thiel had criticized in his convention speech, just for different reasons. A more deliberate, ethical Thiel might have seen that sooner, or avoided it altogether, no matter how tempting or satisfying it had been to see his bet cashed.

Thiel and Mr. A and Charles Harder had each acquired their own types and levels of power. Thiel was a power broker, Mr. A was the most valuable kind of operator now—a proven and private one—and Harder had a growing practice and new kinds of clients he could represent. They had experienced these powers at levels previously inconceivable to them and now quite naturally would look for more opportunities to wield them. What will power do to them? Will it corrupt them? "He who traffics with a tyrant becomes his slave," Sophocles reminds us, "though he goes to him a freeman." I would think of this quote myself as I wrote this book—these people I am talking with, what are they capable of? How will they respond to the publication of a book they do not control?

Once one forges oneself into a hammer of justice and feels the power of crushing one's enemies, driving them before one and taking their possessions as one's own, does one become addicted to it? It can become a cycle without end. It can change you, ruin you. One of the worst things that can ever happen to a leader is to unconsciously associate resistance and criticism with opportunity. When everyone tells you you're wrong and you turn out to be right, you learn a dangerous lesson: *Never listen to warnings.* And so the reason that few conspiracies are followed by additional successful conspiracies is because of this process and the changes that power produces.

As for Denton, what would he learn? What would he take away from it all? It would happen that he would turn to Stoic philosophy, detox from his media obsession, return to Europe, and in many ways become a better person. The joke about Denton had been that he was becoming happier, becoming human, but it really was true. It would be absurd to say he was grateful for what happened. No one enjoys seeing his life's work undone. But there was an element of relief to it. He had come to understand what the Stoics meant by *amor fati*—loving, embracing the good in what has happened. A.J., too, was given a kind of fresh start. He left Gawker in 2012 but had never really been able to leave it, for the lawsuit had tied him to his former employer, keeping him in a state of arrested development. He would struggle now, in the face of this massive failure, to maintain his sobriety. He had spent his journalistic career attacking other people's egos, he would tell me, but in defeat and adversity had come to terms with his own, and was doing the humble, quiet work of ridding himself of it. "I have to step back and just say, 'Yeah this happened, but there is the rest of my life that I have to focus on.' It definitely changed me in ways that I don't particularly like and I will never find any inner peace except if I do it myself."

Neither Nick nor A.J. emerged from this story powerful or victorious, but one could make the argument—as is often true in conspiracies of this nature—that they may have gotten the better end of it. There is at least character in their struggle, as there is in all adversity. It would improve them. If their journey to this catastrophic judgment was defined by a lack of self-awareness, for Nick and for A.J., it is not without some irony to see them gain some from the ordeal. Denton, whom I had met many years before any of this occurred, was humbled by what happened. He was made more introspective, fairer, more compassionate. He found that other part of himself again, the one that had been swallowed by Gawker—the insatiable monster of his own creation. If it is not a bridge too far, it may even be said that there is a kind of greatness in surviving such a calamity, however self-invited it was, and to be made better by it.

There is little of that kind of character or introspection with winning. There rarely is. Hogan, once again a champion in the eyes of the public, found himself absolved of his sins—whether he deserved to be or not. The fake hero of wrestling was turned into the real hero of the legal system, at least to some. There is nothing like a large sum of money and the passage of time to make other people, and most of all yourself, forget the horrible scandal of what you have said or done. Still, the phone doesn't ring for Hogan much these days, not for work anyway. He doesn't need the money, but he does have that chain of beach shops he owns, including the one in Clearwater which takes him past the Sandpearl Resort. When fans approach him to congratulate him on smashing Gawker, it doesn't feel the same as when they would cheer him for body-slamming André the Giant. He feels his pain tighten in his back, it brings back all the memories, the betrayal, the humiliation, the darkness that was inside him, all that he lost. But he is proud of what he did in the case, and not wrong to think that few would have had the determination to stay in it through to the end. He says he prays for Nick and A.J. both now, that they might find some good in what happened and put their talents to greater use. But there is clearly a part of him that hopes to find that for himself, too. Lyndon Johnson would famously conspire to steal a Senate election from Coke Stevenson in 1948, which put him on the path to the presidency. But given how it went, and the fact that Coke died an old man, surrounded by people who loved and admired him, who is to say that LBJ really won?

Perhaps the most interesting unintended consequences, however, were the obvious ones. The ones that no one seriously thought could happen. First, the sex tape actually disappeared. Try to find it—I dare you. You can't. The Streisand Effect now has at least one exception. *Trying doesn't always backfire*.

Goethe would say that many who clamor for freedom of the press do so in order to abuse it. Gawker undoubtedly had. For all the claims that what Peter had done was personal and unethical and wrong, that he had made the world a worse place and horribly wronged a group of journalists, something surprising happened: Media actually did change. *Because they knew they needed to*. A former Gawker writer—the one who had taken the forbidden photo at Denton's wedding—would admit this somewhat painfully, even if he could not credit the cause. As the years passed, he began to reflect on the body of work he had produced at Gawker, and he found himself in 2017 sitting down to interview a movie star he had once gleefully published an upskirt photo of. He wrote:

> It was just another piece of content that came and went as soon as I hit publish. Our understanding of celebrity and its limits was different then—earlier that year, Gawker had published paparazzi pictures of Kate Middleton topless, as well as footage from a Hulk Hogan sex tape, both to viral popularity. (Little did we know of the reckoning that would ensue regarding the latter story.) It's hard to remember now, but paparazzi shots of celebs getting out of cars in skirts sans underwear were enough of a regularity in the mid- and late-aughts to make the whole thing seem like not a big deal at all. Revenge porn laws were then scarce. It wasn't until before the so-called "Fappening" of 2014, in which several celebrities' private nude photos were exposed, that the broader culture came to understand just how fucked up it was. Granted, it was always fucked up—it just took people a while to realize it. I'm one of those people, and I'm

ashamed and embarrassed about that. This is not an excuse—there is no excuse—but an explanation.

While this introspection is interesting, it's more interesting what's missing from it. The writer can admit that his past behavior had been thoughtless, that it had hurt people, but besides his self-pitying confession, he has no sense that there should have been any consequences for it. I would ask Charles Harder if this awareness was the kind of change he had hoped to bring about. He would have just one question: "Why did it take so long?" Still, there must have been some satisfaction, after all that fighting, all those motions which had been met with so much defiance and incredulity, to see *someone* finally get it, even if it was just a single blogger out of so many. Whether more apologies, more realizations followed would remain to be seen. Not that Harder was particularly aggrieved or broken up about it. He had a couple million reasons to be soothed.

Denton had said in his deposition that he was only the publisher, that it was for others to decide the ethical and legal norms for writers to follow. Well, that had happened. Peter and a team of conspirators and a judge and a jury in Florida had spoken. They said: We don't want to live in a world where the media can publish someone having sex—even if it's just the "highlights"—simply because that person has talked about his sex life in public. The begrudging acknowledgment from one Gawker writer might not have been enough for Charles Harder, but it was progress. They had set new norms and the very people who had sworn to resist, to fight it forever, had at least begun to follow them. And on top of that they were reminded of another lesson: *that actions have consequences*. Fair or unfair. That not everything can be solved with apologies or spankings, as Denton had put it.

Do these new norms constitute a "chilling effect" on free speech?

Perhaps, and we don't yet know what a more cautious media will look like. As Denton would tell me, "The pressure for journalists to show empathy has a cost." They may hold powerful people less accountable, they may tell the truth less directly. This could ripple through a democracy in dangerous ways. There's no question that Gawker's style occasionally yielded results. But their destruction also means fewer surreptitiously recorded sex tapes, fewer pointless "glints of meanness," and fewer gratuitous invasions of privacy. Nobody, not even racists, deserves cameras in their bedroom. And a world where that is possible presents plenty of its own potential for abuse.

Thiel's friend Eric Weinstein would observe that you "can't just exact revenge at no cost to yourself." For Thiel, the unintended consequences were there, and the costs were not cheap. But there was also success. He had done what he had set out to do, and in fact done much more than he could have reasonably anticipated. He had changed media. He had created a pivot point in culture and it had worked. He would end this story at the place so well captured at the end of one of his favorite novels, Arthur C. Clarke's *The City and the Stars:* "There is a special sadness in achievement, in the knowledge that a long-desired goal has been attained at last, and that life must now be shaped towards new ends."

What new ends would he conspire to next? Or was the next plan already under way? What ends would Denton, experiencing a different kind of sadness, the sadness of defeat, conspire to? What would *we* do? *What could our first, next conspiracy be?*

Conclusion

In early 2017, I found myself in Peter Thiel's home in Los Angeles, the same home where he had planned so much of this conspiracy. It was a dinner for twenty, all of whom could be seated comfortably in his dining room, attended by nearly everyone involved in the conspiracy, from the lawyers to Hogan himself. It was the first time they had all been in the same place at the same time. All the guests sat down to eat, we lesser mortals served steaks prepared by Thiel's private chef. Reserved for Hogan and Thiel, sitting across from each other, were hulking tomahawk rib eyes. Five-hundred-dollar bottles of wine were passed freely and with the spirit of a limitless tab. Each of the conspirators talked loudly about what had happened, cheered and toasted what they had done.

Peter was the quietest. At the end, he walked out past his fire pit, onto the balcony with its sweeping views of the city in every direction. In a few minutes he would be leaving, though it was late, to take his plane back to San Francisco for meetings in the morning, and the car was, as always, already running in the driveway. For the moment he was still, standing there, alone, reflecting. Or more likely, his mind had already moved on and he was pondering some trade in oil futures or the company he might fund the next day or some new conspiracy already under way.

I stood a few paces behind and felt myself recalling the line from *Hamlet*:

He was a man, take him for all in all,
I shall not look upon his like again.

It would be a shame if that were true not only of Thiel, but of the nearly unbelievable series of events that began in 2007 and ended ten years later. Events that spanned continents, cost millions of dollars, upended so many assumptions, and will loom large, for better or for worse, in the mind of every journalist sitting down to publish a controversial story as well as in the mind of any person who believes they have been bullied or abused by someone wielding a pen or a blog or any other platform.

These events, or at least the traits which spurred them, need not be so rare. The line from the Obamas was "When they go low, we go high." It's a dignified and impressive mantra, if only because for the most part, whether you liked them or not, it's hard to deny that they followed it. But the now cliché remark should not be taken conclusively, for it makes one dangerous omission. It forgets that from time to time in life, we might have to take someone out behind the woodshed.

How we have lost this. How squeamish we have become. We now blindly demonize what is often one of the most effective forms of action. How vulnerable this ignorance has made us to the few real conspiracies, successful or not, that exist in the world. In this rare occasion, though, we got a glimpse, a peek behind the curtain, as the title of Gawker's last post put it, of *how things work*. Now we know. Peter showed us. And yet our instinct is to turn away, to put our fingers in our ears. It's why not once in nearly a decade of concentrated effort and scheming directed at a single enemy—at an entity who was obsessively covered and followed by the media—by an opponent who publicly stated his undying hatred of that enemy, did a single spectator, victim, or even many of the participants suspect any of what you read in the pages of this book. There is no question that what Thiel did over those years was brilliant, cunning, and ruthless. It is equally true that Gawker mostly beat itself. Denton and company allowed this to happen. Even the most cynical and aggressive media site on the planet had missed what was happening right in front of them; they did nothing to save themselves. "The idea of a conspiracy," Thiel would say to me, "is linked with intentionality, with planning, working towards longer-term goals. In a world where you don't have conspiracies maybe also those things disappear." The truth is that Gawker already believed we lived in that world. And so do far too many people.

Regardless of any personal opinions I might have, that was the tragic and absurd message of this book. We live in a world where only people like Peter Thiel can pull something so intentional and long-term off—and it's not because, as Gawker has tried to make it seem, he's rich. It's because he's one of the few who believes it can be done. To borrow a line from *Zero to One*, to believe in conspiracies is an effective truth. To dismiss anything as impossible is as well.

I said in the introduction that we might live in a world of too few conspiracies, not too many. We have plenty of opinions—plenty of histrionic complaints about how terrible and awful and stuck we are—but not enough people with the patience, coordination, and ambition to do anything about it. We used to throw bombs, now we throw tantrums—or worse, tweets. In ancient times it was the foolish sophists who believed that every problem could be talked through, that the logical, obvious, and right thing would simply come about if explained well enough. It's the realists who know that this isn't how things actually work, who know that realpolitik is how things actually get done.

I have gone back and forth many times in the research and

writing of this book about whether I agree with what Peter Thiel did to Gawker. I thought about it out on his balcony, as I watched him watch this last celebratory, conspiratorial night slip toward the dawn. I thought about it as I spent time, as the great Robert Caro advises all writers, not just with the man who wielded the sword, but with the people whom that sword was wielded against—and I was sympathetic to and often convinced by what I heard from them. I have thought about it from a hundred other angles. What if Peter Thiel had funded Shirley Sherrod, the USDA employee terribly slandered and mistreated by the website *Breitbart*, in her court case? What if *Breitbart* had been shut down? What would the ripple effect of that conspiracy have been? The unintended consequences? Might many people in the media have celebrated the exact same thing that outraged them about the Gawker lawsuit? What if the defendant Thiel had backed against Gawker had not been Hogan, but the probable rape victim on the bathroom floor, the one whom A.J. and Gawker had basically told to rub some dirt on it and walk it off? What if the catastrophic verdict hadn't been for Hogan but for the married executive at Condé Nast whom Gawker had outed in 2015, the kind of story that its editors had so proudly published that they resigned when Denton pulled it? Or what if, after the verdict, Thiel's libertarian impulses had been triggered and he'd used the lessons learned in Florida to *stop* Trump instead of supporting him? Would that change how you saw this? Would it change how I saw it?

A mutual friend of Denton's and Thiel's, not unsympathetic to either side, had described the scenario as follows: You believe a restaurant across the street from your house is mistreating its employees, serving tainted food to its customers. You try to speak to the owner and are rebuffed. You reach out to the local authorities and hear nothing. You reach out to the local press and their stories have no impact. Might you then decide to take matters into your own hands? Less than one-third of 1 percent of his net worth—that's what Peter Thiel spent going after Gawker. A fraction of the interest his fortune would earn in a few days if it were in a bank account instead of under the purview of Mr. A or on its way to the accounts receivable department at Charles Harder's new law firm. Would it be wrong for you to spend a relatively trivial sum to do something you thought was important? And if you did, might it be called philanthropic?

Still, it became clear to me that a referendum on the merits of a specific conspiracy would be somewhat pointless. To paraphrase the great Margaret Atwood's line, I decided not to make a final statement but chose instead to deal in tactics. I rounded no rough edges and I'll leave it to other experts to sort through exactly what the implications of this case are. Still, I suspect if Thiel's victory is truly unjust and contrary to what people want, it will not last long. Peter Thiel's claim that destroying Gawker was "one of the most philanthropic" things he has ever done can be challenged (for what it's worth, Dumas has the Count of Monte Cristo, as he sought his revenge, refer to himself as a "kind of philanthropist," too), but what is indisputable is that he saw his actions as a kind of social good and there is something to be admired in that. He felt the world would be better if freed of a certain menace and he set out to change it, he *conspired* to change it, well within the letter and the spirit of the law. (There are many underhanded and vindictive ways for someone with unlimited resources to act. Not telling the person you're suing that you're suing him doesn't strike me as one of them.) So I concerned myself, then, with the *how* of it.

For those who are upset and angry about what happened here, it's worth asking: What are you really mad about? That a man, when attacked by a media outlet, pursued legal means of recourse in the justice system? Or are you upset that the media outlet would be so stupid as to flagrantly violate someone's sexual privacy—contradicting its own grandstanding on the topic—and then not only refuse to apologize and make the situation right, but mount an aggressive but self-defeating legal strategy that gave a judge and jury no choice but to hold it accountable to the laws passed by the voters of Florida? Even with whatever good work Gawker's reporters had done, is that recklessness and arrogance so worth protecting that it should come at the cost of Peter Thiel's and Hulk Hogan's access to the law? We should deprive them of their rights because they are rich? Because they have strange personal lives? Because we don't like their politics?

There are almost certainly better uses for Peter Thiel's money: more pressing causes, worse bullies, worse dampeners on culture than Gawker. The world would have probably benefited more had someone as brilliant as Peter spent his time on more productive projects. But that's not really a reason to have *not* done something here, to have tolerated the status quo as Thiel found it in 2007. Which is the point. What would the world look like if more people tried to change things, *conspired* to change things they found unjust, unfair, immoral?

Was the founding of America not a kind of conspiracy? ("We must, indeed, all hang together, or, most assuredly, we shall all hang separately.") Did Lincoln not conspire to pass the Thirteenth Amendment, knowing it was his only chance, that it was the only way? Was America's entry into the Second World War not a conspiracy between FDR and Churchill? Was it not a conspiracy that took down Nixon, an unstable tyrant whose use of the hidden hand was too heavy to bear? Wasn't there a conspiracy, led by several obscure colonels and captains in the late seventies and eighties, that rebelled against the bloat and the bureaucracy in the Pentagon, reformed military procurement, and created the F-16 and F-18 fighters? Wasn't it a conspiracy to challenge gay marriage in the courts that brought into being what legislation had been unable to accomplish, just as it was a noble but unsuccessful conspiracy involving a mixed-race man named Homer Plessy that challenged segregation? Didn't Branch Rickey and Jackie Robinson conspire to integrate baseball—against the objections of many, both black and white? Are we not to hope that Elon Musk's public advocacy for sending a man to Mars is dwarfed by the secret plans, the backroom deals and complicated steps that will actually get us there?

Sure, Roosevelt also conspired to stack the Supreme Court. There was the so-called Business Plot that tried and failed to install fascism in America. The assassination of Lincoln was a successful conspiracy to prop up white supremacy and counteract the sacrifice of so many Union soldiers. Those who conspired to assassinate Hitler were not exactly heroes—many were upset with how incompetently he was running the war. There have been too many shameful maneuverings in South America to count, as well as disastrous conspiracies by the CIA in the Middle East. More recently, in my own world, Apple and the Big Five book publishers conspired to beat back Amazon in the online book market and were caught and fined by the Justice Department. And there are countless conspiracies to cover up criminal behavior, to hurt other people, and to take more than one's fair share.

When it comes to conspiracies, there are good ones and terrible ones and complicated ones. As I said in the introduction, the word is neutral, the application is not.

The ultimate irony of Peter Thiel's support of Donald Trump, which looks like more and more of a mistake as each day passes, is that Peter has also given those who oppose the president a playbook for doing something about it. Yet this sense of powerlessness over our future and a naïve certainty that the good guys always win remains. This is dangerous, contradictory nonsense. If you want to have a different world, it is on you to make it so. It will not be easy to do it—it may even require things that you are reluctant to consider. It always has. Moreover, that is your *obligation* if you are called to a higher task. To do what it takes, to see it through.

"It's a question," Thiel would say to me a little over a year after the verdict in one of our final interviews, "whether people want to learn lessons or want to teach lessons. Many of the people who have written about this would much rather *teach* lessons than learn lessons." Nick would tell me, in one of our almost weekly chats that I had come to enjoy so much, that the lesson he had learned was that free speech was not necessarily noble by itself, that it needed to be paired with compassion and understanding. Reflecting on Gawker's approach, he would say that "one person's liberation can become another's oppression," which Thiel would almost certainly agree with. It's true on another level that Thiel and Hogan's version of liberation may come at the constraint of the speech of others, as Denton had certainly experienced.

The cleanest or at least the clearest lesson, illustrated in word but mostly in deed by Thiel, is in the power of secrecy, of coordination, and of pushing past those situations where "nothing can be done." In a time when computers are replacing many basic human functions, it will eventually come to be that audaciousness, vision, courage, creativity, a sense of justice—these will be the only tasks left to us. A computer can't practice secrecy or misdirection, a computer can't feel an urge to remake the world.

Only humans can be that crazy.

What you will do with this lesson, what ends you will put it to, are up to you. All I can say is that it is in these times of flux and upheaval that we may need that ambition most.

Acknowledgments and a Note on Sources

This book was the result of the unexpected and unprecedented access I was granted by many of the figures involved in this book, particularly both Nick Denton and Peter Thiel. The vast majority of what is in this book comes from those conversations, but since the media loves nothing more than to cover itself, there was plenty of real-time coverage for me to draw from as well. I would like to thank both Peter and Nick for the time they took to talk with me for this book, as well as to A. J. Daulerio. Our conversations were not only helpful to this book but stimulating and interesting to me—and gave me much to think about beyond whatever might appear in these pages. Charles Harder, Terry Bollea, Mr. A, and Owen Thomas were also generous with their time. Each gave me previously unknown insights about the events so many had previously covered. Many of the quotes and details in this book are from those exclusive interviews (some on and some off the record), from my reading of the many thousands of legal documents, and from other excellent reporting done by journalists at many outlets. I owe a debt of gratitude to many people for this work and have cited them in the pages that follow. Although I will say, I was disappointed that only the Gawker writers and the Gawker lawyers, the ones who had made such a public case for transparency and honesty, declined to be interviewed, despite many requests and an offer to let them name their terms.

Thank you to Nils Parker for his many long conversations about this book and his edits, to my agent Stephen Hanselman and his wife, Julia Sebrinsky, for their support of the project and their suggestions, and to my truly talented researcher and fact checker Hristo Vassilev. Thank you to my partners at Brass Check for their help and support. A special thank-you to my wife, Samantha, who rolled her eyes and said, yes of course, it makes sense to try to squeeze another book in while we're having our first child. Clark—this book is basically the same age as you. I find that unbelievably cool.

And finally, thank you to everyone, especially my editor and publisher at Portfolio, who helped me keep the secrets of this book over the last year and a half. It was our little conspiracy.

Sources

A Word

Eisenhower, Dwight D. *At Ease: Stories I Tell to Friends*. Doubleday, 1967.

Fitzgerald, F. Scott. *The Great Gatsby*. Scribner, 2013.

Klein, Ezra. "Washington Is Bad at Scheming." *Washington Post*, March 4, 2011, http://voices.washingtonpost.com/ezra-klein/2011/03/washington_is_bad_at_scheming.html.

Introduction

Lamb, Harold. *Genghis Khan: Emperor of All Men*. Bantam Books, 1995.

Machiavelli, Niccolò. *The Discourses*. Penguin, 1970.

PART I: THE PLANNING

Chapter 1: The Inciting Incident

abalk. "Stubborn Jew Rolled by More Stubborn Jewier Jew." *Gawker*, July 17, 2007, http://gawker.com/279169/stubborn-jew-rolled-by-more-stubborn-jewier-jew.

abalk2. "Joe Dolce: Portrait of an Asshat." *Gawker*, October 24, 2006, http://gawker.com/209822/joe-dolce-portrait-of-an-asshat.

Beale, Scott. "Nick Denton Takes Over Valleywag." *Laughing Squid*, November 13, 2006, http://laughingsquid.com/nick-denton-takes-over-valleywag.

Biddle, Sam. "It's OK to Be a Hater Because Everything Is Bad." *Gizmodo*, August 10, 2012, http://gizmodo.com/5933688/its-ok-to-be-a-hater-because-everything-is-bad.

Boutin, Paul. "Peter Thiel Is Totally Objectivist, People." *Gawker*, December 20, 2007, http://gawker.com/336024/peter-thiel-is-totally-objectivist-people.

Choire. "Andy Dick Gets The Beat-Down We've All Craved." *Gawker*, July 17, 2007, http://gawker.com/279165/andy-dick-gets-the-beat-down-weve-all-craved.

Cicero, Marcus Tullius. *On Moral Ends*. Cambridge University Press, 2013.

De La Rochefoucauld, François duc. *Reflections; Or, Sentences and Moral Maxims*. Brentano's, 1871.

Eells, George. *Hedda and Louella*. Warner Paperback Library, 1973.

Goethe, Johann Wolfgang von. *Faust I & II*. Princeton University Press, 1994.

Gould, Emily. "Nightmare Online Dater John Fitzgerald Page Is the Worst Person in the World." *Gawker*, October 11, 2007, http://gawker.com/309684/nightmare-online-dater-john-fitzgerald-page-is-the-worst-person-in-the-world.

Grigoriadis, Vanessa. "Everybody Sucks—Gawker and the Rage of the Creative Underclass." *New York*, October 14, 2007, http://nymag.com/news/features/39319.

Grove, Lloyd. "The Gospel According to Nick Denton—What Next for the Gawker Founder?" *Daily Beast*, December 14, 2014, http://thedailybeast.com/the-gospel-according-to-nick-dentonwhat-next-for-the-gawker-founder.

Jessica. "Fred Durst: Touch My Balls and My Ass and Then Sue Gawker." *Gawker*, March 4, 2005, http://gawker.com/035041/fred-durst-touch-my-balls-and-my-ass-and-then-sue-gawker.

———. "Gawker Stalker: Elijah Wood Emphatically Not a Gay." *Gawker*, September 14, 2005, http://gawker.com/125547/gawker-stalker-elijah-wood-emphatically-not-a-gay.

Juzwiak, Rich. "On Outing, Not Outing, and Working for Gawker." July 21, 2015, http://richjuz.kinja.com/on-outing-not-outing-and-working-for-gawker-1719014904.

Kaus, Mickey. "The Shame of the Whitney." *Slate*, May 11, 2004, http://slate.msn.com/id/2099881.

Lehman, Ernest. *Sweet Smell of Success, and Other Stories*. New American Library, 1957.

Levy, Steven. "How Can I Sex Up This Blog Business?" *Wired*, June 1, 2004, http://wired.com/2004/06/blog.

Luscombe, Belinda. "Gawker's Nick Denton: Peter Thiel, Rupert Murdoch and Trolls." *Time*, June 22, 2016, http://time.com/4375643/gawker-nick-denton-peter-thiel.

Mangalindan, JP. "So Who's Making Money Publishing on the Web?" *Fortune*, May 10, 2013, http://fortune.com/2013/05/10/so-whos-making-money-publishing-on-the-web.

Nolan, Hamilton. "Morley Safer Is a Huge Asshole." *Gawker*, February 14, 2011, http://gawker.com/5759958/morley-safer-is-a-huge-asshole.

O'Brien, Sara Ashley. "Who Is Silicon Valley Billionaire Peter Thiel?" *CNNMoney*, May 26, 2016, http://money.cnn.com/2016/05/25/technology/who-is-peter-thiel/index.html.

O'Connor, Maureen. "Peaches Geldof's Heroin-Fueled One-Night Stand at Hollywood's Scientology Center—with Pictures." *Gawker*, March 25, 2010, http://gawker.com/5502453/peaches-geldofs-heroin-fueled-one-night-stand-at-hollywoods-scientology-centerwith-pictures.

Roderick, Kevin. "Gawker Way to Blog, by the Book." *LA Observed*, February 14, 2008, http://laobserved.com/archive/2008/02/gawker_way_to_blog_by_the.php.

Rosenberg, Scott. *Say Everything: How Blogging Began, What It's Becoming, and Why It Matters*. Three Rivers Press, 2009.

Seko, Mobutu Sese. "It's Not That Adam Carolla Isn't Funny, It's That Adam Carolla Is a Dumbfuck." *Gawker*, June 21, 2012, http://gawker.com/5920141/its-not-that-adam-carolla-isnt-funny-its-that-adam-carolla-is-a-dumbfuck.

Silver, James. "Gawk, Don't Talk." *Guardian*, December 11, 2006, http://theguardian.com/technology/2006/dec/11/news.mondaymediasection.

Stein, Joshua. "Danyelle Freeman Sucks: The Marrow Out Of Life, In General." *Gawker*, November 20, 2007, http://gawker.com/324827/danyelle-freeman-sucks-the-marrow-out-of-life-in-general.

———. "Elijah Pollack Is Going to Be a Horror." *Gawker*, September 27, 2007, http://gawker.com/304568/elijah-pollack-is-going-to-be-a-horror.

Stein, Joshua David. "Which NYC Food Critic Is an Idiot? (Hint: Danyelle Freeman!)." *Gawker*, January 15, 2008, http://gawker.com/5002264/which-nyc-food-critic-is-an-idiot-hint-danyelle-freeman.

Thomas, Owen. "Does Nick Denton Wish He Were Peter Thiel?" *Gawker*, July 11, 2008, http://gawker.com/5024376/does-nick-denton-wish-he-were-peter-thiel.

———. "Peter Thiel Is Totally Gay, People." *Gawker*, December 19, 2007, http://gawker.com/335894/peter-thiel-is-totally-gay-people.

———. "Peter Thiel to Move His Hedge Fund to New York." *Gawker*, January 16, 2008, http://gawker.com/345811%2Fpeter-thiel-to-move-his-hedge-fund-to-new-york.

Trow, George W. S. *My Pilgrim's Progress: Media Studies, 1950–1998*. Vintage, 2000.

Yarow, Jay. "Gawker Reports Earnings!" *Business Insider*, July 2, 2015, http://businessinsider.com/gawker-revenue-profits-2015-7.

Chapter 2: Deciding to Act

Arrington, Michael. "Engadget Knocks $4 Billion Off Apple Market Cap on Bogus iPhone Email." *TechCrunch*, May 16, 2007, http://techcrunch.com/2007/05/16/engadget-knocks-4-billion-of-apple-market-cap-on-bogus-iphone-email.

Branson, Richard. "The Fears Are Paper Tigers." *Virgin*, November 6, 2015, http://virgin.com/richard-branson/fears-are-paper-tigers.

DeNuccio, Kyle. "Silicon Valley Is Letting Go of Its Techie Island Fantasies." *Wired*, May 16, 2015, http://wired.com/2015/05/silicon-valley-letting-go-techie-island-fantasies.

Gabler, Neal. *Winchell: Gossip, Power and the Culture of Celebrity*. Vintage Books, 1995.

Kierkegaard, Søren. *The Present Age, and Of the Difference Between a Genius and an Apostle*. Translated by Alexander Dru, Harper Torchbooks, 1962.

Loizos, Connie. "Peter Thiel on Valleywag: It's the 'Silicon Valley Equivalent of Al Qaeda.'" PE Hub, May 18, 2009, http://pehub.com/2009/05/peter-thiel-on-valleywag-its-the-silicon-valley-equivalent-of-al-qaeda.

McKelway, St. Clair. "Gossip Writer." *New Yorker*, June 15, 1940, http://newyorker.com/magazine/1940/06/15/gossip-writer.

"'Out' Magazine Releases Power List, Underestimates 'Times' Gaiety." *Daily Intelligencer* (blog), *New York*, April 7, 2008, http://nymag.com/daily/intelligencer/2008/04/out_magazine_releases_power_li.html.

Packer, George. "No Death, No Taxes." *New Yorker*, November 28, 2011, http://newyorker.com/magazine/2011/11/28/no-death-no-taxes.

Tate, Ryan. "Facebook Backer Peter Thiel Escapes New York." *Gawker*, June 17, 2010, http://gawker.com/5566532/facebook-backer-peter-thiel-escapes-new-york.

Thiel, Peter. "The Education of a Libertarian." *Cato Unbound*, April 13, 2009, http://cato-unbound.org/2009/04/13/peter-thiel/education-libertarian.

Thomas, Owen. "Facebook Backer Wishes Women Couldn't Vote." *Gawker*, April 28, 2009, http://gawker.com/5231390/facebook-backer-wishes-women-couldnt-vote.

———. "Peter Thiel to Move His Hedge Fund to New York." *Gawker*, January 16, 2008, http://gawker.com/345811%2Fpeter-thiel-to-move-his-hedge-fund-to-new-york.

Thucydides. *History of the Peloponnesian War.* Translated by Rex Warner with an Introduction and Notes by M. I. Finley (Revised, with a new introduction and appendices). Penguin, 1972.

Tiku, Nitasha. "Peter Thiel's Dream of a Lawless Utopia Floats On." *Gawker*, September 23, 2013, http://valleywag.gawker.com/peter-thiel-s-dream-of-a-lawless-utopia-floats-on-1368141049.

Warren, Samuel D., and Louis D. Brandeis. "The Right to Privacy." *Harvard Law Review*, vol. 4, no. 5 (1890): 193–220.

Chapter 3: Turning to Conspiracy

Benner, Erica. *Be Like the Fox: Machiavelli in His World.* W. W. Norton, 2017.

Bercovici, Jeff. "'Gawker Is Snarkier Than I'd Like': Outtakes from My Playboy Interview with Nick Denton." *Forbes*, February 28, 2014, http://forbes.com/sites/jeffbercovici/2014/02/28/gawker-is-snarkier-than-id-like-outtakes-from-my-playboy-interview-with-nick-denton.

Creasy, Edward Shepherd. *Fifteen Decisive Battles of the World: From Marathon to Waterloo.* Da Capo, 1994.

Denton, Nick. "How Things Work." *Gawker*, August 22, 2016, http://gawker.com/how-things-work-1785604699.

Dumas, Alexandre. *The Count of Monte Cristo.* Penguin, 2006.

Ferriss, Timothy. "Eric Weinstein." *Tools of Titans: The Tactics, Routines, and Habits of Billionaires, Icons, and World-Class Performers.* Houghton Mifflin Harcourt, 2017.

Lopez, German. "Meet the 16-Year-Old Canadian Girl Who Took Down Milo Yiannopoulos." *Vox*, February 24, 2017, http://vox.com/policy-and-politics/2017/2/24/14715774/milo-yiannopoulos-cpac-pedophile-video-canada.

Machiavelli, Niccolò. *The Discourses*. Penguin, 1970.

———. *The Portable Machiavelli*. Translated by Peter Bondanella, Penguin, 2005.

McGrath, Ben. "Search and Destroy." *New Yorker*, October 18, 2010, http://newyorker.com/magazine/2010/10/18/search-and-destroy-ben-mcgrath.

Schmidt-Häuer, Christian. *Gorbachev: The Path to Power*. Pan Books, 1986.

Silver, James. "Gawk, Don't Talk." *Guardian*, December 11, 2006, http://theguardian.com/technology/2006/dec/11/news.mondaymediasection.

Silverman, Craig. "How Lies Spread Faster Than Truth: A Study of Viral Content." *MediaShift*, February 18, 2015, http://mediashift.org/2015/02/how-lies-spread-faster-than-truth-a-study-of-viral-content.

Thomas, Owen. "Does Nick Denton Wish He Were Peter Thiel?" *Gawker*, July 11, 2008, http://gawker.com/5024376/does-nick-denton-wish-he-were-peter-thiel.

Chapter 4: Assembling the Team

Brown, Mick. "Peter Thiel: The Billionaire Tech Entrepreneur on a Mission to Cheat Death." *Telegraph*, September 19, 2014, http://www.telegraph.co.uk/technology/11098971/Peter-Thiel-the-billionaire-on-a-mission-to-cheat-death.html.

Caro, Robert A. *The Path to Power: The Years of Lyndon Johnson*. Vintage, 1983.

Cieply, Michael. "Guard Dog to the Stars (Legally Speaking)." *New York Times*, May 21, 2011, http://nytimes.com/2011/05/22/business/22singer.html.

Cohen, Rich. *The Fish That Ate the Whale: The Life and Times of America's Banana King*. Picador, 2013.

Freedman, Lawrence. *Strategy: A History*. Oxford University Press, 2015.

Stevens, Laura Roe. "Spurned New Hires Have Their Say." *New York Times*, July 31, 2001, http://nytimes.com/2001/08/01/jobs/spurned-new-hires-have-their-say.html.

Wolfe, Alexandra. *Valley of the Gods: A Silicon Valley Story*. Simon & Schuster, 2017.

Chapter 5: Finding the Back Door

Baker, Jesse. "Gawker Wants to Offer More than Snark, Gossip." NPR, January 3, 2011, http://npr.org/2011/01/03/132613645/Gawker-Wants-To-Offer-More-Than-Snark-Vicious-Gossip.

Clausewitz, Carl von. *On War*. Princeton University Press, 1989.

Daulerio, A. J. "Brett Favre's Cellphone Seduction of Jenn Sterger (Update)." *Deadspin*, October 7, 2010, http://deadspin.com/brett-favres-cellphone-seduction-of-jenn-sterger-upda-5658206.

Denton, Nick. "To quote the great Marty Singer—Eric Dane's lawyer—if you don't want a sex tape on the internet, 'don't make one!'" Twitter, September 23, 2009, http://twitter.com/nicknotned/status/4325607614.

Freedman, Lawrence. *Strategy: A History*. Oxford University Press, 2015.

Goodwin, Liz. "Silicon Valley Billionaire Funding Creation of Artificial Libertarian Islands." *Yahoo! News*, August 16, 2011, http://yahoo.com/news/blogs/lookout/silicon-valley-billionaire-funding-creation-artificial-libertarian-islands-140840896.html.

Greenstein, Fred I. *The Hidden-Hand Presidency: Eisenhower as Leader*. Johns Hopkins University Press, 1994.

Hudson, John. "Nick Denton's Done Defending Himself." *Atlantic*, March 8, 2011, http://theatlantic.com/entertainment/archive/2011/03/nick-denton-done-defending-himself/348665.

Juzwiak, Rich. "On Outing, Not Outing, and Working for Gawker." July 21, 2015, http://richjuz.kinja.com/on-outing-not-outing-and-working-for-gawker-1719014904.

Liddell Hart, B. H. *Strategy: The Indirect Approach*. Pentagon Press, 2012.

Marsh, Julia. "Gawker's Internal Emails Show Callous Response to 'Rape' Victim." *New York Post*, March 11, 2016, http://nypost.com/2016/03/11/blah-blah-blah-gawker-editor-blew-off-woman-who-begged-him-to-remove-possible-rape-video.

Moylan, Brian. "Anderson Cooper Is a Giant Homosexual and Everyone Knows It." *Gawker*, October 29, 2009, http://gawker.com/5392766/anderson-cooper-is-a-giant-homosexual-and-everyone-knows-it.

———. "10 People Who Need to Finally Come Out of the Closet." *Gawker*, March 29, 2010, http://gawker.com/5504885/10-people-who-need-to-finally-come-out-of-the-closet.

O'Connor, Maureen. "Christina Hendricks Says These Giant Naked Boobs Aren't Hers, but Everything Else Is." *Gawker*, March 5, 2012, http://gawker.com/5890527/christina-hendricks-says-these-giant-naked-boobs-arent-hers-but-everything-else-is.

Serpe, Gina. "McSteamy Sex Tape Goes Offline . . . Forever." *E! News*, August 4, 2010, http://eonline.com/ca/news/193659/mcsteamy-sex-tape-goes-offline-forever.

Chapter 6: Tear Out Your Heart

Bilton, Nick. *American Kingpin: The Epic Hunt for the Criminal Mastermind Behind the Silk Road*. Portfolio/Penguin, 2017.

Deutsch, Harold. *The Conspiracy Against Hitler in the Twilight War*. University of Minnesota Press, 1970.

Dumas, Alexandre. *The Count of Monte Cristo*. Penguin, 2006.

Jackson, Eric M. *The PayPal Wars: Battles with eBay, the Media, the Mafia, and the Rest of Planet Earth*. WND Books, 2012.

James, William. *The Letters of William James: 2 Volumes Combined*. Cosimo, 2008.

Kibbe, Matt. *Don't Hurt People and Don't Take Their Stuff: A Libertarian Manifesto*. William Morrow Paperbacks, 2015.

McKelway, St. Clair. "Gossip Writer." *New Yorker*, June 15, 1940, http://newyorker.com/magazine/1940/06/15/gossip-writer.

Sherman, William T. "Letter to James M. Calhoun, et al., September 12, 1864." Wikisource, http://en.wikisource.org/wiki/Letter_to_James_M._Calhoun,_et_al.,_September_12,_1864.

Chapter 7: Seizing the Sword

Bixenspan, David. "31 Moments That Led to Hulk Hogan's Bankrupting Gawker Media." *Death and Taxes*, June 15, 2016, http://deathandtaxesmag.com/290581/hulk-hogan-bankrupting-gawker-timeline.

Chong, Celena. "Nick Denton Is Confident Gawker Will Win Its $100 Million Lawsuit over Hulk Hogan's Sex Tape." *Business Insider*, June 17, 2015, http://businessinsider.com/nick-denton-confident-gawker-will-win-hulk-hogan-sex-tape-lawsuit-2015-6.

Daulerio, A. J. "Some Additional Notes About the Hulk Hogan Sex Tape We Should All Take Into Consideration as Things Fall Apart." *Gawker*, October 5, 2012, http://gawker.com/5949317/some-additional-notes-about-the-hulk-hogan-sex-tape-we-should-all-take-into-consideration-as-things-fall-apart.

DeadspinVideos. "NBC Rock Center 7 March 2012 Feature on Gawker Media's Nick Denton." YouTube, March 7, 2012, http://youtube.com/watch?v=ferrE5gSeeY.

Finn, Natalie. "Hulk Hogan Sex Tape a Best-Seller? Adult Video Honcho Thinks It Could Be!" *E! News*, March 8, 2012, http://eonline.com/ca/news/299792/hulk-hogan-sex-tape-a-best-seller-adult-video-honcho-thinks-it-could-be.

Folkenflik, David. "On the Demise of Gawker.com: Unsparing, Satiric and Brutal." NPR, August 19, 2016, http://npr.org/sections/thetwo-way/2016/08/19/490657591/on-the-demise-of-gawker-com-unsparing-satiric-and-brutal.

Gawker. "Hulk Hogan's Sex Tape Is the Heavyweight Champion . . ." Facebook, October 4, 2012, http://facebook.com/Gawker/posts/431273250268865.

———. "It's Probably Time You Watched This Snippet from . . ." Facebook, October 4, 2012, http://facebook.com/Gawker/posts/454145771295146.

Harder, Charles. Transcribed from press conference on Monday, October 15, 2012, at the United States Courthouse in Tampa, Fla.

Hogan, Hulk. *My Life Outside the Ring*. Hodder & Stoughton, 2011.

———. "Now my actions will speak louder than my words. HH." Twitter, October 15, 2012, http://twitter.com/hulkhogan/status/257870787346853889.

"Hulk Hogan Betrayed by Best Friend: 'I'm Sick to My Stomach'." *TMZ*, October 9, 2012, http://tmz.com/2012/10/09/hulk-hogan-tmz-live-sex-tape-bubba-the-love-sponge.

"Hulk Hogan: I Have NO IDEA Who My Sex Tape Partner Is." *TMZ*, March 7, 2012, http://tmz.com/2012/03/07/hulk-hogan-sex-tape-partner-tmz-live.

"Hulk Hogan: I'm the VICTIM in a Sex Tape Setup." *TMZ*, March 7, 2012, http://tmz.com/2012/03/07/hulk-hogan-i-had-no-idea-sex-was-being-filmed.

"HULK HOGAN Sex Tape Being Shopped." *TMZ*, March 7, 2012, http://tmz.com/2012/03/07/hulk-hogan-sex-tape.

Johnson, Mike. "Complete Details on Hulk Hogan's $100 Million Lawsuit Against Gawker Media and Others, Why Gawker Didn't Pull the Sex Tape Footage and Much More." *PWInsider*, October 19, 2012, http://pwinsider.com/article/72757/complete-details-on-hulk-hogans-100-million-lawsuit-against-gawker-media-and-others-why-gawker-didnt-pull-the-sex-tape-footage-and-much-more.html.

Juzwiak, Rich. "I'm Not Straight, But My Boyfriend Is." *Gawker*, February 14, 2013, http://gawker.com/5983927/im-not-straight-but-my-boyfriend-is.

Machiavelli, Niccolò. *The Portable Machiavelli*. Translated by Peter Bondanella, Penguin, 2005.

Marshall, Matt. "Why Valleywag's Nick Douglas Got Fired: He Wanted Lawsuit." *VentureBeat*, November 15, 2006, http://venturebeat.com/2006/11/15/why-valleywags-nick-douglas-got-fired-he-wanted-lawsuit.

Moore, Tracy. "Trans Woman Commits Suicide amid Fear of Outing by Sports Blog." *Jezebel*, January 18, 2014, http://jezebel.com/trans-woman-commits-suicide-amid-fear-of-outing-by-spor-1503902916.

Munzenrieder, Kyle. "Bubba the Love Sponge: 'F*ck Haiti.'" *Miami New Times*, January 20, 2010, http://miaminewtimes.com/news/bubba-the-love-sponge-f-ck-haiti-6561737.

O'Connor, Maureen. "Christina Hendricks Says These Giant Naked Boobs Aren't Hers, but Everything Else Is." *Gawker*, March 5, 2012, http://gawker.com/5890527/christina-hendricks-says-these-giant-naked-boobs-arent-hers-but-everything-else-is.

———. "Olivia Munn's Super Dirty Alleged Naked Pics: 'Lick My Tight Asshole and Choke Me'." *Gawker*, March 5, 2012, http://gawker.com/5890506/olivia-munns-super-dirty-alleged-naked-pics-lick-my-tight-asshole-and-choke-me.

Read, Max. "Ladies: 8,000 Creeps on Reddit Are Sharing the Nude Photos You Posted to Photobucket." *Gawker*, August 8, 2012, http://gawker.com/5932702/ladies-8000-creeps-on-reddit-are-sharing-the-nude-photos-you-posted-to-photobucket.

Romanesko, Jim. "Gawker's Nick Denton: We Hire People Who Detest Bullshit." *JimRomanesko* (blog), October 15, 2012, http://jimromenesko.com/2012/10/15/gawkers-nick-denton-we-hire-people-who-detest-bullshit.

Sherman, Gabriel. "Gawker Ex-Editor A.J. Daulerio: The Worldwide Leader in Sextapes." *GQ*, January 19, 2011, http://gq.com/story/aj-daulerio-deadspin-brett-favre-story.

Trotter, J. K. "This Is Why Billionaire Peter Thiel Wants to End Gawker." *Gawker*, May 26, 2016, http://gawker.com/this-is-why-billionaire-peter-thiel-wants-to-end-gawker-1778734026.

PART II: THE DOING

Chapter 8: Prepare for Setbacks

Bazilian, Emma. "In Experiment, Gawker Goes 'Traffic Whoring'." *Adweek*, January 31, 2012, http://adweek.com/digital/experiment-gawker-goes-traffic-whoring-137801.

Benner, Erica. *Be Like the Fox: Machiavelli in His World*. W. W. Norton, 2017.

Biddle, Sam. "Tech Bros' Google-Sponsored Trip to India Turns into Naked Beach Romp [UPDATE]." *Gawker*, February 18, 2013, http://gawker.com/5985094%2Ftech-bros-google-sponsored-trip-to-india-turns-into-naked-beach-romp.

Bustillos, Maria. "FBI Documents Strongly Suggest Hulk Hogan Lied in Court." *Death and Taxes*, March 21, 2016, http://deathandtaxesmag.com/284541/fbi-documents-hulk-hogan-lied-gawker-sex-tape.

Cairnes, William E., editor. *Napoleon's Military Maxims*. Translated by Lt. Gen. Sir George C. D'Aguilar, Dover Publications, 2004.

Carroll, Paul, and Chunka Mui. *Billion-Dollar Lessons: What You Can Learn from the Most Inexcusable Business Failures of the Last 25 Years*. Penguin, 2010.

Carus, Titus Lucretius. *The Nature of Things*. Translated by A. E. Stallings, Penguin, 2007.

Chen, Andrew. "After the Techcrunch Bump: Life in the 'Trough of Sorrow.'" *@andrewchen* (blog), September 10, 2012, http://andrewchen.co/after-the-techcrunch-bump-life-in-the-trough-of-sorrow.

Clausewitz, Carl von. *On War*. Princeton University Press, 1989.

Cook, John. "A Judge Told Us to Take Down Our Hulk Hogan Sex Tape Post. We Won't." *Gawker*, April 25, 2013, http://gawker.com/a-judge-told-us-to-take-down-our-hulk-hogan-sex-tape-po-481328088.

Dodero, Camille. "Many People Asked This Hulk Hogan Cosplayer About His Sex Tape This Weekend." *Gawker*, October 15, 2012, http://gawker.com/5951695/many-people-asked-this-hulk-hogan-cosplayer-about-his-sex-tape-this-weekend.

Frieswick, Kris. "Why Hulk Hogan's Sex Tape Might Undo Gawker Media." *Inc.*, January 20, 2016, http://inc.com/magazine/201602/kris-frieswick/how-gawkers-nick-denton-is-stepping-into-the-ring-against-hulk-hogan.html.

Gardner, Eriq. "Gawker Beats Hulk Hogan: Appeals Court Reverses Sex Tape Injunction." *Hollywood Reporter*, January 17, 2014, http://hollywoodreporter.com/thr-esq/gawker-beats-hulk-hogan-appeals-671950.

———. "Hulk Hogan Brings Second Lawsuit Against Gawker." *Hollywood Reporter*, May 2, 2016, http://hollywoodreporter.com/thr-esq/hulk-hogan-brings-second-lawsuit-889386.

———. "Why Hulk Hogan Is Likely to Lose Sex Tape Lawsuit Against Gawker (Analysis)." *Hollywood Reporter*, January 4, 2013, http://hollywoodreporter.com/thr-esq/why-hulk-hogan-is-lose-408595.

"Keith A. Davidson Attorney Bio." Albertson & Davidson, LLP, http://aldavlaw.com/attorneys/keith-a-davidson.

Scocca, Tom. "Is the *New York Post* Edited by a Bigoted Drunk Who Fucks Pigs?" *Gawker*, April 18, 2013, http://gawker.com/5994999/is-the-new-york-post-edited-by-a-bigoted-drunk-who-fucks-pigs.

Thompson, Paul. "Hulk Hogan Branded 'Ultimate, Lying Showman' as Former Best Friend Accuses Wrestler of Being Behind Leak of Sex Tape." *Daily Mail Online*, October 16, 2012, http://dailymail.co.uk/tvshowbiz/article-2218646/Hulk

-Hogan-branded-ultimate-lying-showman-best-friend-accuses-wrestler-leak-sex-tape.html.

Weaver, Caity. "The Most Deranged Sorority Girl Email You Will Ever Read." *Gawker*, April 18, 2013, http://gawker.com/5994974/the-most-deranged-sorority-girl-email-you-will-ever-read.

Chapter 9: Know Thy Enemy

Carlson, Nicholas. "Gawker Sued for $1 Million over McSteamy Sex Tape." *Business Insider*, September 23, 2009, http://businessinsider.com/gawker-sued-for-1-million-over-mcsteamy-sex-tape-2009-9.

Cook, John. "A Judge Told Us to Take Down Our Hulk Hogan Sex Tape Post. We Won't." *Gawker*, April 25, 2013, http://gawker.com/a-judge-told-us-to-take-down-our-hulk-hogan-sex-tape-po-481328088.

Gardner, Eriq. "Dr. Phil Sues Gawker for Copyright Infringement." *Hollywood Reporter*, May 6, 2013, http://hollywoodreporter.com/thr-esq/dr-phil-sues-gawker-copyright-501905.

———. "Gawker's Nick Denton Explains Why Invasion of Privacy Is Positive for Society." *Hollywood Reporter*, May 22, 2013, http://hollywoodreporter.com/thr-esq/gawkers-nick-denton-explains-why-526548.

Grove, Lloyd. "A. J. Daulerio Doesn't Regret Child Sex Quip at Hogan-Gawker Trial." *Daily Beast*, March 23, 2016, http://thedailybeast.com/aj-daulerio-doesnt-regret-child-sex-quip-at-hogan-gawker-trial.

Herodotus. *The Histories*. Penguin, 2015.

Horgan, Richard. "Slandered Schwarzenegger Flight Attendant Goes After Gawker." *Adweek*, August 4, 2011, http://adweek.com/digital/arnold-schwarzenegger-love-child-gawker-john-cook-tammy-tousignant-lawsuit.

Kaplan, Sarah. "Gawker on Trial: Hulk Hogan Sex Tapes 'Very Amusing' and 'Newsworthy.'" *Washington Post*, March 11, 2016, http://washingtonpost.com/news/morning-mix/wp/2016/03/10/gawker-on-trial-hulk-hogan-sex-tapes-very-amusing-and-newsworthy.

Knappenberger, Brian, director. *Nobody Speak: Trials of the Free Press*. Netflix & First Look Media, 2017.

Koblin, John. "Nick Denton's Secret Weapon: Gaby Darbyshire Is Gawker's Chief Enforcer." *Observer*, July 7, 2010, http://observer.com/2010/07/nick-dentons-secret-weapon-gaby-darbyshire-is-gawkers-chief-enforcer.

Lowrey, Brandon. "Gawker Editors Scrutinized in Hulk Hogan Privacy Trial." Law360, March 14, 2016, http://law360.com/articles/771169/gawker-editors-scrutinized-in-hulk-hogan-privacy-trial.

McGrath, Ben. "Search and Destroy." *New Yorker*, October 18, 2010, http://newyorker.com/magazine/2010/10/18/search-and-destroy-ben-mcgrath.

Sun Tzu. *The Art of War*. Filiquarian, 2006.

Thielman, Sam. "Nick Denton Grilled in Gawker-Hogan Trial: 'We're Dependent on Leaks'." *Guardian*, March 15, 2016, http://theguardian.com/media/2016/mar/15/nick-denton-testimony-gawker-hulk-hogan-sex-tape-trial.

Walshe, Shushannah. "HarperCollins Sues Gawker: What's Their Case?" *Daily Beast*, November 22, 2010, http://thedailybeast.com/harpercollins-sues-gawker-whats-their-case.

Wolf, Gary. "Utopian Pessimist Calls on Radical Tech to Save Economy." *Wired*, January 25, 2010, http://wired.com/2010/01/st_thiel.

Chapter 10: The Power of Secrets

Brown, Anthony Cave. *Bodyguard of Lies*. Harper & Row, 1975.

De La Rochefoucauld, François duc. *Reflections; Or, Sentences and Moral Maxims*. Brentano's, 1871.

Freud, Sigmund. *Dora: An Analysis of a Case of Hysteria*. Simon & Schuster, 1997.

Frontinus. *The Stratagems: And the Aqueducts of Rome*. Translated by Charles Edwin Bennett, Harvard University Press, 1925.

Greene, Robert. *The 33 Strategies of War*. Profile, 2008.

Loizos, Connie. "Peter Thiel on Valleywag; It's the 'Silicon Valley Equivalent of Al Qaeda.'" PE Hub, May 18, 2009, http://pehub.com/2009/05/peter-thiel-on-valleywag-its-the-silicon-valley-equivalent-of-al-qaeda.

Machiavelli, Niccolò. *The Portable Machiavelli*. Translated by Peter Bondanella, Penguin, 2005.

Malcolm, Janet. *The Journalist and the Murderer*. Knopf Doubleday, 2011.

Smith, Ben. "Uber Executive Suggests Digging Up Dirt on Journalists." *BuzzFeed*, November 17, 2014, http://buzzfeed.com/bensmith/uber-executive-suggests-digging-up-dirt-on-journalists.

Stock, Jon. "JK Rowling Unmasked: The Lawyer, the Wife, Her Tweet—and a Furious Author." *Telegraph*, July 21, 2013, http://telegraph.co.uk/culture/books/10192275/JK-Rowling-unmasked-the-lawyer-the-wife-her-tweet-and-a-furious-author.html.

Tate, Ryan. "Peter Thiel: 'Valleywag Is the Silicon Valley Equivalent of Al Qaeda'." *Gawker*, March 18, 2009, http://gawker.com/5259805/peter-thiel-valleywag-is-the-silicon-valley-equivalent-of-al-qaeda.

Thiel, Peter A., and Blake Masters. *Zero to One: Notes on Startups, or How to Build the Future*. Crown Business, 2014.

Zweig, Stefan. *Magellan*. Pushkin, 2011.

Chapter 11: Sow Confusion and Disorder

"Adobe Distances Itself from Gawker After Writer's Gamergate Tweet." *Recode*, October 22, 2014, http://recode.net/2014/10/22/11632146/adobe-distances-self-from-gawker-after-writers-gamergate-tweet.

Barakat, Christie. "Gawker's Unpaid Intern Saga: Do as I Say, Not as I Do." *Adweek*, May 30, 2014, http://adweek.com/digital/gawker-unpaid-intern-lawsuit.

Blumenthal, Jeff. "Mitch Williams Sues MLB Network, Deadspin, Gawker for Defamation." *Philadelphia Business Journal*, September 24, 2014, http://

bizjournals.com/philadelphia/news/2014/09/24/mitch-williams-sues-mlb-network-deadspin-gawker.html.

Breuer, William B. *The Secret War with Germany: Deception, Espionage, and Dirty Tricks, 1939–1945*. Jove Books, 1989.

Carr, Paul Bradley. "Disgruntled Former Gawker Exec: Nick Denton Is a Coward, Here Are the Company's Financials." *Pando*, June 4, 2015, http://pando.com/2015/06/04/disgruntled-former-editorial-boss-nick-denton-is-a-coward-here-are-gawkers-financials.

———. "Gawker Is Being Sued for Trying to Scam Its Own Legal Insurers (Here Are the Court Docs)." *Pando*, August 5, 2014, http://pando.com/2014/08/05/gawker-is-being-sued-for-trying-to-scam-its-own-legal-insurers-here-are-the-court-docs.

———. "Gawker No Longer Even Trying to Pretend It's Not Grotesquely Hypocritical on Tax." *Pando*, July 25, 2014, http://pando.com/2014/07/25/gawker-no-longer-even-trying-to-pretend-its-not-grotesquely-hypocritical-on-tax/essays+montaigne.

———. "Revealed: Gawker's Sworn Affidavits Explaining Why Its Greedy Interns Didn't Deserve to Be Paid." *Pando*, February 21, 2014, http://pando.com/2014/02/21/revealed-gawkers-sworn-affidavits-explaining-why-its-greedy-interns-didnt-deserve-to-be-paid.

Cook, John. "Here Is Lena Dunham's $3.7 Million Book Proposal [UPDATE]." *Gawker*, December 7, 2012, http://gawker.com/5966563/here-is-lena-dunhams-37-million-book-proposal.

Demosthenes. *Complete Works of Demosthenes*. Delphi Classics, 2011.

Drange, Matt. "Peter Thiel's War on Gawker: A Timeline." *Forbes*, June 21, 2016, http://forbes.com/sites/mattdrange/2016/06/21/peter-thiels-war-on-gawker-a-timeline/#fb9c6d51c591.

Freedman, Lawrence. *Strategy: A History*. Oxford University Press, 2015.

Gardner, Eriq. "Quentin Tarantino Files New Gawker Lawsuit over 'Hateful Eight' Script Leak." *Hollywood Reporter*, May 1, 2014, http://hollywoodreporter.com/thr-esq/quentin-tarantino-files-new-gawker-700605.

Johnson, Charles C. "I Want to Make You a Promise: Gawker . . ." Facebook, October 17, 2015, http://facebook.com/charles.c.johnson/posts/10205138719487766.

Kafka, Peter. "Gawker Media Shuffles Org Chart, Names Tommy Craggs Top Editor." *Recode*, December 10, 2014, http://recode.net/2014/12/10/11633692/gawker-media-shuffles-org-chart-names-tommy-craggs-top-editor.

Kludt, Tom. "Hulk Hogan Sex Tape Trial Could Destroy Gawker." *CNNMoney*, June 18, 2015, http://money.cnn.com/2015/06/17/media/hulk-hogan-gawker-lawsuit/index.html.

Machiavelli, Niccolò. *The Discourses*. Penguin, 1970.

Mahler, Jonathan. "Gawker's Moment of Truth." *New York Times*, June 12, 2015, http://nytimes.com/2015/06/14/business/media/gawker-nick-denton-moment-of-truth.html.

McAlone, Nathan. "Now the Daily Mail Is Suing Gawker." *Business Insider*, September 4, 2015, http://businessinsider.com/now-the-daily-mail-is-suing-gawker-2015-9.

Nickols, Fred. "Eight Maxims of Strategy from Sir Basil H. Liddell-Hart." Distance Consulting, 2012, http://nickols.us/strategy_maxims.htm.

Nwanevu, Osita. "Gamergate Showed How to Kneecap a Website. Now This Group Is Trying to Do the Same to Breitbart." *Slate*, December 14, 2016, http://slate.com/articles/news_and_politics/politics/2016/12/sleeping_giants_campaign_against_breitbart.html.

Prochilo, Dan. "Gawker's Unpaid Interns Are Legally Employees, Suit Says." Law360, June 24, 2013, http://law360.com/articles/452365/gawker-s-unpaid-interns-are-legally-employees-suit-says.

Read, Max. "Did I Kill Gawker?" *New York*, August 19, 2016, http://nymag.com/selectall/2016/08/did-i-kill-gawker.html.

———. "How We Got Rolled by the Dishonest Fascists of Gamergate." *Gawker*, October 22, 2014, http://gawker.com/how-we-got-rolled-by-the-dishonest-fascists-of-gamergat-1649496579.

Sola, Katie. "Conservative Blogger Sues Gawker For $66 Million Over Public Pooping Rumors." *HuffPost*, June 19, 2015, http://huffingtonpost.ca/entry/chuck-johnson-sues-gawker_n_7616756.

Staff, Gawker Media. "Gawker Media Votes To Unionize." *Gawker*, June 4, 2015, http://gawker.com/gawker-media-votes-to-unionize-1708892974.

Sun Tzu. *The Art of War*. Filiquarian, 2006.

Wingfield, Nick. "Intel Pulls Ads from Site After 'Gamergate' Boycott." *New York Times*, October 2, 2014, http://bits.blogs.nytimes.com/2014/10/02/intel-pulls-ads-from-site-after-gamergate-boycott.

Chapter 12: The Ties That Bind

Abad-Santos, Alex. "The Gawker Meltdown, Explained." *Vox*, July 21, 2015, http://vox.com/2015/7/21/9011045/gawker-outing-resignations.

Denton, Nick. "The Purpose of Gawker." *Gawker*, October 15, 2012, http://gawker.com/5951868/the-purpose-of-gawker.

Godkin, E. L. "The Rights of the Citizen." *Scribner's Magazine*, July 1890.

Kaufman, Rachel. "The Real Reason John Cook Left Yahoo?" *Adweek*, September 23, 2010, http://adweek.com/digital/the-real-reason-john-cook-left-yahoo.

Machiavelli, Niccolò. *The Discourses*. Penguin, 1970.

Mahler, Jonathan. "Gawker's Moment of Truth." *New York Times*, June 12, 2015, http://nytimes.com/2015/06/14/business/media/gawker-nick-denton-moment-of-truth.html.

Manchester, William. *The Last Lion Box Set: Winston Spencer Churchill, 1874–1965*. Little, Brown, 2012.

Murphy, Samantha. "Gawker's Nick Denton Instates 'No Social Media' Rule at His Wedding." *Mashable*, May 14, 2014, http://mashable.com/2014/05/14/gawker-nick-denton-wedding-no-social-media.

Scocca, Tom. "How Can You Mend a Broken Shitheart?" *Special Projects Desk*, October 13, 2017, http://specialprojectsdesk.kinja.com/how-can-you-mend-a-broken-shitheart-1819115519.

Stelter, Brian. "Founder of Gawker Media Nick Denton: '. . . In This Particular Instance, the Judgment Call Was Wrong, and I Had It Reversed.'" CNN, July 26, 2015, http://cnnpressroom.blogs.cnn.com/2015/07/26/founder-of-gawker-media-nick-denton-in-this-particular-instance-the-judgment-call-was-wrong-and-i-had-it-reversed.

Sterne, Peter. "Gawker's Denton: 'This Is Not the Company I Built'." *Politico*, July 20, 2015, http://politico.com/media/story/2015/07/gawkers-denton-this-is-not-the-company-i-built-003979.

Chapter 13: The Testing of Faith

Baysinger, Tim. "Gawker Removes Gossip Item That Outed Condé Nast CFO." *Adweek*, July 17, 2015, http://adweek.com/digital/gawker-removes-gossip-item-outed-cond-nast-cfo-165954.

Catton, Bruce. *Grant Moves South*. Castle Books, 2000.

Denton, Nick. "Hulk v. Gawker, the Story So Far." *Nick Denton* (blog), July 10, 2015, http://nick.kinja.com/hulk-v-gawker-the-story-so-far-1716479711.

———. "Taking a Post Down." *Nick Denton* (blog), July 17, 2015, http://nick.kinja.com/taking-a-post-down-1718581684.

Gardner, Eriq. "Hulk Hogan Sex Tape Trial Delayed After Appeals Court Intervenes." *The Hollywood Reporter*, July 2, 2015, http://hollywoodreporter.com/thr-esq/hulk-hogan-sex-tape-trial-806550.

———. "Hulk Hogan's Lawyers Seize on Nick Denton Blog Post in Bid for More Secrecy." *Hollywood Reporter*, July 14, 2015, http://hollywoodreporter.com/thr-esq/hulk-hogans-lawyers-seize-nick-808679.

Knappenberger, Brian, director. *Nobody Speak: Trials of the Free Press*. Netflix and First Look Media, 2017.

Manchester, William. *The Last Lion Box Set: Winston Spencer Churchill, 1874–1965*. Little, Brown, 2012.

Marsh, Julia. "Hulk Suing Gawker for Allegedly Leaking His Racist Tirade." *New York Post*, May 2, 2016, http://nypost.com/2016/05/02/hulk-hogan-hits-gawker-with-another-lawsuit.

Rafferty, Scott. "Hulk Hogan Fired by WWE Over 'Racial Tirade'." *Rolling Stone*, July 24, 2015, http://rollingstone.com/sports/news/hulk-hogan-fired-by-wwe-over-racial-tirade-20150724.

Toobin, Jeffrey. "Gawker's Demise and the Trump-Era Threat to the First Amendment." *New Yorker*, December 19, 2016, http://newyorker.com/magazine/2016/12/19/gawkers-demise-and-the-trump-era-threat-to-the-first-amendment.

Trotter, J. K. "Hulk Hogan Refers to 'Fucking Niggers' in Leaked Transcript." *Gawker*, July 24, 2015, http://gawker.com/hulk-hogan-refers-to-fucking-niggers-in-leaked-transc-1719933145.

———. "Tommy Craggs and Max Read Are Resigning from Gawker." *Gawker*, July 20, 2015, http://gawker.com/tommy-craggs-and-max-read-are-resigning-from-gawker-1719002144.

Chapter 14: Who Wants It More?

Abrams, Dan. "Might a Gawker Hater Be Covering Hulk Hogan's Legal Bills?" *LawNewz*, March 9, 2016, http://lawnewz.com/high-profile/might-an-anti-gawker-benefactor-be-covering-hulk-hogans-legal-bills.

Amit, Reut. "That Type of Girl Deserves It." *Gawker*, September 27, 2014, http://gawker.com/that-type-of-girl-deserves-it-1639772694.

Caro, Robert A. *The Path to Power: The Years of Lyndon Johnson*. Vintage, 1983.

Chernow, Ron. *Titan: The Life of John D. Rockefeller Sr.* Little, Brown, 1999.

Ingram, Mathew. "Gawker Gets Its First Outside Investment Ever, from a Russian Oligarch." *Fortune*, January 20, 2016, http://fortune.com/2016/01/20/gawker-funding.

Knappenberger, Brian, director. *Nobody Speak: Trials of the Free Press*. Netflix and First Look, 2017.

Lehman, Ernest. *Sweet Smell of Success, and Other Stories*. New American Library, 1957.

Neuhaus, Les, and Julia Marsh. "'We Needed to Send a Message': Hogan Jury Slams 'Arrogant' Gawker." *New York Post*, March 24, 2016, http://nypost.com/2016/03/24/we-needed-to-send-a-message-hogan-jury-slams-arrogant-gawker.

Sterne, Peter. "Gawker in the Fight of Its Life with Hulk Hogan Sex-Tape Suit." *Politico*, June 12, 2015, http://politico.com/media/story/2015/06/gawker-in-the-fight-of-its-life-with-hulk-hogan-sex-tape-suit-004004.

PART III: THE AFTERMATH

Chapter 15: The Battle for Hearts and Minds

Hogan, Hulk. "All is well. HH." Twitter, March 7, 2016, http://twitter.com/hulkhogan/status/706782227905060864.

Keneally, Meghan. "Erin Andrews Awarded $55 Million in Lawsuit." *ABC News*, March 7, 2016, http://abcnews.go.com/US/erin-andrews-jury-set-deliberate-75-million-lawsuit/story?id=37460110.

Madigan, Nick. "Gawker Editor's Testimony Stuns Courtroom in Hulk Hogan Trial." *New York Times*, March 9, 2016, http://nytimes.com/2016/03/10/business/media/gawker-editors-testimony-stuns-courtroom-in-hulk-hogan-trial.html.

Neuhaus, Les. "Ex-Gawker Editor Backs Off Testimony in Hulk Hogan Case." *New York Times*, March 14, 2016, http://nytimes.com/2016/03/15/business/media/ex-gawker-editor-backs-off-testimony-in-hulk-hogan-case.html.

Pilkington, Ed. "Tyler Clementi, Student Outed as Gay on Internet, Jumps to His Death." *Guardian*, September 30, 2010, http://theguardian.com/world/2010/sep/30/tyler-clementi-gay-student-suicide.

Sherman, Gabriel. "Gawker Ex-Editor A.J. Daulerio: The Worldwide Leader in Sextapes." *GQ*, January 19, 2011, http://gq.com/story/aj-daulerio-deadspin-brett-favre-story.

Chapter 16: Managing the Aftermath

Bowles, Nellie, and Danny Yadron. "Billionaire's Revenge: Facebook Investor Peter Thiel's Nine-Year Gawker Grudge." *Guardian*, May 25, 2016, http://www.theguardian.com/technology/2016/may/25/peter-thiel-gawker-hulk-hogan-sex-tape-lawsuit.

Cernovich, Mike. "Why Peter Thiel Is a Hero #ThankYouPeter." *Danger & Play*, May 26, 2016, http://www2.dangerandplay.com/2016/05/26/why-peter-thiel-is-a-hero-thankyoupeter.

Clausewitz, Carl von. *On War*. Princeton University Press, 1989.

Crile, George. *Charlie Wilson's War: The Extraordinary Story of How the Wildest Man in Congress and a Rogue CIA Agent Changed the History of Our Times*. Grove Press, 2007.

Eckholm, Erik. "Legal Experts See Little Effect on News Media from Hulk Hogan Verdict." *New York Times*, March 19, 2016, http://nytimes.com/2016/03/20/business/media/legal-experts-see-little-effect-on-news-media-from-hulk-hogan-verdict.html.

Fitzgerald, F. Scott. *The Great Gatsby*. Scribner, 2013.

Gajda, Amy. "The Threat to Dignity Should Be the Criterion in Privacy Cases Like Hulk Hogan's." *New York Times*, March 18, 2016, http://nytimes.com/roomfordebate/2016/03/18/should-the-gawker-hulk-hogan-jurors-decide-whats-newsworthy/the-threat-to-dignity-should-be-the-criterion-in-privacy-cases-like-hulk-hogans.

Grove, Lloyd. "Gawker Hit by Another Lawsuit—This Time from a Journalist." *Daily Beast*, January 20, 2016, http://thedailybeast.com/gawker-hit-by-another-lawsuitthis-time-from-a-journalist.

Hackett, Robert. "Gawker Sued for Defamation by Fran Drescher's Husband." *Fortune*, May 12, 2016, http://fortune.com/2016/05/12/gawker-lawsuit-shiva-ayyadurai.

Hiltzik, Michael. "Peter Thiel, Gawker, and the Risks of Making the Courthouse a Private Sandbox for the Wealthy." *Los Angeles Times*, May 25, 2016, http://latimes.com/business/hiltzik/la-fi-hiltzik-thiel-gawker-20160525-snap-story.html.

Hogan, Hulk. "Praying HH." Twitter, March 18, 2016, http://twitter.com/HulkHogan/status/710899185768382467.

Hyde, Marina. "Peter Thiel's Mission to Destroy Gawker Isn't 'Philanthropy'. It's a Chilling Taste of Things to Come." *Guardian*, May 27, 2016, http://theguardian

.com/commentisfree/2016/may/27/peter-thiel-gawker-philanthropy-paypal-mogul-secret-war-billionaire.

James, Brendan. "Most Americans Don't Care That Peter Thiel Crushed Gawker." *VICE News*, August 9, 2016, http://news.vice.com/article/most-americans-dont-care-that-peter-thiel-crushed-gawker.

Knappenberger, Brian, director. *Nobody Speak: Trials of the Free Press*. Netflix and First Look Media, 2017.

Mac, Ryan. "This Silicon Valley Billionaire Has Been Secretly Funding Hulk Hogan's Lawsuits Against Gawker." *Forbes*, May 24, 2016, http://forbes.com/sites/ryanmac/2016/05/24/this-silicon-valley-billionaire-has-been-secretly-funding-hulk-hogans-lawsuits-against-gawker/1.

Machiavelli, Niccolò. *The Portable Machiavelli*. Translated by Peter Bondanella, Penguin, 2005.

Neuhaus, Les, and Julia Marsh. "'We Needed to Send a Message': Hogan Jury Slams 'Arrogant' Gawker." *New York Post*, March 24, 2016, http://nypost.com/2016/03/24/we-needed-to-send-a-message-hogan-jury-slams-arrogant-gawker.

Sorkin, Andrew Ross. "Gawker Founder Suspects a Common Financer Behind Lawsuits." *New York Times*, May 23, 2016, http://nytimes.com/2016/05/24/business/dealbook/gawker-founder-suspects-a-common-financer-behind-lawsuits.html.

———. "Peter Thiel, Tech Billionaire, Reveals Secret War with Gawker." *New York Times*, May 25, 2016, http://nytimes.com/2016/05/26/business/dealbook/peter-thiel-tech-billionaire-reveals-secret-war-with-gawker.html.

Thiel, Peter. "Peter Thiel: The Online Privacy Debate Won't End with Gawker." *New York Times*, August 15, 2016, http://nytimes.com/2016/08/16/opinion/-thiel-the-online-privacy-debate-wont-end-with-gawker.html

Thiel, Peter A., and Blake Masters. *Zero to One: Notes on Startups, or How to Build the Future*. Crown Business, 2014.

Chapter 17: The Art of Settling

Bowles, Nellie. "Jeff Bezos on Peter Thiel: 'Seek Revenge and You Should Dig Two Graves'." *Guardian*, June 1, 2016, http://theguardian.com/technology/2016/jun/01/jeff-bezos-on-peter-thiel-seek-revenge-and-you-should-dig-two-graves.

Denton, Nick. "A Hard Peace." *Nick Denton.org* (blog), November 2, 2016, http://nickdenton.org/a-hard-peace-e161e19bfaf.

———. "An Open Letter to Peter Thiel." *Gawker*, May 26, 2016, http://gawker.com/an-open-letter-to-peter-thiel-1778991227.

———. "How Things Work." *Gawker*, August 22, 2016, http://gawker.com/how-things-work-1785604699.

Downs, Jim. "Peter Thiel Shows Us There's a Difference Between Gay Sex and Gay." *Advocate*, October 14, 2016, http://advocate.com/commentary/2016/10/14/peter-thiel-shows-us-theres-difference-between-gay-sex-and-gay.

Drange, Matt. "A. J. Daulerio to Peter Thiel: Do You Want My Rice Cooker and Dishes?" *Forbes*, August 23, 2016, http://forbes.com/sites/mattdrange/2016/08/23/a-j-daulerio-to-peter-thiel-do-you-want-my-rice-cooker-dishes-and-books.

———. "Former Gawker Editor Lashes Out at Peter Thiel, Calls Freeze on His Checking Account 'Ludicrous'." *Forbes*, August 18, 2016, http://forbes.com/sites/mattdrange/2016/08/18/former-gawker-editor-lashes-out-at-peter-thiel-calls-freeze-on-his-checking-account-ludicrous.

Ember, Sydney. "Gawker and Hulk Hogan Reach $31 Million Settlement." *New York Times*, November 2, 2016, http://nytimes.com/2016/11/03/business/media/gawker-hulk-hogan-settlement.html.

———. "Gawker Is Said to Be Sold to Univision in a $135 Million Bid." *New York Times*, August 16, 2016, http://nytimes.com/2016/08/17/business/media/gawker-sale.html.

Gardner, Eriq. "Peter Thiel Objects to Investigation into How He Funded Gawker's Demise." *Hollywood Reporter*, April 19, 2017, http://hollywoodreporter.com/thr-esq/peter-thiel-objects-investigation-how-he-funded-gawkers-demise-995400.

Greene, Robert. *The 48 Laws of Power*. Profile, 2010.

Kosoff, Maya. "Peter Thiel Wants to Inject Himself with Young People's Blood." *Vanity Fair*, August 1, 2016, http://vanityfair.com/news/2016/08/peter-thiel-wants-to-inject-himself-with-young-peoples-blood.

Lat, David. "Peter Thiel Had No Reason to Be Angry at Gawker for Writing That He's Gay." *Washington Post*, May 27, 2016, http://washingtonpost.com/posteverything/wp/2016/05/27/peter-thiel-had-no-reason-to-be-angry-at-gawker-for-writing-that-hes-gay.

"Longform Podcast #213: A. J. Daulerio." *Longform*, September 28, 2016, http://longform.org/posts/longform-podcast-213-a-j-daulerio.

Machiavelli, Niccolò. *The Discourses*. Penguin, 1970.

Raftery, Brian. "How Can We Make You Happy Today, Peter Thiel?" *Wired*, May 25, 2016, http://wired.com/2016/05/three-cheers-for-peter-thiel.

Randles, Jonathan. "Gawker Adviser to Market Potential Claims Against Peter Thiel." *Wall Street Journal*, November 2, 2017, http://www.wsj.com/articles/gawker-adviser-to-market-potential-claims-against-peter-thiel-1509658396.

Roberts, Jeff John. "Gawker's Nick Denton Is Set to Exit Bankruptcy." *Fortune*, March 23, 2017, http://fortune.com/2017/03/23/gawker-nick-denton-peter-thiel-2.

Sorel, Nancy Caldwell. "When Hearst Met Welles." *Independent*, September 22, 1995, http://independent.co.uk/life-style/when-hearst-met-welles-1602576.html.

Sorkin, Andrew Ross. "Peter Thiel, Tech Billionaire, Reveals Secret War with Gawker." *New York Times*, May 25, 2016, http://nytimes.com/2016/05/26/business/dealbook/peter-thiel-tech-billionaire-reveals-secret-war-with-gawker.html.

Winchell, Walter. *Winchell Exclusive: Things That Happened to Me and Me to Them*. Prentice-Hall, 1975.

Zaretsky, Staci. "Too Poor to Pay Million-Dollar Judgment, Former Gawker Editor Offers Up Rice Cooker, Dishes." *Above the Law*, August 24, 2016, http://abovethelaw.com/2016/08/too-poor-to-pay-million-dollar-judgment-former-gawker-editor-offers-up-rice-cooker-dishes.

Chapter 18: There Are Always Unintended Consequences

Bastiat, Frédéric. *That Which Is Seen, and That Which Is Not Seen. Frédéric Bastiat* (blog), originally published July 1850. http://bastiat.org/en/twisatwins.html.

Byers, Dylan. "Vox Suspends Editor for Encouraging Riots at Donald Trump Rallies." *CNNMoney*, June 3, 2016, http://money.cnn.com/2016/06/03/media/vox-editor-suspended-trump-riots/index.html.

Caro, Robert A. *The Path to Power: The Years of Lyndon Johnson*. Vintage, 1983.

Cohen, B. R. "The Confidence Economy: An Interview with T. J. Jackson Lears." *Public Books*, May 7, 2013, http://publicbooks.org/the-confidence-economy-an-interview-with-t-j-jackson-lears.

Girard, René. *The Scapegoat*. Johns Hopkins University Press, 1992.

"Hillary Clinton: Public Will Find Out President Is Innocent." CNN, January 28, 1998, http://cnn.com/ALLPOLITICS/1998/01/28/hillary.gma.

Holiday, Ryan. "Peter Thiel's Reminder to the Gawker Generation: Actions Have Consequences." *Observer*, May 27, 2016, http://observer.com/2016/05/peter-thiels-reminder-to-the-gawker-generation-actions-have-consequences.

Juzwiak, Rich. "Consider the Hathaway." *The Muse* (blog), *Jezebel*, April 3, 2017, http://themuse.jezebel.com/consider-the-hathaway-1793960148.

Kosoff, Maya. "Jeff Bezos: Peter Thiel Is 'a Contrarian,' and Contrarians 'Are Usually Wrong.'" *Vanity Fair*, October 20, 2016, http://vanityfair.com/news/2016/10/jeff-bezos-peter-thiel-trump-contrarian.

Nazaryan, Alexander. "Meet Charles Harder, the Gawker Killer Now Working for Melania Trump and Roger Ailes." *Newsweek*, October 14, 2016, http://newsweek.com/charles-harder-gawker-melania-trump-roger-ailes-people-magazine-509926.

Percy, Walker. *Lancelot*. Picador, 1999.

Plutarch. *Age of Caesar: Five Roman Lives*. W. W. Norton, 2017.

Rensin, Emmett. "Anybody want to fund a covert lawsuit to destroy @Ryan Holiday? Don't worry, he approves of such 'consequences'." http://T.co/qz7hqZSvaV." Twitter, May 26, 2016, http://twitter.com/emmettrensin/status/735931850623975424.

Republican National Convention. "Peter Thiel, Full Speech, 2016 Republican National Convention." YouTube, July 21, 2016, http://youtu.be/UTJB8AkT1dk.

Thompson, Edward Palmer. *Zero Option*. Merlin Press, 1982.

Scocca, Tom. "Gawker Was Murdered by Gaslight." *Gawker*, August 22, 2016, http://gawker.com/gawker-was-murdered-by-gaslight-1785456581.

Statt, Nick. "Reporting on Donald Trump's Hair Might Get You Sued." *Verge*, June 14, 2016, http://theverge.com/2016/6/14/11938310/gawker-media-donald-trump-hair-report-lawsuit.

Conclusion

Atwood, Margaret. *Morning in the Burned House*. McClelland & Stewart, 2009.

Dumas, Alexandre. *The Count of Monte Cristo*. Penguin, 2006.

Shakespeare, William. *Four Tragedies: Hamlet, Othello, King Lear, and Macbeth*. Penguin, 1996.

More From Me

Every week I write something. About getting better. About good books to read. About issues in the media. About marketing. About ancient philosophy. If you want to follow along and read more writing from me, sign up here at ryanholiday.net/articles.

You can also get monthly book recommendations (plus a list of my all-time favorites to right now) from me at ryanholiday.net /reading-newsletter

Or you can just shoot me a note with "Email list" in the subject line at ryanholiday@gmail.com and I'll sign you up.